The Seattle Sound

1990

Seattle's Music Scene

Distorts

As 80s Glam

Goes 90s Grunge

[Book One – The Seattle Sound Series]

By Michael Edward Browning

LinkeBook
Publishing
1750 30th Street, #365
Boulder, CO, USA

MOTHER LOVE BONE
WITH ALICE IN CHAINS
MAY 4th 8 PM
OZ
131 TAYLOR N.
Reserved $7 advance $9 at door
Produced by ECI

Intro

MOTHER LOVE BONE
May 4, 1989
The OZ Nightclub

We stepped into the Oz just as Love Bone stormed the tiny stage with the first song from their EP, Thru Fade Away. Jeff's bass intro filled the hall with as much power as any band who plays the Coliseum, and you can bet (your sweet ass) that these guys are arena-bound.

Looming larger than life, center stage was Dallas super fan, Andrew Wood, sporting a Cowboy's jersey and the ever present chartreuse green. Bruce and Stone both were looking unusual in the night's unusual heat with their hair gathered up in a top-side tail.

They broke into a set of material I presume will be on the album currently being recorded down in California. Included were; Come Bite the Apple, [Bone] China, and the surreal rocker, This Is Shangri-La, which, by the way, is just a killer song - it's still runnin' thru my skull.

When they played KISW's hit single, Half-Ass Monkey Boy, the crowd really got into it and the slam-dancers up front opened the pit, keeping the numerous fine skirts there on the outskirts. To settle things down a bit, they countered with a personal favorite, Crown of Thorns. Landrew the Love Child then introduced Capricorn Sister as 'the bonus track' (like it appears on the tape). Rounding out the set were a couple more unreleased tunes; Holy Roller and Stardog [Champion].

Then it was Queen's I'm in Love With My Car for a well-received, glitzy encore. Tho they got loads of flash, they're no flash in the pan, like Wood's exiting words of wisdom,

"Love reigns supreme!"

As does Love Bone.

Watch for the LP later this summer, in the meantime, pick up Shine and keep an eye out for Andy and the boys' next local show. They are a *must-see* event!

Mother Love Bone are: Vocals; Andrew Wood, Guitars; Stone Gossard and Bruce Fairweather, Bass; Jeff Ament, Percussion; Greg Gilmore.

# # #

KarenMasonBlair.com

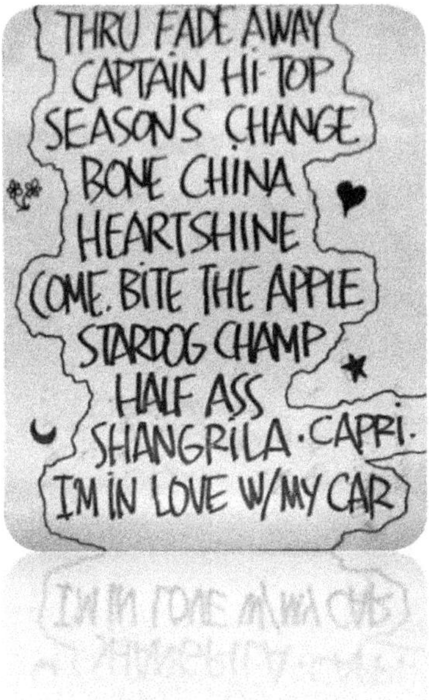

At the OZ that night, I bought my first Seattle band t-shirt - "Do What You Do" featuring the **Shine** EP cover art - at the merch table. This show review is the first music article I ever had published.

Good evening Stardogs! Looks like Jupiter is rising in the west, hence the Shine campaign, through Landry's demise and the rise of the Bickerstaff project, the Mothers of Love Bone by all means are out and about spreading a little Shangri-La to those who can cop the new ultra love vibe, if you know what I mean?

DO WHAT YOU DO
1989

Boston ∞ New Haven ∞ Providence ∞ Brooklyn ∞ Montreal ∞ Toronto ∞ New York ∞ Washington DC ∞ Baltimore ∞ Philadelphia ∞ Pittsburgh ∞ Detroit ∞ Cleveland ∞ Milwaukee ∞ Chicago ∞ Minneapolis ∞ St. Louis ∞ Lawrence ∞ Norman ∞ San Antonio ∞ Houston ∞ Dallas ∞ Austin ∞ Albuquerque ∞ Phoenix ∞ Los Angeles ∞ San Francisco ∞ Portland ∞ Seattle

Wore that shirt out over the years (later, at the Apple release party in Belltown, Jeff Ament gave me one of the "Air Love Bone" white long sleeves that instantly became my absolute favorite shirt, alas, <u>all gone now</u>).

A few months later, I was so struck by **Shine** and the power coming from the scene (actually arriving at venues in time to see Alice In Chains open for MLB - both at The Central Tavern in Pioneer Square and down at The Satyricon in Portland) that when they played the big stage at Bumbershoot that Labor Day weekend in 1989, I set up on the patio of my East Lake apartment painting a cardboard sign honoring the EP's artwork and combining the titles of my favorite song(s).

In the following YouTube video, you can see my orange-painted "Chloe's Crown" sign make a cameo at the beginning.

Mother Love Bone - Chloe Dancer / Crown Of Thorns - Live 1989

After I swam thru the crowd and chucked it onstage, Andy picked it up and positioned it - just before sitting down to the piano for the signified, unified tracks.

I was already deeply enamored with the man and his message:

"Love Rock awaits you people! Lo and behold!"

Get YOUR Free Gift Copy

of ***City Heat, Seattle's Music Magazine***

December 1990 Issue

MichaelEdwardBrowning.com/Heart1990

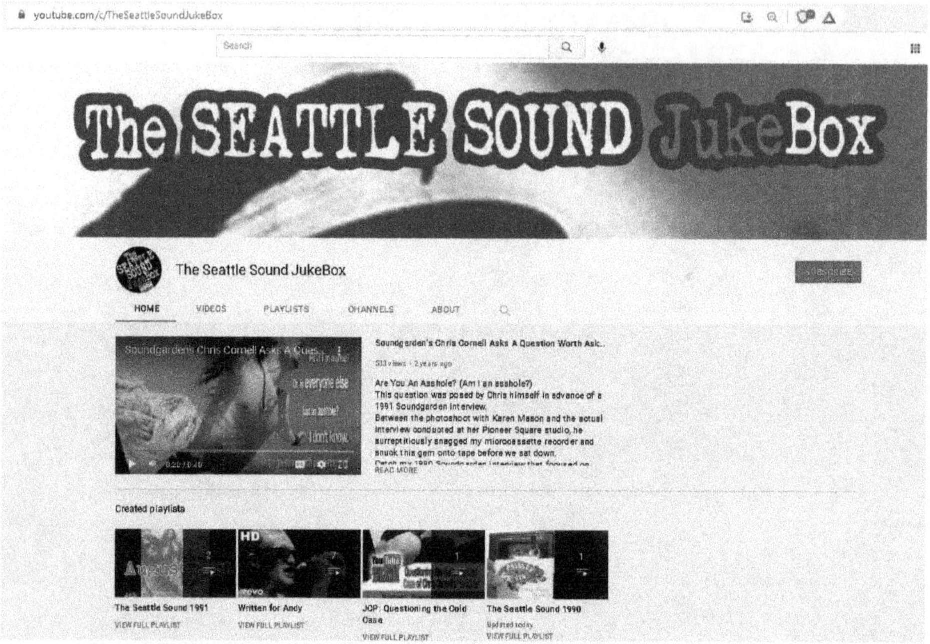

Listen to original interviews, demo tapes and other priceless relics of The Seattle Sound, from its 1990's heyday!

Search "*The Seattle Sound JukeBox*" on YouTube.

https://www.youtube.com/c/TheSeattleSoundJukeBox

"Through his exclusive interviews with the main Seattle bands in the late '80s and early '90s, Michael has been an eye-witness to one of the last, yet one of the most amazing, rock revolutions the world has seen.

As I was in the process of writing my book on Andy Wood and Mother Love Bone, I found in Michael a unique and reliable source. Specifically, he has been essential in providing some relevant material I was in search of, namely the contents of the last interview Andy Wood ever did. Indeed, Michael was the very last journalist to ever talk to Andy.

That long and extensive conversation is a precious and moving document Michael was willing to share with me, showing a deep sense of cooperation. The inclusion of his interview details made my book even richer. For that, I will be forever grateful."

Valeria Sgarella, Italian Author

Andy Wood, The Guy Who Made "Grunge" Happen:
Life (and Death) in Seattle Before Pearl Jam Came Along

plus, others surrounding the Seattle scene.

Amazon Author Page

https://www.amazon.com/Michael-Edward-Browning/e/B00IEDWV5M

"Michael is not only a rock historian, who's been in a lot of the right places at the right times, but his writing style has always dug in for a deeper dive – revealing a sense of the place and time he was writing about, along with his subjects.

Now more than ever, his stories hit home with renewed relevance and a reminiscence of some of those times and places, in the early days of some very familiar faces.

Michael was able to interview Andrew Wood only days before his departure from this earth. I'm grateful for his considerate sharing of that event with me, and for the grace with which he's carried it. That interview was a big part of the inspiration that kept me moving forward in telling Andy's story with my own work.

Cheers on diving into The Seattle Sound Series, starting right here in 1990! Great work, music historians. Enjoy the ride!"

Scot Barbour, Author, Director

Man of Golden Words: *The Biography of Andrew Wood*

Landrew's Love Notes: *A Collection of Lyrics From Andrew Wood*

Malfunkshun: *The Andrew Wood Story*

"…and the story continues!"

Link **eBook Publishing**
1750 30th Street, #365
Boulder, CO, 80301 USA

Book Design by Michael Edward Browning
http://michaeledwardbrowning.com

Original Mother Love Bone & Soundgarden Photography by Karen Mason-Blair
See more at **http://karenmasonblair.com**

For information about exclusive discounts for classrooms,
groups, or bulk purchasing options, please contact

Link **eBook** Publishing at (720) 772-9172.
Digitally manufactured in the United States of America.

ISBN: 978-0-9758900-0-4

Library of Congress Control Number: 2021922496

Library of Congress Cataloging-in-Publication Data
Browning, Michael Edward.
The Seattle Sound 1990: Seattle's Music Scene Distorts As 80's Glam Goes 90's Grunge / Michael Edward Browning

1. American Folklore.
2. Music – History.
3. Culture – Grunge.
4. Travel – Seattle, WA, USA.
5. Publishing – History, Zines.

Also from MEB:

Jesus Christ Pose: *You Tube Independent Journalists Questioning the Curiously Cold Case of Chris Cornell's "Suicide"*

Other books *edited* by Michael:

Time For The Talk: *Talking to Your Doctor Or Patient About Medical Cannabis* *by Dr. Regina Nelson with Michael Edward Browning*

Growing Your Own Medical Cannabis: *5 Core Concepts to Cultivation Success for the Absolute Beginner* *by Sugary Tips and Friends*

The Medical Cannabis Recommendation: *An Integral Exploration of Doctor/Patient Experiences* *by Dr. Regina Nelson*

Co-Creating Good, Healthy Relationships*: Living Life "The WeWay" With Everyone, Every Day* *by Wendy Foxworth*

The Secret World of Poker Progressives: *A History and How-To of Video Poker Slot Teams in Las Vegas* *by Frank Kneeland*

The SEATTLE SOUND Juke Box

PARENTAL ADVISORY EXPLICIT CONTENT

Contents

Acknowledgments

First off, I'd be remiss not to thank Robert Barr for publishing my first piece for City Heat back in 1989. That was a review of Mother Love Bone and Alice In Chains' show at The Oz Nightclub. If anyone has a copy of that, please hit me up!

Bob then assigned me a feature on Paisley Sin, included – at least visually – below. After that I was expressively on deadline every month, just as I was getting my feet economically in the big Pugetropolis. I owe him all I know of Adobe PageMaker!

Next up is my true-blue City Heat crew, Jeff Lageson & Karen Mason, both of whom were instrumental resources in helping to get this book into pixels [and now paper]. Both of whom are still considered dear friends. Both of who were always the ones I could count on "back in the day".

Please visit their sites, you'll be glad you did!

Publishing my book (books really, but it all starts with the first one, right?) was something that hung out there for me for the past twenty years until I met a talented watercolor artist in Albuquerque. I was blessed and privileged to have Karin Pitman as my accountability partner over a couple of seasons on this project. It is to her persistent support that I owed my own ability to initially publish this title back in 2012. Thanks again!

Finally, and firstly, LB^3, this first one's for you. Probably wouldn't have been able to do this without your inspiration in my life. I love you, son! Always remember to stay true - to you.

Author's Note

For those few gray haired readers thinking, "I remember Michael's articles. What's with the *Edward* all of a sudden?"

"Punk."

I just want to say that the reason is simply IMDB.

Yes, I've been interested in - and flirting with - the movie industry for years. Seems there's at least a couple other Michael Brownings who have as well. The middle moniker addition was precipitated by my ego's need for distinction in an industry I have yet to crack.

Lame, huh?

Oh, well. It also made my signature easier & shorter - for all these autographed copies!

Thank you, Rawk-Mart shoppers!

Some of you also might notice my proclivity for brevity. Except for syllabically.

In my bid to write more with less, I have attempted to further the campaign already in motion to shorten American spellings of English words "Through" to "Thru" and "Though" to "Tho".

Ya know?

Why not?

I have better things to do than reaching for a bunch of useless, UGH-ly characters across my keyboard, don't you? Even tho they *are* all centrally located.

LinkeBook

Within these pages you'll find many names, places and phrases underlined.

Each of the links adds time, detail and audio/visual context to the overall historic value contained here.

The **LinkeBook** version on any Kindle e-reader device is the best method to get full color image zoom, audio and video enjoyment from this title.

If you have purchased a paperback or hardbound copy, just send me an email, and address it to linkebook@michaeledwardbrowning.com with some proof of purchase and I'll send you the **LinkeBook** digital version by return email, gratis!

LinkeBook

...and the story continues!

amazon

kindle

www.MichaelEdwardBrowning.com/TheSeattleSoundSeries

Outside Insider

That May 1989 Love Bone show basically marked my first year in Seattle. I had started working with (and going to concerts under press credentials for) a tiny club magazine called **Rumors and Raggs**. I answered an ad like this, tho I don't think Seaun Richards ever published a single word in his Puget Sound entertainment guide.

Not any words of mine at least. After writing concert reviews of Boston, Van Halen, Scorpions, David Lee Roth, nada.

The Love Bone Oz review was the first piece **City Heat** published of mine - in June of '89.

For the next issue, Publisher, Bob Barr (or it might have been Editor Guy Lacey, yet another one of Seattle's great guitarists, see War Babies in **The Seattle Sound 1991: Seattle's Music Scene *Changes the Face* of The Music Industry**) assigned a combined show review/interview that turned into my first band feature, published in July 1989.

IMHO, it's a genuine interest in the stories of individual humans - and the hidden wisdom within those stories - that makes the deeper truths surface in an engrossing interview.

Can we talk?

Admittedly, on this first go, I didn't quite know how to present actual quotes from the band members cohesively. This is really just a well informed show review. Hopefully you'll see a progression with the passage of pages.

Paisley Sin

You'll be Glad You Did

By Michael Browning

Given the chance, these guys (and gal) will blow you away. Seattle's most underrated band is back with a strong line-up and a long list of inventive, original tunes. In the midst of a west coast tour and with an EP due out soon, Paisley Sin has returned to make a believer out of you.

Formed in 1984 by Sylvan Smith and Findle McBliss, Paisley Sin won the Hall of Fame Battle of the Bands in 1985. It looked like a great start to a promising career. But, shit happens. After a few hiatuses and personnel changes they solidified and went into the studio. Working together for the past six months, Smith and McBliss along with Jeanine Cunningham, Bill Ackerlund, Robert Middleton and John Passarelli have put together an eight song EP titled "It's Not Just a Hobby, It's a Hassle." As you can tell, this band has a healthy sense of humor--a necessity to survive the club circuit.

And clubbing is just what they've been doing for the past five years. But they've decided, and I'm inclined to agree, that now is the time for success. Hoping to spark label interest with the EP, you could be seeing Paisley Sin on vinyl very soon. With Seattle's current level of interest and over 50 songs in their catalog, an LP shouldn't pose any problems for them. And being fortunate enough to preview the tape, I can say they've got what it takes, now if someone would just take notice.

I took notice when they rocked the walls of the O.K. Hotel on the 16th. Never having heard them before, I wasn't sure what to expect. But now I can tell you to expect a variety of damn good music. With roots in punk, soul, funk, pop and classic ole rock n' roll, this group never lacks for variations. The show started with McBliss singing "Can't Find It," a triumphant but sorry testimonial on interpersonal relationships. Then it went to semi-improvised blithering rap on the verses of "Whiskey For Me" (Fresh Whores for the Boys)", a duet by Jeanine and Findle.
A couple more highlights with

(Cont. on page 17)

July City Heat 15

Paisley Sin
(Cont. from Page 15)

McBliss singing were the punky "Frat Boy" and the funky, tongue-in-cheek "This is the Life!". Jeanine then did a fantastic cover of Tina Turner's "Can't Stand the Rain." For the remainder of the show, Sylvan had the vocal spotlight. Some stand outs of his were "Used to Know," about love lost, "I've Been Watchin'", "Lonely Streets", and the show ending "Out and Down."

It was a diverse sixteen song set that came off the stage with power and emotion. Smith and McBliss shared bass duties, and vocal chores are shared between them and Cunningham. Of the two guitarists, Ackerlund and Passarelli, it seemed like Passarelli took care of most leads. a special note must be made here about Passarelli's guitar performance. His animated facial expressions and lively performance make for an enjoyable show. Even though there's six members this band is on a common wavelength and plays super-tight; tighter than most trios or quartets. They really seem to enjoy getting up there and it comes across in the live performance. They're having fun and so will you when you see them play. After having as good a time as I did seeing them in arguably the worst hall in town, (the stage faces a wall),e you can be certain of fully enjoying them when they play a larger place. Or, if you're really on top of it, you can catch them tonight (July 1st) at the Central.

Whether you first see them live or check out the tape, give 'em a chance. You'll be glad you did.

To obtain Paisley Sin's EP, "It'Not Just a Hobby, It's a Hassle" contact Jill Cunningham at 329-8939.

Given the chance, these guys (and gal) will blow you away. Seattle's most underrated band is back with a strong line-up and a long list of inventive, original tunes. In the midst of a west coast tour and with an EP due out soon, Paisley Sin has returned to make a believer out of you.

Formed in 1984 by Sylvan Smith and Findle McBliss, Paisley Sin won the Hall of Fame Battle of the Bands in 1985. It looked like a great start to a promising career. But, shit happens. After a few hiatuses and personnel changes, they solidified and went into the studio. Working together for the past six months, Smith and McBliss along with Jeanine Cunningham, Bill Ackerlund, Robert Middleton and John Passarelli [brother of Lipstick's Paul Passarelli, as seen on Northwest Metalfest, one of my early vinyl purchases in Oregon] have put together an eight song EP titled It's Not Just a Hobby, It's a Hassle. As you can tell, this band has a healthy sense of humor - a necessity to survive the club circuit.

And clubbing is just what they've been doing for the past five years. But they've decided, and I'm inclined to agree, that now is the time for success. Hoping to spark label interest with the EP, you could be seeing Paisley Sin on vinyl very soon. With Seattle's current level of interest and over 50 songs in their catalog, an LP shouldn't pose any problems for them. And being fortunate enough to preview the tape, I can say they've got what it takes, now if someone would just take notice.

I took notice when they rocked the walls of the O.K. Hotel on the 16th. Never having heard them before, I wasn't sure what to expect. But now I can tell you to expect a variety of damn good music. With roots in punk, soul, funk, pop and classic ole rock n' roll, this group never lacks for variations. The show started with McBliss singing *Can't Find It*, a triumphant but sorry testimonial on interpersonal relationships. Then it went to semi-improvised blithering rap on the verses-of *Whiskey For Me (Fresh Whores for the Boys)*, a duet by Jeanine and Findle. A couple more highlights with McBliss singing were the punky *Frat Boy* and the funky, tongue-in-cheek *This is the Life!* Jeanine then did a fantastic cover of Tina Turner's *Can't Stand the Rain*. For the remainder of the show, Sylvan had the vocal spotlight. Some stand outs of his were *Used to Know*, about love lost, *I've Been Watchin'*, *Lonely Streets*, and the show ending, *Out and Down*.

It was a diverse sixteen-song set that came off the stage with power and emotion. Smith and McBliss shared bass duties, and vocal chores are shared between them and Cunningham. Of the two guitarists, Ackerlund and Passarelli, it seemed like Passarelli took care of most leads, a special note must be made here about Passarelli's guitar performance. His animated facial expressions and lively performance make for an enjoyable show.

Even though there's six members this band is on a common wavelength and plays super-tight; tighter than most trios or quartets. They really seem to enjoy getting up there and it comes across in the live performance. They're having fun and so will you when you see them play. After having as good a time as I did seeing them in arguably the worst hall in town (the stage faces a wall), you can be certain of fully enjoying them when they play a larger place.

Or, if you're really on top of it, you can catch them tonight (July 1st) at the Central.

Whether you first see them live or check out the tape, give 'em a chance… You'll be glad you did.

To obtain Paisley Sin's EP, It's Not Just a Hobby, It's a Hassle, contact Jill Cunningham at 329-8939.

Hair Metal. I'll readily admit I was an avid consumer.

The polished production of 80's butt rock gives way at the end of the "me" decade to lo-fi DIY. Never mind the bullocks.

Massive CFC discharges from hair spray succumb (under the infamous environmentalism pressures of the Pacific Northwest) to a "greening" society that leads to "grungy" art products - in the vein of Bed Head messiness replacing AquaNet prettiness.

Seattle wasn't above the influence. But we were molding it for our own intentions.

Keep the hair, ditch the hairspray. Punks and posers alike.

Over time.

There'll still be some glitz-ches to work thru, some glam-age to be done.

I traveled north towards the turn of the decade from Oregonic origins. Scorps, Lep, Priest and Crue were what I loved and knew. Van Halen's debut was the first vinyl album to grace my quadraphonic stereo, a second-hand gift for my 12th birthday.

Luckily, I later got a turn as Music Director at KRVM 97.1 for North Eugene High School where our daytime slot ran **Alt Rock** programming. That exposed me also to PiL, Hoodoo Gurus & Husker Du. I pulled a Tuesday afternoon extended slot that shred metallic goodness on the populace, crazy international stuff like Saxon, Raven, Tsunami and Accept, but those school day morning slots really pushed my angst as a high school teen.

The "Rat Fuk" skater crowd I sometimes ran with - to Eugene's south side and UofO campus - expanded it further with Dead Kennedys, The Smiths and Descendants. I was personally at the nexus we were at culturally in America after the spike haired feed from the U.K. A long simmering ('70s) punk ethos was getting mainlined by U.S. record execs (including John & Bruce at Sub Pop) and getting prepped for mass domestic consumption.

Meanwhile...

Real punks embraced real pain on Seattle streets, dancing the city's mainline along Skid Row and beyond as the CIA importation machine pumped ever more cheap heroin up America's urban veins.

Thru music, community, and cannabis, we clung together. Of course there was always the ubiquitous cheer of abundant beer.

We start our tour of the Seattle Sound in 1990 with Sedated Souls, a finely styled example of Seattle's twist on where the music world was heading - as we came out of the Reagan era into the undercurrents of Operation Desert Storm and the (First) Gulf War.

S.O.S.

We chose then and there to let the Sounds Of Seattle *Save Our Souls.*

Within a year or so, the whole world was humming "our" tunes.

1990

JFMAMJJASOND

Sedated Souls – Feature, City Heat

At first glance, one might think that these guys are from the glam capital, Los Angeles, but the fact of the matter is that they're all hard-core Washingtonians, born and bred around the Puget Sound area.

And quite frankly, damn proud of it!

> *"One thing I would like to make very clear; we are a Seattle band. We realize that we're in Seattle, not in L.A. and we have a Seattle sound,"*

Explains vocalist, Trevor.

From very early on, these four dudes knew what they wanted to do and learned plenty from local heroes and role models. Since then, they have looked to the south for inspiration in style and attire, but have never lost sight of their home. This uninhibited openness to fresh concepts, sights and sounds has broadened the base on which their career currently sits.

One could get a very lop-sided view of their music if limited to the visual presentation. That's why it's important to recognize that this is a *performance* band whose image is meant to be taken in as a whole while they're playing live. Indeed, one look at them will stick in your mind, but one listen will give you a much more focused picture.

• BY Michael Browning

At first glance, one might think that these guys are from the glam capital, Los Angeles, but the fact of the matter is that they're all hard core Washingtonians, born and bred around the Puget Sound area. And quite frankly, proud of it. "One thing I would like to make very clear, we are a Seattle band. We realize that we're in Seattle, not in L.A., and we have a Seattle sound," explains vocalist, Trevor.

From very early on, these dudes knew what they wanted to do and learned plenty from local heroes and role models. Since then, they have looked to the south for inspiration in style and attire, but have never lost sight of their home. This uninhibited openness to fresh concepts, sights and sounds has broadened the base on which their career currently sits. One could get a very lop-sided view of their music if limited to the visual presentation. That's why it's important to recognize that this is a performance band whose image is meant to be taken in as a whole while they're playing live. Indeed, one look at them will stick in your mind, but one listen will give you a much more focused picture.

The evolution of their style and sound of today can be traced back to the earliest origins of the friendship between guitarist, Jeff Angel and bassist, Jeff Berns. The two Jeffs started kickin' it back in junior high when Berns got an axe for Christmas. They put together a punk outfit and were playing Tacoma's Community World by the ripe old age of 14. After being in numerous bands and personnel changes, they've wound up together again. Along the way, they've experimented with different styles and genres and it's culminated into a sound that lies somewhere between dark, dancable alternative and a real heavy grunge. At times it's both, but it's always your basic rock 'n roll. When asked if they prefer the bubble gum lightness or the deeper material, they respond logically. "We try to have the widest audience possible. Go for serious dread, yet keep it dancable and appealing to girls. If you can please both sides of the street, hell . . . do it."

Berns, the accomplished musician, plays drums, cello, upright bass, as well as his Charvel electric. His formal education includes a couple of years in orchestra and jazz choir, which makes him the only member musically literate enough to read and write page music. While Angel, on the other hand, is basically self-taught. He did, however, get his start on an acoustic with the help of Roy Clark's Learn to Play Handbook. Since then, he's been learning the language of Gibson by ear. Their completely different methods make them seem like strange bedfellows, (just an expression), but they're actually old pals and the best of friends.

Sedated Souls originally was formed in May '89 with another bass player and Angel's drummer from the now defunct Marilyn Was Murdered. Eric Knudsen played the snare drum in his school's stage band and wanted to expand, so he bought a Pearl set and has been playing for three years now. Like Angel and Berns, he's played a variety of styles in different bands and likes what he's doing now best (although he is deathly shy of make up and hair sprayl. Trevor, who'd been around Seattle's scene for years, made the group a foursome by contributing his tough, throaty

CITY HEAT February 14

The evolution of their style and sound of today can be traced back to the earliest origins of the friendship between guitarist, Jeff Angell, and bassist, Jeff Berns. The two Jeffs started kickin' it back in junior high when Berns got an axe for Christmas. They put together a punk outfit and were playing Tacoma's Community World by the ripe old age of 14.

After being in numerous bands and personnel changes, they've wound up together again. Along the way, they've experimented with different styles and genres and it's culminated into a sound that lies somewhere between dark, danceable alternative and a real heavy grunge. At times it's both, but it's always your basic rock 'n roll.

When asked if they prefer the bubblegum lightness or the deeper material, they respond logically.

> *"We try to have the widest audience possible. Go for serious dread; yet keep it danceable and appealing to girls. If you can please both sides of the street, hell... do it!"*

Berns, an accomplished musician, plays drums, cello, and upright bass as well as his Charvel electric. His formal education includes a couple of years in orchestra and jazz choir, which makes him the only member musically literate enough to read and write page music.

While Angell, on the other hand, is basically self-taught. He did, however, get his start on an acoustic with the help of *Roy Clark's Learn to Play Handbook*.

Since then, he's been learning the language of Gibson by ear. Their completely different methods make them seem like strange bedfellows, (just an expression!) but they're actually old pals and the best of friends.

Sedated Souls originally was formed in May '89 with another bass player and Angel's drummer from the now defunct Marilyn Was Murdered. Eric Knudsen played the snare drum in his school's stage band and wanted to expand, so he bought a Pearl set and has been playing for three years now. Like Angell and Berns, he's played a variety of styles in different bands and likes what he's doing now best (although he is deathly shy of makeup and hair spray).

Trevor, who'd been around Seattle's music scene for years, made the group a foursome by contributing his tough, throaty brand of vocals. When he and Angell were at a choral recital last fall, they heard someone that convinced them to make it a quintet.

A powerful solo by a demure little lady enlightened them to the something extra they were looking for.

> *"Trevor and I just looked at each other when she'd finished and said, 'We've got to have her!' and then we got her,"*

Angell remarks.

Apparently, it wasn't too hard to convince Yolanda Adams, who's got a long history of gospel and choir activity, to try something drastically contemporary. Sedated Souls now had a unit with backing vocals that helped capture the sound of rock's roots in the '50s and '60s, with lyrics centered on life in the '90s.

When a gradual difference in musical direction led to an amicable parting with the original bassist (after their first big breakthrough gig with Junkyard and Dangerous Toys) the group had to lay low for a couple of weeks while they brought in Berns to learn the songs and get into the studio.

While at E.S.P. Studios, they recorded a single called *I Remember* and will be back in the studio this month to record a five-song demo. It's still undecided, but there's a good chance that some part of that demo will be available to the public.

Until then, you can treat yourself to one of their frenetic, captivating shows, as they'll be playing several in the next few weeks.

They've been gigging steadily since last summer, and have amassed a solid south end draw but have yet to really crack Seattle, mostly for lack of venue. Although after opening for both Mother Love Bone and Vain last month, we doubt they'll have much trouble now.

In the event you don't hear of any dates here, at the end of this month they're with Mudhoney at Legends in Tacoma and hey, the town's only a short drive away.

Check it out!

Sedated Souls
(cont. from page 14)

brand of vocals. When he and Angel were at a choral recital last fall, they heard someone that convinced them to make it a quintet.

A powerful solo by a demure littlelady enlightened them to the something extra they were looking for. "Trevor and I just looked at each other when she'd finished, and said, 'We've got to have her,' and then we got her," Angel remarks. Apparently, it wasn't too hard to convince Yolanda Adams, who's got a long history of gospel and choir activity, to try something drastically contemporary. SS now had a unit with backing vocals that helped capture the sound of rock's roots in the fifties and sixties, centered around life in the nineties.

When a gradual difference in musical direction led to an amicable parting of the original bassist, after their first big breakthrough gig with Junkyard and Dangerous Toys, the group had to lay low for a couple of weeks while they brought in Berns to learn the songs and get into the studio. While at E.S.P., they recorded a single called "I Remember" and will be back in the studio this month to record a five-song demo. It's still undecided, but there's a good chance that some part of that demo will be available to the public. Until then, you can treat yourself to one of their frenetic, captivating shows, as they'll be playing several in the next few weeks. They've been gigging steadily since last summer, and have amassed a solid southend draw but have yet to really crack Seattle, mostly for lack of venue. Although after opening for both Mother Love Bone and Vain last month we doubt they'll have much trouble now. In the event you don't hear of any dates here, at the end of this month, they're with Mudhoney at Legends in Tacoma and hey, the town's only a short drive. Check it out. ⊕ ⊕

1990
JFMAMJJASOND

CITY HEAT
Seattle's Music Magazine
$0.00
MOTHER LOVE BONE ★ BATHTUB GIN
TRIBAL THERAPY ★ ANDREW WOOD REMEMBERED

LOCAL DIRT

By J. Hollywood

March was an eventful month for local music with the top story being the untimely death of **"Mother Love Bone"** vocalist **Andrew Wood,** more details in this issue. CITY HEAT magazine was well represented at this years **NAMA** convention. If you didn't make it down this year make it a point next year - if you're serious about your music. This month also seems to be the month for bands changing their names. Before a star struck crowd last month at the 99 Club **"Gypsy Rose"** announced that they will now call themselves **"Dazzler"** . **"Topcat Dancer"** has announced at a recent show at Meckers that they will be called **"Mother Earth."** Marty "The electric" Shalk has rejoined **"Troubled Valentine"** and also did a showcase a Meekers last month. Remember that Tuesdays are original showcase nights at Meeker's, and Sundays the 99 Club in the south and the "Riv" in the north are the places to be for original showcase music, show your support!

The band to watch locally is the **"Joseph Lee Wood "** band who recently appeared at Meeker's with **"Fire Choir"**. The band consists of **"Joseph Lee Wood"** on lead vocals, Greg Fox on keys, Monty Smith on lead guitar, Marty Randles on Bass and Chris Leighton on drums. The band played a flawless show of original, commercial hard rock that has several major labels interested, watch for them! Former **"Vice Versa"** members Jon Rydeen, Brent Olson and Keith Crocker have joined former **"Pretty Boy"** guitarist Kelly Burke to form **"Robyn Cradle"**. **NASTYMIX** Records announced the signing of splatter kings **"The Accused"**, their debut is titled "Grinning Like an Undertaker", and will be available this summer . In other NASTYMIX news the label has signed 3 new Rap artists, **"BOB & THE MOB"**, **"AMERICAS MOST WANTED,"** and **"SIDE F-X."**

The third annual **NAMA** Awards will take place April 9, 1990 at the Moore Theatre at 7:00pm tickets are $10.00 at the door and through Ticketmaster. The Hall of fame inductees are **Larry Coryell, "The Dynamics," "The Frantics," "Heart** (original band members)," **Paul Revere** and **"The Ventures."** It's all ages and everyone is welcome to this unique Northwest music celebration. Congrats are due to staff writer **Jimmy St. Bitchin** for his one year anniversary of the infamous **"Bitchins Corner."** Remember, if you have any **"LOCAL DIRT"** send it to **J. Hollywood** c/o City Heat Magazine and remember, stay clean, you'll feel better!

CITY HEAT
An Aird Hooker Publication
Executive Publisher
Matthew Aird
Publisher
Robert E. Barr
Editor in Chief
Jeff Lageson
Associate Editor
Michael Browning
Contributing Writers
Katie McMillan
Jimmy St. Bitchin
Michelle Klossner
Andrea Long
David Sterling
Rob Moitoza
Linnea Freed
Fashion Editor
A.R. Stuart
Photography
Charles Hoselton
Karen Mason
Graphic artist
Glen Mulvey
Cover Design
Doug Kammerer
Concert Desk
Rita O'Harren
Distribution Manager
Ted Treichler
Computer Layout
Doug Kammerer
Color Separations
WIZYWIG

CITY HEAT is published monthly at 929 SW 152nd St. Seattle, WA 98166. CITY HEAT accepts no responsibility for unsolicited materials. Subscriptions are available for $12/year U.S., $15/year first class or foreign. All inquiries please phone (206) 242-3952

What you see here in the margins is a _Capricorn Sister_ homage when inscribing a "collectible" gift for my loving father's 61st birthday. He was the reason I had come up to Seattle, why I was here. Thirty-some years later, it is indeed a collectible. See eBay.

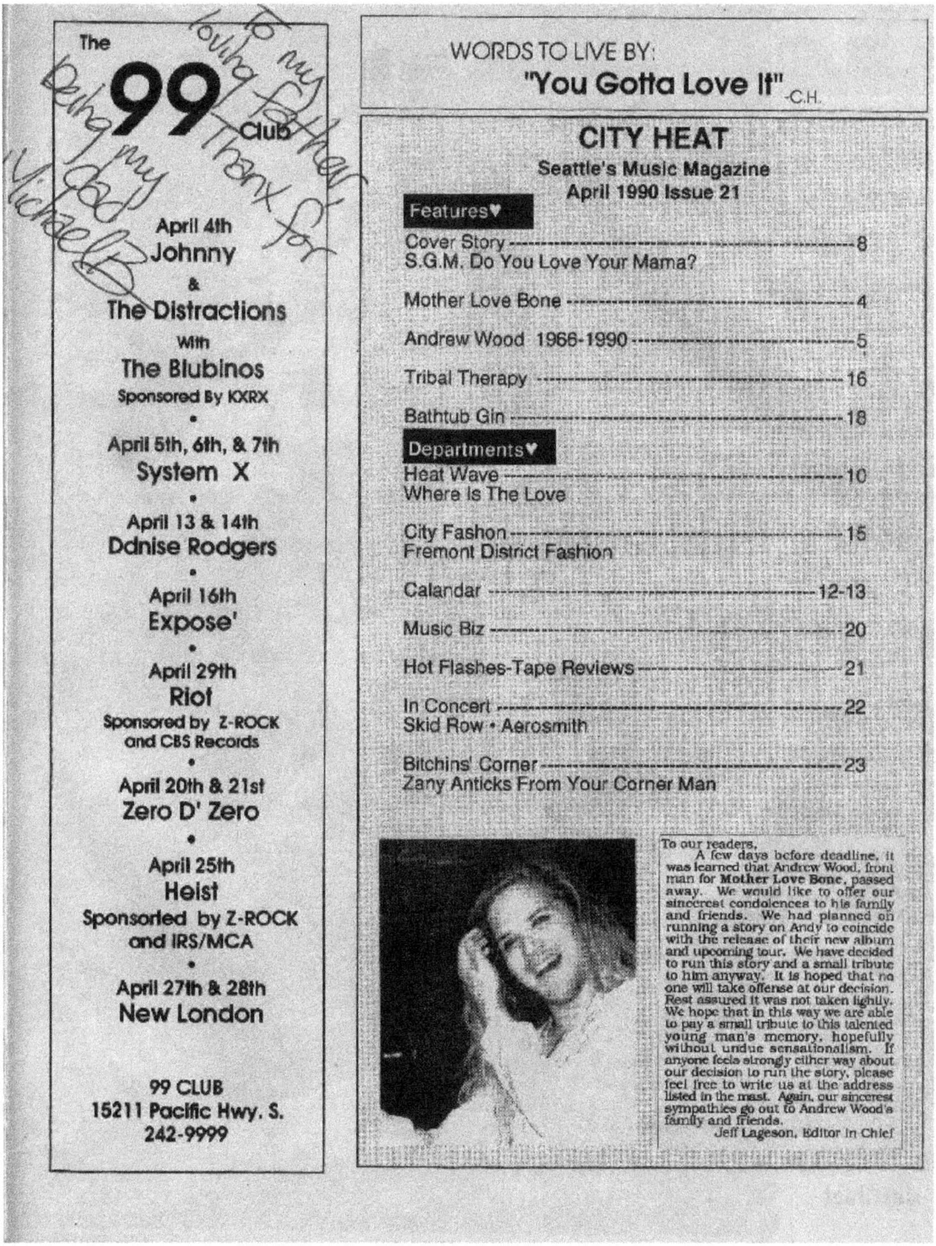

To my loving father, Thanx for being my dad Michael

The **99** Club

April 4th
Johnny & The Distractions
With
The Blubinos
Sponsored By KXRX
•
April 5th, 6th, & 7th
System X
•
April 13 & 14th
Ddnise Rodgers
•
April 16th
Expose'
•
April 29th
Riot
Sponsored by Z-ROCK and CBS Records
•
April 20th & 21st
Zero D' Zero
•
April 25th
Heist
Sponsorled by Z-ROCK and IRS/MCA
•
April 27th & 28th
New London

99 CLUB
15211 Pacific Hwy. S.
242-9999

WORDS TO LIVE BY:
"You Gotta Love It" -C.H.

CITY HEAT
Seattle's Music Magazine
April 1990 Issue 21

Features♥

Cover Story ---------- 8
S.G.M. Do You Love Your Mama?

Mother Love Bone ---------- 4

Andrew Wood 1966-1990 ---------- 5

Tribal Therapy ---------- 16

Bathtub Gin ---------- 18

Departments♥

Heat Wave ---------- 10
Where Is The Love

City Fashon ---------- 15
Fremont District Fashion

Calandar ---------- 12-13

Music Biz ---------- 20

Hot Flashes-Tape Reviews ---------- 21

In Concert ---------- 22
Skid Row • Aerosmith

Bitchins' Corner ---------- 23
Zany Anticks From Your Corner Man

To our readers,
A few days before deadline, it was learned that Andrew Wood, front man for **Mother Love Bone**, passed away. We would like to offer our sincerest condolences to his family and friends. We had planned on running a story on Andy to coincide with the release of their new album and upcoming tour. We have decided to run this story and a small tribute to him anyway. It is hoped that no one will take offense at our decision. Rest assured it was not taken lightly. We hope that in this way we are able to pay a small tribute to this talented young man's memory, hopefully without undue sensationalism. If anyone feels strongly either way about our decision to run the story, please feel free to write us at the address listed in the mast. Again, our sincerest sympathies go out to Andrew Wood's family and friends.
Jeff Lageson, Editor In Chief

Somewhat stupidly, none of us on the editorial staff caught the syllabic faux pas in the first sentence. Or the redundancies.

We were all in shock, gasping for air inside our own local scene's J.F.K. moment.

To Our Readers:

A few days before deadline, we learned that Andrew Wood, front man for Mother Love Bone, passed away. We would like to offer our sincerest condolences to his family and friends. We had planned on running a story on Andy to coincide with their new album and upcoming tour. We have decided to run this story and a small tribute to him anyway.

It is hoped that no one will take offense at our decision. Rest assured, it was not taken lightly. We hope that in this way we are able to pay a small tribute to this talented young man's memory, hopefully without undue sensationalism. If anyone feels strongly, either way, about our decision to run the story, please feel free to write us at the address listed in the mast.

Again, our sincerest sympathies go out to Andrew Wood's family and friends.

Jeff Lageson, Editor in Chief

Do You Love Your Mama?

S.G.M.

"Dear City Heat, do a story on us or we will find you and kill you. Love, Cole/SGM We luv you guys!"

Hmmmm ... how now could we resist such a tempting offer?

Actually, we had planned on doing a story on SHOT GUN MAMA anyway, so we can conveniently avoid their thinly veiled threat.

For those of you out there who haven't seen an SGM show, or are only familiar with them from their punk-oriented "Aggression" album, you're in for a surprise. A few personnel changes have taken place and they're still a serious group of musicians who just want to play Rock-n-Roll, kick a little ass, and take names, but the sound has evolved. So, in an era where we have WARRANT running around in their cute little white leather outfits and winking at video cameras, and the NEW DORKS ON THE BLOCK being themselves, we find a band with integrity.

Integrity?

An odd thought for the 90s, isn't it?

Yep, as children of the 80s the five guys (**Adam Cziesler** - Vox, **Rico Credo** - Guitar, **Chris Quinn** - Guitar, **Cole Peterson** - Bass, and **Pablo Uhlir** - Drums) who make up SGM experienced a variety of musical influences, which permeate their sound. It's music with only one appropriate label, "Rock-n-Roll."

But what about the name SHOT GUN MAMA? They've been called SGM for a long time and they always changed what it stood for. One night it would be one thing and another night it would be another. After countless names and perhaps some [illegible] soul-searching, they finally decided on SHOT GUN MAMA.

The name has caused some confusion. Many in Seattle know them just as SGM, while those in the south know them as SHOT GUN MAMA. So get this straight everybody, it's SGM and it stands for SHOT GUN MAMA.

Got it?

Good.

When "Aggression" came out a few years ago the evolution in their sound had already begun. The personnel changes and whatnot got the band moving in some other directions. The album "Aggression" is actually a collection of a couple of demo tapes that the label decided to release as is. Although the response was good and fans still call out for some of those tunes, the experience with their label was not a positive one. Or, as Pablo so succinctly put it, "It was a nightmare."

So, to ensure that things work out better for the future the band is taking a more careful approach. They're looking to sign but they're taking their time, recording more demos, and rehearsing several nights a week for their live act. I caught up with them one night at their hell-to-find rehearsal space at the foot of the West Seattle Bridge and we chatted in between songs like "Shoot" and "1st and Pike."

Live, of course, is where the real SGM comes out. They love to play live and they've travelled high and low to do [illegible] road trips down the west coast and to Las Vegas. The first time they went to Vegas, for instance, was an awesome experience. They helped to open a new club and the whole thing went well. But times aren't always that great on the road. By the time they returned to play another show, the club had closed down and they had no place to play. The evening was a mass state of confusion while they and their fans waited to find out when, where, and if they would be playing.

PHOTO SHOT IN THE DARK

The west coast has been pretty consistent though. They've had good response playing all the way south in San Diego and have had good luck in San Francisco, where they freaked out a friends mom by staying there and all using the bathroom to clean up. But life on the road is eventually what these guys want. They want to play some day in big arenas like the Tacoma Dome and play before huge audiences. Because getting a good vibe live is where it's at in rock.

Locally, things have been picking up as well. SGM has been playing with a lot of regularity lately, headlining on their own at places like the Backstage and opening for national acts like Vain this past January.

But what about the songs?

A band can't make it today without strong original material (NEW DORKS excluded). For the most part Adam writes the words. While what the words say is important, "It's not just the words but the sounds they make," he said, "like a 'T' sound followed by a cymbal crash." And, as band members come up with new riffs or a new idea and it sounds good, they bring it in and work with it. In this way new songs are always being worked on. It's not just "Let's sit down and write a new hit song," but something that comes along more naturally and that everybody is involved in.

Now, I'm probably making it sound like these guys are the next demi-gods of rock, ready to conquer the territory of the Stones. But, let's get this straight, they rock.

The question for SGM and the other bands trying to get signed who deserve attention though, is can they last for the long haul? Although that question really can't be answered and depends on a lot of intangibles and the quirks of consumers' tastes, there is and hopefully always will be a market for good rock.

If things do work out and SGM is able to score it big we can expect an evolution of sound to continue. Change is healthy and it can be expected from them. It's not like we'll hear a sequel to the next album all the time. But not to get too far ahead of ourselves here, that will all come in due time.

They seem to be realistic. That sort of success is rare. They admit it would be nice to see it happen and all and that's why they practice so hard. But right now it's important to play tight live and as Chris says to "get a good vibe with an audience," as well as recording some songs, and trying to get signed to a label they can trust.

In the meantime we can always catch them live, spreading their "love vibes" around the Great Northwest.

This is your friendly neighborhood failed guitarist turned writer signing off for now.♥♥♥

City Heat

Mother Love Bone – Feature, City Heat

Hello and welcome, babies!

Let me plug you into this feeling known as Mother Love Bone, whose mission it is to let their love rock energy shine down on the waiting populace.

As many of you are well aware, Mother Love Bone is one of Seattle's prize exports of late and on the eve of the release of their PolyGram LP, Apple, City Heat had the opportunity to speak with the 'Bone about their feelings on recording albums, the record itself and anticipation.

So, without further ado, *who loves you?*

Mother Love Bone came about thru the friendship and collaboration between Andrew Wood (then in Malfunkshun with Regan Hagar and Kevin Wood) with Stone Gossard and Jeff Ament (both in Green River with Mark Arm and Alex Shumway) a year before the conception of Mother Love Bone.

Jeff Ament uncovers the beginnings,

> *"Andy and [Malfunkshun's drummer] Regan, and me and Stone all knew each other kind of as friends, so a year before Green River even broke up, we got together and learned about six covers. Zeppelin and Aerosmith stuff, just us four. At that point we were called Lords Of The Wasteland."*
>
> *"We totally just did it to have fun and do things we'd never do inside our respective bands. Then when me and Stone were trying to get something going after Green River... I don't know, things just kind of fell into place."*
>
> *"Within a month we were jamming with Greg [Gilmore] and Bruce [Fairweather]. At that point we already had six or seven new songs. Then by late January, early February [1988], we went in and just live...cut five songs in four or five hours for our demo, purely for us to get shows."*

The sticky part was that Green River was officially past tense, whereas Malfunkshun had yet to be discussed. When Wood parted ways with his best friend and his brother, he made a very tough decision.

Hagar tells me,

MOTHER LOVE BONE
BY MICHAEL BROWNING
PHOTO BY KAREN MASON

Hello and welcome babies! Let me plug you into this feeling known as Mother Love Bone, whose mission it is to let their love rock energy shine down on the waiting populace. As many of you are well aware Mother Love Bone is one of Seattle's prize exports of late and on the eve of the release of their PolyGram LP, Apple, City Heat had the opportunity to speak with the Bone about their feelings on recording albums, the record itself and anticipation. So without further ado, who loves you?

Mother Love Bone came about thru the friendship and collaboration between Andrew Wood (then in Malfunkshun with Regan Hagar and Kevin Wood) and Stone Gossard and Jeff Ament (both in Green River with Bruce Fairweather, Mark Arm, and Alex Shumway) a year before the conception of MLB. Jeff Ament uncovers the beginnings. "Andy and their drummer, Regan, and me and Stone all knew each other kind of as friends, so a year before Green River even broke up, we got together and learned about six covers, Zeppelin and Aerosmith stuff, just for fun, at that point we were called Lords of the Wasteland. We totally just did it to have fun and do things we'd never do inside our respective bands. Then when me and Stone were trying to get something going after Green River...I don't know, things just kind of fell into place. Within a month we were jamming with Andy and Regan, and a month after that we ended up jamming with Greg Gilmore and Bruce. At that point we already had six or seven new songs. Then by late January, early February [88] we went in and just live...cut five songs in four or five hours for our demo, purely for us to get shows." The sticky part was that Green River was officially past tense whereas Malfunkshun had yet to be dismissed. When Wood parted ways with his best friend and his brother he made a very tough decision, Hagar tells me. "Andy really felt terrible about replacing me and that's kind of too bad, because I understood that it was a business decision and the very best one he could make then." The group enlisted the considerable percussive talents of Greg Gilmore, best known for his work with The Living and Ten-Minute Warning. Returning from Asia in late 1987 Gilmore says, "The very day I came back to Seattle, I ran into Stone up on Broadway after being in town just a few hours. He asked me if I wanted to come play sometime. I did a couple, three weeks later and that was it." He adds, "At the time I didn't really know what was going on. The first or second time I was there and Regan showed up was when I learned that Regan had been playing with them. Because all of a sudden everybody was very uncomfortable and silently started to put their guitars away. We were still just in the 'come down and jam with us' phase, and see what we all think. It was only the second time and even then it was kinda happening already."

It was that magic in the combination of members that began to manifest itself in some fantastically creative songs that would soon capture the attention of everyone who heard them. When recording their first demo that Ament mentioned earlier, he adds "...even when we were recording, I think we knew that it was something pretty special. It was just totally spontaneous, jingling in the studio most of the time. But we just knew what was happening...It was just...it's cool. Definitely something special." Now, with a minimum of tribulation, they had cemented their line up and were getting shows. The next year was spent being courted by labels, looking at signing with Geffen, only to end up with Polygram in one of the biggest contracts ever for a band with no released material.

Cont. page 20

In Loving Memory of

Andrew Wood

January 8, 1966 • March 19, 1990

1980 to 1987 was a highly creative period for Andy Wood, in which he performed solo, billed as L'Andrew the Love Child, simultaneously fronting Malfunkshun, and later Lords of the Wasteland.

From 1987 to 1990, Andy involved himself in the project we know as the band Mother Love Bone. It was this vehicle that brought Andy the recognition that his dreams knew would come.

At 24, his talent had only begun to be tapped.

"I just hope that there are some other people out there that, you know, see what happened to him and hopefully realize that their pain is fleeting and the pain that they feel from it, you know, is over in a matter of days, but other people will be in pain for a lot longer until it's kind of a selfish thing. It's a real tragedy." - Bruce Fairweather

"It's just like anybody else, things get you screwed out, you go have a beer. Whatever. There's really not a whole lot of difference, other than one drug is instantly deadly and the other one isn't. They're both addictions." Jeff Ament

"Just check out what Andy had to say and think about it." - Greg Gilmore

"There were so many things he did that were so great, and he had such a positive effect on so many peoples lives with his attitude, that everything you could write or say is not really going to explain what he meant to us and to everyone who really knew him." - Stone Gossard

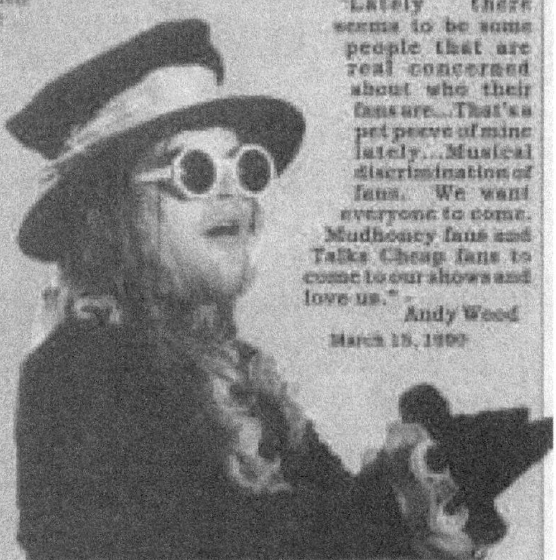

"Lately there seems to be some people that are real concerned about who their fans are...That's a pet peeve of mine lately...Musical discrimination of fans. We want everyone to come. Mudhoney fans and Talks Cheap fans to come to our shows and love us." - Andy Wood

March 15, 1990

5 City Heat

> *"Andy felt really terrible about replacing me and that's kind of too bad because I understood that it was a business decision, and the very best one he could make then."*

The group enlisted the considerable percussive talents of Greg Gilmore, best known for his work with The Living and Ten-Minute Warning. Returning from Asia in late 1987, Gilmore says,

> *"The very day I came back to Seattle, I ran into Stone up on Broadway after being in town just a few hours. He asked me if I wanted to come play sometime. I did a couple, three weeks later and that was it."*

He adds,

> *"At the time I didn't really know what was going on. The first or second time I was there and Regan showed up was when I learned that Regan had been playing with them, because all of a sudden everybody was very uncomfortable and silently started to put their guitars away. We were still just in the 'come down and jam with us' phase and see what we all think. It was only the second time and even then, it was kinda happening already."*

It was that magic in the combination of members that began to manifest itself in some fantastically creative songs that would soon capture the attention of everyone who heard them.

When recording their first demo that Ament mentioned earlier, he adds,

> *"...even when we were recording, I think we all knew it was something pretty special. It was just totally spine tingling in the studio most of the time. We just knew what was happening...it was just...it's cool. Definitely something special."*

Now, with a minimum of tribulation, they had cemented their line up and were getting shows. The next year was spent being courted by labels, looking at signing with Geffen, only to end up with PolyGram in one of the biggest contracts ever for a band with no released material.

I asked Wood about the reputed seven record, quarter million dollar deal.

> *"I don't really know the whole logistics of it. I know we got signed for $250,000 and seven albums, and I know now that we're broke and that we could also get dropped at any point."*

He added that depending on the success of this release they could renegotiate everything anyway. So the original deal could still be pointless, but speaking of the record, let's.

Tracked last fall [1989] at The Plant in Sausalito and completed in January at London Bridge, Apple is a huge album in sound, style and content. Wood paints poignant lyrical pictures within Love Bone's distinctive instrumental fabric. Produced in connection with local session star Terry Date and mixed by a Brit, Wood tells us about the finished product.

> *"It's a really weird album because when we finished it with Terry it sounded completely different than what it sounds like now because a guy by the name of Tim Palmer got to mix it. He's a guy from England, I've never met, who worked with*

MUSIC BIZ

By David Sterling & Wendy Cook

Music business people have been converging all over the Northwest in the last few weeks. NAMA, the Northwest Area Music Association, recently presented a very successful Music Business Conference that attracted major and independent label representatives to Seattle.

During the three-day event, over a thousand music people from all over the region assembled at the Washington State Convention & Trade Center to shmooz, discuss current topics, and learn about many aspects of the industry. The keynote address was given by Ron Fell, publisher of the Gavin Report, who discussed the need for music people to create new and innovative music markets. There were several discussions concerning promotion and publicity, songwriting, legal negotiations, A&R, music publishing, and the censorship issue. Major record labels such as Warner Brothers, Sire, A&M, Hollywood, Columbia, SBK, Island, and Capitol were in attendance. It was a great opportunity to meet with these representatives, exchange ideas, and to learn new and innovative techniques to promote your musical career.

With the success of the conference behind them, NAMA is now preparing for the Third Annual Northwest Area Music Awards to be held Monday, April 9 at the Moore Theatre in downtown Seattle at 7:00 pm.

This is the evening where major stars from the Northwest and music industry professionals get together to celebrate and acknowledge the best of the Northwest. This year's show promises to be the best ever, with performances by Forced Entry, High Performance, The Olson Brothers, Ginny Reilly, Jr. Cadillac, Brydge, the Carlton Jackson Band, and the Hall of Fame showcase by the Viceroys. Special appearances will be made by all of this year's Hall of Fame inductees, which include Heart, Paul Revere, The Ventures, The Frantics, and The Dynamics with Jimmy Hanna. This year's non-performance inductee is Lou Lavinthal, and Pat O'Day will be inducted as the foremost radio personality.

You don't want to miss this night if you have anything to do with the music scene in the Northwest. Tickets are $10 and are available through Ticketmaster. For more information contact NAMA at (206) 525-5322. ♥♥♥

David Sterling is Vice President of International Marketing and Wendy Cook is Director of Publishing/A&R for Northwest International Entertainment, Inc.

MOTHER LOVE BONE

Cont. From Page 5

I asked Wood about the reputed seven album, quarter million deal. "I don't really know the whole logistics of it. I know we got signed for $250,000 and seven albums, and I know now that we're broke and that we could also get dropped at any point." He added that depending on the success of this release they could renegotiate everything anyway so the original deal could still be pointless. But speaking of the record, let's.

Recorded last fall at The Plant in Sausalito, and completed in January at London Bridge, Apple is a huge album in sound, style and content. Wood paints poignant lyrical pictures within Love Bone's distinctive instrumental fabric. Produced in connection with local session star Terry Date and mixed by a brit named Tim Palmer, Wood tells us about the finished product. "It's a really weird album because when we finished it with Terry it sounded completely different than what it sounds like now because a guy by the name of Tim Palmer got to mix it. He's a guy from England, I've never met, who worked with Robert Plant's Now and Zen record and Tin Machine's album and he did an amazing mixing job on it. It sounded completely different. I don't know if Terry was very pleased - it was Terry's baby and he was like 'what did he do to my project' - but he made it really spacey. It sounds like I would have mixed it." Others were so glad to just have it completed finally after spending so much time and money that their opinions reflect almost relief. Gilmore on the final mix, "I don't know if I'm really happy with it. I'm satisfied. At first I thought, 'that's fine', I didn't care. Then I started listening to it, first time, I was 'whatever', second time I'm like 'I really don't dig it', now I'm thinkin' it's alright. It's not what..." I interject, "not the way you envisioned it?" "Ideally, no. But Tim Palmer was the one guy that we all agreed on without hesitation on anyone's part. He happened to be available, fine give it to him, let's do it. If we don't just go with this we're gonna end up monkeyfucking the thing until the fall of 1992."

They've spent a lot of time over this past year waiting, waiting for things to happen. As soon as this does then that will. Before their January show at Legends - just after Gilmore had cut his hair - I asked about how waiting and the anticipation was affecting them. Gilmore: "It's been pretty tedious lately. It's been a lot of waiting." Wood: "A lot of hurry up and wait." MB: "Is that what caused you to shave your hair Greg?" Gilmore: "Actually it might have had an effect on my hairdo." Wood: "Some of us are more anxious than others. Myself, I'm kind of really happy about this time we have right now before the tour starts, because I've got things to do as far as getting myself together. When we got back from Sausalito I went into rehab for 30 days. So I'm pleased to have time to feel a little more stable in the real world before we go out and assault. And then others of us are really chomping at the bit because it is a lot of sitting around." MB: "But that's really nothing new to you guys is it?" Gilmore: "No, signing, finding a producer, recording, can all take more time than you could possibly think. The one thing, I can say in our whole career so far, that happened on schedule was recording the EP, which pretty much went down on time like we had talked about it. I think we even started on it before we were signed. But then we waited for the EP to come out, we waited to go on tour, we started to look for a producer for the LP before the tour of the EP, before the release of the EP." Wood: "We did that real cheaply and real fast - in like five days. Now it sounds like we recorded it in five days." MB: "So is the fact that you recorded Shine in five days and then spent over three months on Apple going to be pretty noticable?" I think you will find that, yes, definately." MB: "Okay!" Wood: "Without question!"

Apple has 13 songs totaling about an hour of music, including new mixes of two songs from Shine, Capricorn Sister (originally titled Mother Love Bone) and Crown of Thorns (minus Chloe Dancer). The other guitar ballad Stargazer and two piano ballads - Man of Golden Words and Gentle Groove - are prime examples of Wood's haunting lyrics and immense talent as a songwriter. While the whole album is compelling, these close glimpses are captivating. Stardog Champion and Captain Hi-Top provide rich, over-the-top anthems to sing along with, and Heartshine as well as This Is Shangrila are good tunes just to groove to. April 17 and April 30 have both come up as release dates, love rock awaits you people. Don't hesitate. Pick up Apple and give it a listen, and always remember...

love reigns supreme.

Hot Flashes

Street Romeo -

Some decent pop metal/ hard rock from STREET ROMEO. The music is reminiscent of most top 40 type metal/hard rock bands around today (just where do you draw the line on that anyway?). Guitarist Jeff Cameron has a few snazzy little leads during "Let Me Go" and the intro to "Want You Dead" and gives the band's sound a decent edge. The five songs are kind of predictable and although the lyrics get a little silly on songs like "Want You Dead" and "Broken Heart Avenue" the overall quality of the tape is all right.

♥♥♥

Slippin' Lizard -

Not bad. This four song tape by SLIPPIN' LIZARD is pretty cool. Vocalist Chris T. Hooker's at times raspy vocals blend well with the band's guitar driven metal sound and gives SLIPPIN' LIZARD a solid edge. They're not thrash, just solid metal. Songs like "Nothing" and "Bloody Murder" come across pretty well when played very loud, but the best tune is the last one, "Season of the Witch." I'll have to check these guys out live to see how good they really are.

♥♥♥

Mr. Yuk -
"Keep Out of Reach of Children"

Well now. In the mood for screeching and basically indecipherable lyrics with a punk sound? Songs with titles like "Public Restroom Nightmare," "Blue Balls," and "Beesting On My Head" sound compelling? They at least sound interesting to me. If so, then it's time for you to meet MR. YUK. If not, then keep it out of your reach as well as children.

Actually, this tape was a blast to listen to. The pseudo-ballad "Girls Fart" and the cover of "One Way Or Another" are gems. I suppose if I got really hammered and cranked this I'd understand it better.

Fun tape guys.

♥♥♥

Heaven's Gun -

I liked this tape from the first song. Actually I started on side two, but that's not that important. HEAVEN'S GUN has a strong hard rock sound with keyboard overlays that don't overpower the rock end of the sound. The songs are well-written and flow well. Of special note are "I'll Wait For You" and "Route To Paradise."

Good things will happen to HEAVEN'S GUN.

♥♥♥

Green Pajamas -
"Book of Hours" -
Green Monkey Records

Definitely a change o' pace for me, but I enjoyed it thoroughly. GREEN PAJAMAS is a good "alternative". The sound is quite experimentative with what are obviously varying influences with the mixing of guitars and keyboards as leads. At times perhaps a hint of later Beatles and maybe even some early 80s pop. It seems to work well as a mix, whatever it is. Lyrically, the songs are quite interesting and seem to be well thought out. My personal favorite would have to be "The Night Miss Sundby Died."

Overall, this tape is an "A" and a good Rock n' Roll recording.

♥♥♥

Leonard The Dog
"Day By Day" -
Recovery Records

Good Rock n' Roll. LEONARD THE DOG's "Day By Day" is a good mix of various styles of rock. The band doesn't seem to be scared to mix in some metal guitar and some reggae rhythms like in the song "Sea of Life," which is my favorite, for their sound. Although this type of a mix could have had them falling flat on their face, they seem to pull it off. It's a very professional recording and the production is clean.

An interesting album with a good message in regards to abuse and recovery. Fortunately, it's not pounded into you, but the message is strong and is allowed to speak for itself.

♥♥♥

Tape Reviews
By Jeff Lageson

> *Robert Plant's Now And Zen record and Tin Machine's album and he did an amazing mixing job on it. It sounds completely different." "I don't know if Terry was very pleased. It was Terry's baby and he was like, 'what did he do to my project?' But he made it really spacey. It sounds like if I would have mixed it."*

Others were so glad to just have it completed [finally!] after spending so much time and money that their opinions reflect... almost relief.

Gilmore opines on the final mix,

> *"I don't know if I'm really happy with it. I'm satisfied. At first I thought, 'that's fine', I didn't care. Then I started listening to it. First time, I was 'whatever'. Second time, I'm like, 'I really don't dig it'. Now I'm thinkin' it's alright. It's not what..."*

I interject,

> *"Not the way you envisioned it?"*

> *"Ideally, no. But Tim Palmer was the one guy that we all agreed on without hesitation on anyone's part. He happened to be available, fine give it to him, let's do it. If we don't just go with this, we're gonna end up monkeyfucking the thing until the fall of 1992."*

They've spent a lot of time over this past year waiting, waiting, waiting for things to happen. As soon as *this* does, then *that* will.

Before their January show at Legends - just after Gilmore had cut his hair - I asked about how waiting and the anticipation was affecting them.

Gilmore: "It's been pretty tedious lately. It's been a lot of waiting."

Wood: "A lot of hurry up and wait."

Browning: "Is that what caused you to shave your head, Greg?"

Gilmore: "Actually, it might have had an effect on my hairdo!"

Wood: "Some of us are more anxious than others. Myself, I'm kind of really happy about this time we have right now before the tour starts, because I've got things to do as far as getting myself together. When we got back from Sausalito I went into rehab for thirty days, so I'm pleased to have time to feel a little more stable in the real world before we go out and assault. Then, others of us are really chomping at the bit because it is a lot of sitting around."

Browning: "But that's really nothing new to you guys is it?"

Gilmore: "No, signing, finding a producer, recording can all take more time than you could possibly think. The one thing, I can say in our whole career so far, that happened on schedule was recording the EP, which pretty much went down on time like we had talked about it. I think we even started on it before we were signed. But then we waited for the EP to come out, we waited to go on tour, we started to look for a producer for the LP before the tour of the EP, before the release of the EP."

Wood: "We did that real cheaply and real fast, in like, five days. Now it sounds like we recorded it in five days."

Browning: "So is the fact that you recorded ***Shine*** *in five days and then spent over three months on Apple going to be pretty noticeable?"*

Wood: "I think you will find that, yes, definitely."

Browning: "Okay!"

Wood: "Without question!"

Photo Credits
Karen Mason, Lance Mercer, Todd Hottell, Paul Hernandez Xana LaFuente, Kelly Curtis, James Bland, Mother Love Bone, and their archivist, Denny

City Heat
6

Apple has thirteen songs totaling about an hour of music, including new mixes of two songs from Shine, Capricorn Sister (originally titled *Mother Love Bone*) and Crown of Thorns (minus Chloe Dancer). The other guitar ballad, Stargazer, and two piano ballads (Man of Golden Words and Gentle Groove) are prime examples of Wood's haunting lyrics and immense talent as a songwriter. While the whole album is compelling, these close glimpses are completely captivating.

Stardog Champion and Captain Hi-Top provide rich, over-the-top anthems to sing along with as Heartshine and This Is Shangrila are good tunes to just groove to. April 17 and April 30 [1990] have both come up as release dates, love rock awaits you people.

Don't hesitate.

Pick up Apple and give it a listen, always remembering that...*love reigns supreme.*

80s/90s Seattle Alley Graffiti (by Jeff Ament)

Along with the ever-present show postering of wooden telephone poles within the city proper, the even-more urban cultural forms were also being experimented with, unabashedly, by rock bands with no noticeable kinship to the rap artists popularizing graffiti trends on the East Coast. This also elucidates the inclusiveness extended and creative abandon employed by Emerald City artists of that era. A true free-for-all!

A couple years later Pearl Jam enjoyed their own Aerosmith/Run DMC '90s reprise recording "Real Thing" with Cypress Hill for the mashup collection crafted for the soundtrack to the motion picture, **Judgement Night**.

First Avenue.

On the side of **ReBar**, Denny Way.

Andrew Wood Memorial – Tribute, City Heat

In Loving Memory of Andrew Wood

January 8, 1966 to March 19, 1990

1980 to 1987 was a highly creative period for Andy Wood in which he performed solo (billed as Landrew The Love Child) simultaneously fronting Malfunkshun and later, Lords Of The Wasteland.

From 1987 to 1990, Andy involved himself in the project we know as the band Mother Love Bone [a virtual extension of himself]. It was this vehicle that had begun to bring Andy the recognition and fame that his dreams assured him would come.

At 24, his talent had only begun to be tapped.

The band reflects;

> *"I just hope there are some other people out there that, you know, see what happened to him and hopefully realize that their pain is fleeting and the pain that they feel from it, you know, is over in a matter of days, but other people will be in pain for a lot longer and it's kind of a selfish thing. It's a real tragedy."*
>
> *-Bruce Fairweather*

> *"It's just like anybody else. Things get you stressed out, you go have a beer. Whatever. There's really not a whole lot of difference, other than one drug is instantly deadly and the other one isn't. They're both addictions."*
>
> *-Jeff Ament*

> *"Just check out what Andy had to say and think about it."*
>
> *-Greg Gilmore*

> *"There were so many things that he did that were so great and he had such a positive effect on so many people's lives with his attitude, that everything you could write or say is not really going to explain what he meant to us and to everyone who really knew him."*
>
> *-Stone Gossard*

"Lately there seems to be some people that are real concerned about who their fans are. That's a pet peeve of mine lately, musical discrimination of fans. We want everyone to come. We want Mudhoney fans and Talk's Cheap fans to come to our shows and love us!"

-Andy Wood
on the final conscious evening of his life, March 15, 1990

Memorial Photos: Paul Hernandez

1990 Northwest Area Music Association Music Business Conference. My first trade show with City Heat!

FALLING RAIN
PHOTO BY SHOT IN THE DARK

April 1990

Sunday	Monday	Tuesday	Wednesday	Thursday	Friday	Saturday
April Fool's Day Sleaze Room- The Flatulating Cosaks Chinese Junk Lounge- Harry Wang and One Hung Lo The G Spot-Muff 1	Winthrop Elks Club -Mike McGarrah and His Pan Flute (Somewhere My Love) The Beach Hut- Captain Hook and Crotch Itch 2	Smell the Glove Club-Nice and Stinky Open Aire Lounge- Jimmie Gas and the Windbreakers CH Bar - Bob Barr and Mega Studds 3	B.F.- Trixter,Blacken,Rag Doll 4	L.C.-Jangle Town,Scattering Way, My sisters Machine Parkers-Duffy Bishop B.S.- The Subdudes 5	Docs-The Royals B.S.-Electric Bonsai Band L.C.-Catalyst, Troubled Valentine, Fire Choir Parkers-Duffy 6	Doc Maynards-The Royals B.S.-Mary Chapin Carpenter L.C.-Unearth,Eratic Pace,Ingitor,Cyprus Parkers-Duffy 7
Riviera-Sarge, Angel7, Vigilance 8	Leslies-Faultline, Street Survivors, Advent Pier 70-Deuces Wild, X-Caliber,Uslord of Kings 9	Farside-Vicious Regress, Rag Doll,Witch Dokters Pier 70-Medusa,Fire Choir,Heir Apparent New World-Rockandy, 10	B.F.-Liquid Rainbow,Aarge,Catal yst B.S.-Mono Men,Girl Trouble, Marshmallow,Overco at 11	B.S.-Hot Tuna L.S.-Hell Trap,My Name,Sleeping Capsule 12	Noggins Classic Rock Cafe-The Rangehoods B.S.-Crazy Eights Docs-Duffy Bishop, L.S.-Sarge,Jagged Dagger,Kamrun Veil OK Hotel-My 13	Noggins-The Rangehoods B.S.-Crazy Eights Docs-Duffy Bishop L.S.-Island of Kings,X-Caliber,Ham mer Head 14
B.S.-Robin & Linda Williams & Ranch Romance Rivera-Witch Dokters, Gypsy Rose & The Front 15	Leslies-Childzplay,Pi stol Moon & Vigilance Meekers-RocKandy New World-Kry thru 22nd Pier 70-Hammerhead, 16	B.S.-Southern Soul Review Farside-Vicious Syacle, Johane Window, Deuces Wild Meekers-My Sisters Machine 17	B.S.-Garth Brooks B.F.-Vile Boogie, Retik, Vicious Regresss Meekers-Boy Toy 18	Parkers-The Rangehoods B.S.-Scott Lindemuth L.S.-The East &The West, Mad Mad Nomad, Son of Man 19	Parkers-The Rangehoods B.S.-Sundogs Docs-The Hawks L.S.-Condemmed, Vicious Rumors, Bitter End 20	Parkers-The Rangehoods B.S.-Hermeto Pascoal & Group Docs-The Hawks L.S.-Nu Desire, Gypsy Rose, Angel 21
Riviera- Dragon, Whiskey Fix, Vicious Rumors 22	Leslies- Rude Love, Jagged Dagger, Rocking Dogs Pier 70-Street Romeo,Toxx'l Rae,Catalyst 23	Farside-Lickity Split, Liquid Rainbow,Advent New World-Aurora thru 29th Pier 70-Childzplay,Pis 24	B.S.-Jonathan Richman B.F.-X-Caliber, Hammerhead, Faultline 25	L.S.-Street Romeo, Rockin Dogs, Topcat Dancer 26	Docs-The Rangehoods B.S.-Nancy Griffith L.S.-Maelstrom, Kaos,Coven Noggins-Duffy Bishop The Square-Out of the Blue 27	Docs-The Rangehoods B.S.-Rumors of the Big Wave L.S.-Talks Cheap, Whiskey Fix, War Babies Noggins-Duffy 28
B.S.-Negative Land Riviera- Street Survivors, Toxx'l Rae, Havanna Black 29	Leslies-Crystal Rain, X-Caliber, Hammerhead Pier 70-Lickity Split,Diamond Back, Cash R Jail 30					

Created with CalendarMaker™ by CE Software, 515-224-1995

BATHTUB GIN

By Linnea Freed

Their name conjures up images of Louisiana backwoods, coverall-wearing hillbilly bootleggers. Are they? No. Bathtub Gin hails from right here in the Pacific Northwest.

City Heat: "How did you get your name?"

Jeff Hiatt (guitar): "It's from the alcohol that was made during the prohibition. Don't know what it's made of. It's a conglomeration of a bunch of shit and it ends up being good. Sort of like us."

City Heat: "How would you describe your type of music? What are some song themes?"

John Reidt (vocals): "It's about my old man being a heroin addict, about sex, about problems, about good times, bad times, just times. Everything we sing about is all true life. We impose no fiction in our music at all. That's what the blues are about."

Bathtub Gin is a "basic rock n' roll" band with heavy blues influence. The Rolling Stones, Muddy Waters, AC/DC, Chuck Barry, and the Beatles are some influences. Bathtub Gin doesn't stick to a certain fixed style. They're influenced by variety. "If it's good, it's an influence."

City Heat: "Where did Bathtub Gin start in terms of ability?"

Hiatt: "We're all basically self-taught. Gary Jyrack (drums) played for jazz band in high school. Brian Martinez (guitar) started out on trumpet. Troy Hewitt (bass) began playing the sax. I learned how to play (guitar) from books."

Reidt: "I learned to sing from listening to AC/DC records."

Reidt used to play for Tramp Alley and Hiatt is formerly of Dead Flowers. Bathtub Gin formed when Dead Flowers fell apart and Tramp Alley decided "to put on make-up and wear skirts." So whoever was left over, still desired to play and refused to look like a fruit, got together to "just play the blues."

City Heat: "How serious is Bathtub Gin about their music/career?"

Hiatt: "We're very serious. At times we may be sarcastic in our attitude, but not in our music. We

City Heat 18

practice every day, however long it takes, until we're satisfied."

Reidt: "We look at practice as a state of mind. If you've got a good attitude, it will go good."

City Heat: "Tell me some of your long term goals?"

Hiatt: "We'd like to make some money. We're not obsessed with being super rock gods. We just want to be able to eat."

Reidt: "We're not greedy. We played the Iron Lords' (biker gang) twenty year reunion. We told ourselves before we started playing that the most important thing was to turn on older people as well as younger people. That's the main thing. It's one of the reasons why we chose music. We want to be respected. Respect in itself will do a lot for us."

City Heat: "Any tapes, working on anything?"

Reidt: "Too broke." (laughs) "We've been together five months, and I've noticed that the older audiences seem to groove on us harder than the younger audience. People with a bit of culture and taste enjoy us more."

Hiatt: "Most of the audiences who enjoy us are ones that look beyond an image. We don't really have one."

Reidt: "We plan on doing this for awhile. When we turn forty could we actually take ourselves seriously when we look into the mirror and see make-up and spiked hair? Look at John Lee Hooker man, he's been the same guy forever. He just puts on his hat and his blazer and he's ... godlike."

Hiatt: "We don't want to be predictable. We don't want someone to come to a show, then come to another one two weeks later and say 'I saw them two weeks ago, I know what they're gonna do.' 'Cause we won't do it."

Reidt: "My mood depends on the audience. If they're getting heavy into it and starting to sweat, I'll sweat even harder."

City Heat: "What do you think will be your key to success?"

Reidt: "Big smiles, having a good time. Mark my word, I dare you to come and watch us play and I dare you not to smile. At some point you're gonna crack a grin. There will be something to laugh about."

City Heat: "This April issue of City Heat is the 'love' issue. What would you like our readers to remember you by?"

Reidt: (pause) "I think the Beatles said it really, and that is 'all you need is love.' The bottom line is, there are so many assholes in this world that you got to counteract it with a good attitude.

Hiatt: "Two of our songs are about this kind of attitude, 'What She Wants' and 'Hit the Wine.' 'Hit the Wine' is about the love of a good time. Not get drunk and everything will be O.K. It's saying, don't worry whether things are good or bad. If they are bad, they'll eventually get better. Everyone should look on the bright side of things."

Reidt: "Music is an art form, it's not a con game. We play music from the innermost parts of our hearts and soul. It's not about how much money we can make, or how many friends or women we can get. It's what is within yourself."

Bathtub Gin wants to bring back that old feeling that swept the world when rock n' roll was born. They want to give their fans goosepimples and fainting spells in a sense, and they'll accomplish this through playing straight forward blusey rock. No make-up, skirts, butt-gripping leather or any sort of gimmick will shoot them to super stardom, they will earn it.

Bathtub Gin's ultimate goal is to eventually have a fully orchestrated band. In the future they'll be looking for female back-up singers, a blues piano player, a sax player, etc. Interested? Call or write any of the band members at: **Bathtub Gin 3614 S. 299th Place Auburn, Washington 98001 946-6887 ♥♥♥**

"Who loves Ya.." ...C.H.

QUALITY RECORDING
DOESNT HAVE TO COST
A FORTUNE!
NEW
TASCAM TRS-8 8-Trk 1/2" Reel to Reel • $75 Day/$150 Wk
NEW
TASCAM 32 2-Track 1/4" Reel to Reel • $50 Day/$100 Wk
TASACM 312 12-channel Rec./Mixer •$50 Day/$100 Wk
TASCAM M208 8-channel Rec./Mixer • $40 Day/$80 Wk
NEW
TASCAM PORTA 02 4-Track Cas. w/Mix • $35 Day/$40 Wk
TASCAM 202WR Dual Cassette Deck • $25 Day/$50Wk
TASCAM 102 Cassette Deck • $20 Day/$40 Wk
NEW
TASCAM CD40 Compact Disk Player • $30 Day/$60 Wk
PLAYBACK UNITS AVAILABLE
AMERICAN
MUSIC
RENTALS
CALL NOW TO RESERVE
BY PHONE
547-9609

Enjoy The Latest
Link eBook™
Exclusively On
amazonkindle
1990
Seattle's Music Scene
Distorts As 80's Glam Goes 90's Grunge
CITY HEAT
Seattle's Music Magazine
Rock
by Michael Edward Browning

HISTORIC ARTICLES & INTERVIEWS

FEATURING THESE SEATTLE BANDS

Andrew

Alias
Alice In Chains
Andrew Wood
Billy Idol
Breda
Dio
Faith No More
Fire Choir
Heart
Love/Hate
Mother Love Bone
Paisley Sin
Queensryche
Red Platinum
Sedated Souls
SGM
Soundgarden
War Babies

ALICE IN CHAINS

1990
JFMAMJJASOND

LOCAL DIRT

By J. Hollywood

Hello Music Lovers, hope you're enjoying the fine summer we're having!! The new hotspot for musician's and the like is Monday night at **New World** (formerly the China Chef). It's Open Mike Night and it's becoming more successful every week with some great jams from complete bands and just a quick assembling of the proper Guitarist, bassist, drummers and vocalist, it's a bash!!! Check it out!! The event is sponsored by Z-ROCK AM 1590. Also sponsored by Z-ROCK is the SOS (Sounds of Seattle) concert series at the **Mural Amphitheater**, Saturdays from 1:00-3:00 pm, it's a great setting for Rock 'n Roll (weather permitting). Bassist Ben Shepard has been added to Soundgardens line-up and after return from Europe they will join **DANZIG** for a six-week U.S. Tour. Ronny Munroc, former "Paladin" vocalist has joined former "Ray Gunn" bassist Jim Cooper & drummer Mike McNair and lead guitarist Rob Young. They call themselves **"LEGION"** and can be seen on the local circuit soon. **The Squirrels** have just finished recording the new CD titled "WHAT GIVES" and it's due out this fall. With sadness, we note that on June 17, 1990, Ben Sidles, drummer of **"CURIOUS NATURE"** died in a auto accident. On June 23 a memorial service was held at Swan Lake in Kenmore At a gathering of friends and family a tree was planted in his memory. A very warm-hearted, fun loving individual that touched many lives. He will be missed....That's the short but sweet local dirt this month, if you have any you'd like to share, drop a line to J. Hollywood, c/o City Heat. Also, stay clean, you'll be glad you did. ALOHA!!!! till next month.

CITY HEAT
An Aird Hooker Publication

Executive Publisher
Matthew Aird

Publisher
Robert E. Barr

Editor in Chief
Jeff Lageson

Associate Editor
Michael Browning

Account Executive
Stephen Watts

Contributing Writers
Katie McMillan
Jimmy St. Bitchin
Michelle Klossner
Andrea Long
David Sterling
Wendy Cook
Ron Lageson
Linnea Freed
Kristen Bordelon
J. Hollywood
Stephen Watts
Shay McGraw

Fashion Editor
A.R. Stuart

Photography
Charlie Hoselton
Karen Mason

Promotional Director
Kristen Bordelon

Graphic artist
Glen Mulvey

Concert Desk
Rita O'Harran

Distribution Manager
Ted Treichler

Computer Consultants
Doug Kammerer
Dan Stinson

CITY HEAT is published monthly at 929 SW 152nd St. Seattle, WA 98166. CITY HEAT accepts no responsibility for unsolicited materials. Subscriptions are available for $12/year U.S., $15/year first class or foreign. All inquiries please phone 206.242.3952

CITY HEAT MAGAZINE
JUNE 1990 • ISSUE 24

ALICE IN CHAINS

Life In The Chains Gang

"I dare you to try and make an interview out of this!" challenged one pretentious Sean Kinney. We accepted: *City Heat vs. Alice in Chains, today at The Central.*

-ROUND ONE

"Let's start this off right...BEER?!?!" Jerry Cantrell signals to the referee/bartender. We settle in our respective corners, attempting to get some background on these 'Four Stooges', better known as Alice in Chains. Layne Staley, vocalist, opens the round with the first punch. "Jerry (guitar) and I met, and then we met Mike Starr, (bass) and Sean (drums), thought we'd be neat together, we jammed, we all had neat hairdos, so we became a band, and now we're neat." (laughs)

That was 2-years ago. Since then, they have remained undefeated in their rise to the top of the local scene.

Signifying their success is their recent signing to the megalabel CBS Records. Already out is "We Die Young", Alice in Chains' current EP, paving the way for their still untitled LP, to be released in August.

-ROUND TWO

"BELCH!!! Ah...room for more beer..." Sean enthusiastically cries out.

"OK, OK," we urge the battle on, "now tell us about the album and your experience with California...please?!" (We are being pushed in the corner with rapid verbal kidney punches.)

ON SIGNING "We met a publisher at the Music Bank and he thought we were neat. He became an A&R guy with Columbia Records, he signed us, we made an album, and it will be out in August. It took two months to record and we did the basic tracks at London Bridge studios. Buy the record!!!" Sean interrupts, confused, "Wait a minute...I understood there would be no math in this questioning?!" (Yes, we're as puzzled as you are on that last comment...anyway...) Sean continues, "We'll be out on a promo tour soon for the EP, then we'll probably do a video, then the album will be released simultaneously with the video and hopefully we'll jump onto something bigger... with a live broadcast of me in the shower." (laughs)

ON CALIFORNIA "It was big! Big and sweaty. We stayed at the Oakwood Apts in Burbank. L.A. is full of poser pussies. The dorkiest person here is cooler than the coolest person in L.A. It was fun, though.

We got free tickets from Columbia to go to Disneyland, which was cool."

ROUND THREE

Layne briefly leaves the ring to retrieve a third pitcher, giving Jerry time to ponder life in California compared to his Seattle home. "We are from Seattle. We love Seattle. We aren't gonna move to fuckin' L.A. Seattle is really supportive to the music scene. KISW has been really supportive; KING 5 News, the papers. In L.A., you have to pay to play, and up here, everyone's willing to help you

ON NORTHWEST MUSIC "Our favorite Seattle bands are (besides us - ha, ha) Soundgarden, Nirvana, Forced Entry, Bitter End, Unearth, and Son of Man is our number one favorite. There's lots of good bands in Seattle, but we believe we have our own little part of the Seattle sound."

We jokingly question the origin of the Alice in Chains 'look'- (laughing) "It's called thrift store shopping; rehabilitative dressing. Stop drugs and look like shit anyway; look like you're on drugs.

4

up in. Frothy, frilly, occasionally studded. Spikes and arm bands and snakes around the neck."

-ROUND FOUR

With the sound of the bell/ clanking change and crumpled dollar bills hitting the table, Mike stumbles to the bar for the final pitcher. Fighting a losing battle, we press on, trying to continue the interview, with the hopelessness of Tyson in the tenth round, the fight is now in their hands.

ON THEIR FUTURE PLANS

Layne: "All my money blown on drugs, hookers, and Elvis memorabilia, and I hope to be playing the Vogue next year about this time." (laughs)

Sean: "Playing the Ballard Firehouse about a year from now, packing 'em in like sardines. Plus I have my solo project that'll be out in late December, Christmas release. Just hold on, just hold on..."

Jerry: "In five years time I plan to be on a high South American plateau with a small band of natives naked, and participating in a very weird sex ritual. Actually, this is serious: I plan on opening my own trout farm throughout the Northwest because that's basically the most fertile trout waters. Maybe some goat herding later on."

Mike: "Ditto."

I guess you could say we lost the fight, but we did come out of the ring with some knowledge gained about this band. They've come a long way since playing Caine Hall at the University of Washington. Alice in Chains has played all over the Northwest and California, and have opened for the Bullet Boys, Tora Tora, Bang Tango, Great White, and Tesla. Hoping to reach at least the status of these bands, Jerry commented on their goals. "We hope to reach Metallica status. Reach the point where we are comfortable with what we are doing musically, in video, and all press where we are all represented well."

So why should you buy this album and help them achieve this goal? As Jerry states emphatically, "Because our album is hotter, redder wetter, and faster than any other one.

Alice in Chains is a very good and hard-working band who are grateful to the many people who believe in their talent. They especially wanted to thank Dave Jerdan, the albums producer. If their album is as good as we've heard, it will be the fans thanking these guys.

Well, we were dared, we tried. Hope you understood, 'cause we didn't.

Oh, by the way, in case you were wondering how they got the name, Layne offered an explanation. "I made it up. I'm neat. I'm Layne the singer. Hi! I was bored and drunk. We have a cat named Alice and we chained it up and (bleeped) it vigorously. No, no, no... slice that last comment......

By Michele klossner &Andrea Long

5 CITY HEAT

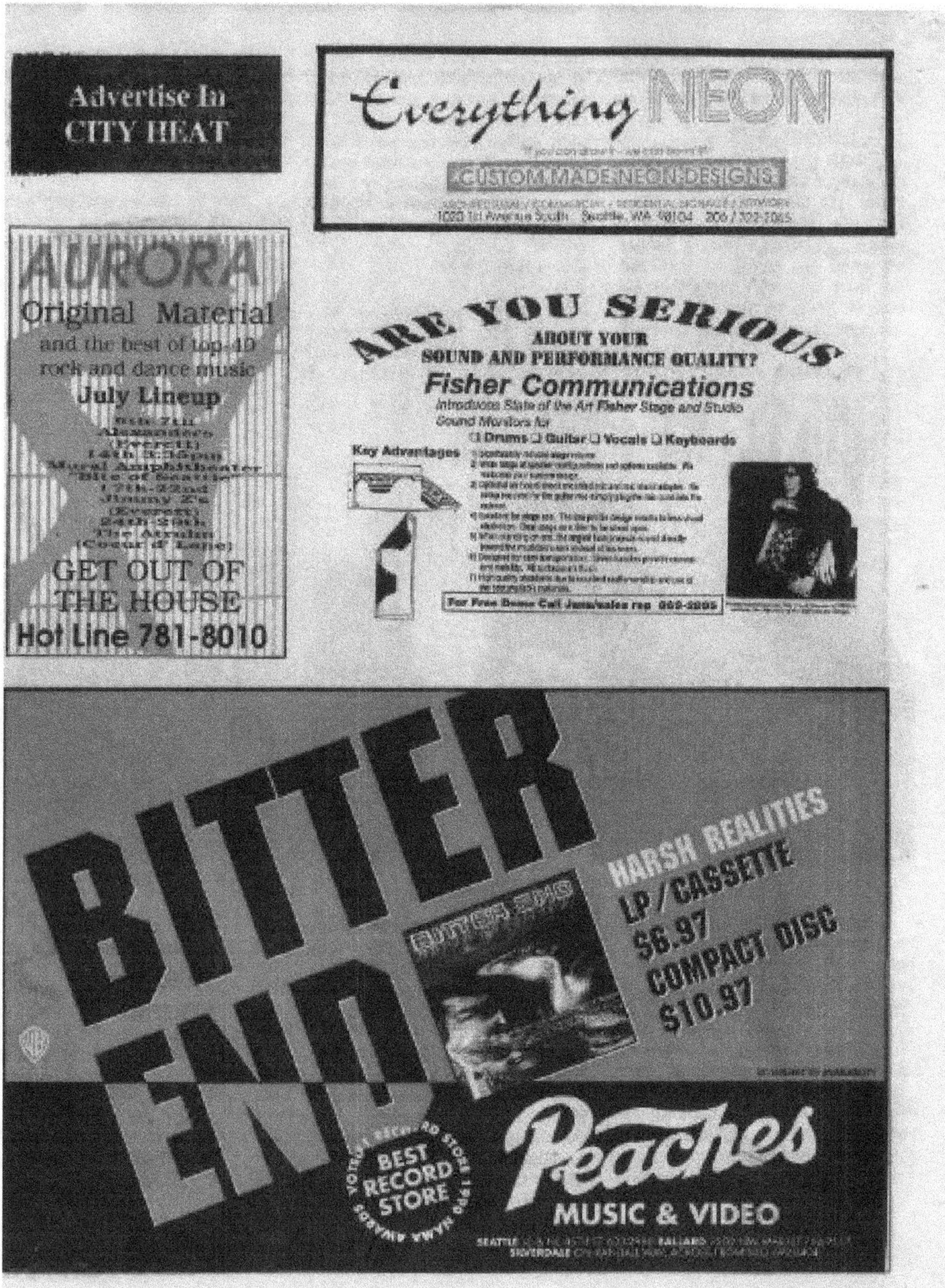
Advertise In
CITY HEAT
Everything NEON
CUSTOM MADE NEON DESIGNS
AURORA
Original Material
and the best of top-40
rock and dance music
July Lineup
GET OUT OF
THE HOUSE
Hot Line 781-8010
ARE YOU SERIOUS
ABOUT YOUR
SOUND AND PERFORMANCE QUALITY?
Fisher Communications
Introduces State of the Art Fisher Stage and Studio
Sound Monitors for
Drums Guitar Vocals Keyboards
Key Advantages
BITTER
END
HARSH REALITIES
LP / CASSETTE
$6.97
COMPACT DISC
$10.97
BEST
RECORD
STORE
Peaches
MUSIC & VIDEO

July 1990

Sunday	Monday	Tuesday	Wednesday	Thursday	Friday	Saturday
BFH: All ages Sunday: The Source, Acid Bride, & Flying Circus RIVIERA: Hurricane W/ Electric Angels & Von Dutch 1	CENTRAL: Caterwaul w/ Suicide Bride NEW WORLD CAFE: Open Mike Nite FARSIDE: Wheels & Tarman Gani 2	BFH: Boom Siang w/ Boy Blue & the Moon CENTRAL: Crop Dusters FARSIDE: All Fall Down, Spaz, & Skeptic Tank 3	HAPPY AND SAFE 4th TO ALL OF YOU!!!!!! CENTRAL: My Sister's Machine 4	BS: Christine Lakeland & Joe Louis Walker BFH: Luna Park & The Fuze CENTRAL: Kristen Barry & Tribal Therapy THE SQUARE ON YESLER: Sad/Happy & The Pickets 5	BS: Chaba Fadela & Cheb Sahraoui BFH: Curtis Salgado & the Stilettos CENTRAL: Young Fresh Fellows, Bedlam Rovers Sonya Hunter FARSIDE: The Chas White Band SQUARE ON YESLER: Jill Sobule SWAN CAFE: Monkey Business & Quigry Stick USB&G: The Defenders 6	BS: Richard Barone BFH: Curtis Salgado & the Stilettos FARSIDE: The Chas White Band SWAN CAFE: Monkey Business & Quigry Stick USB&G: The Defenders 7
RIVIERA: Scatter Brains with Childsplay & Rusty Puppets 8	FARSIDE: Mungers & Strange Cause for Gladness NEW WORLD CAFE: Open Mike Nite RIVIERA: New London 9	BS: Robyn Hitchcock BFH: Silent Night & Negative Earth FARSIDE: The Source RIVIERA: New London 10	BS: That Petrol Emotion FARSIDE: Blues Jam, All Blues Musicians Welcome RIVIERA: New London 11	BS: Long John Baldry & Kathy McDonald BFH: Sleepy LaBeef w/Splinter Party CENTRAL: Rabbit Chorus w/ Young Brians FARSIDE: THE Britin's RIVIERA: New London SQUARE ON YESLER: Violets are Blue 12	BS: Crazy Eights BFH: The Defenders CENTRAL: Splinter Party, Fighting Cocks & Life Ring FARSIDE: The Britin's RIVIERA: New London SWAN CAFE: Jr. Cadillac w/ Lilly Wilde USB&G: The Young Fresh Fellows 13	BS: Crazy Eights BFH: The Defenders CENTRAL: Skin Yard, Coffin Break & Victim's Family FARSIDE: The Britin's RIVIERA: New London SWAN CAFE: Dub Squad USB&G: The Young Fresh Fellows 14
BS: Naral Benefit: Peggy Platt's All Girl Comedy Revue BFH: Charlie Chiblin, Peter Broggs, & Roots Radics--reggae RIVIERA: Heir Apparent w/ Dragon & Advent 15	FARSIDE: Silent Night NEW WORLD CAFE: Open Mike Nite RIVIERA: Missile's End 16	BFH: All Fall Down w/ Crnix & Spaz CENTRAL: A Different Kitchen RIVIERA: Missile's End 17	BS: OK Hotel Benefit CENTRAL: Hard Rain w/ Native Messiah FARSIDE: Blues Jam (Al Welcome) RIVIERA: Missile's End 18	BS: Almighty Dread BFH: Edison Jones CENTRAL: Panic & Forced Entry FARSIDE: The Sorecs RIVIERA: Missile's End SQUARE ON YESLER: Jim Lyon, David, Mark Soittal 19	BS: Lockup, Psychetunkapus, Hungry Crocodiles BFH: Edison Jones CENTRAL: The Life, Kinetics & Rykir Descent FARSIDE: Duffy Bishop & the Rhythm Dogs RIVIERA: Missile's End SWAN CAFE: Seatown USB&G: Walkabouts 20	BS: Bochinche & Latin Expression BFH: Edison Jones CENTRAL: Hungry Crocodiles FARSIDE: Duffy Bishop & the Rhythm Dogs PARAMOUNT: Lyle Lovett RIVIERA: Missile's End SWAN CAFE: Seatown USB&G: Walkabouts 21
BS: Simon Shaheen BFH: All Age Sunday -- Herbivores RIVIERA: Osiris, Miss B. Haven, Cryn Shame 22	RIVIERA: Aurora 23	BFH: Billy Branch & The Sun of the Blues CENTRAL: All Fall Down FARSIDE: Tarman Gani RIVIERA: Aurora 24	BS: Cropdusters w/ Splinter Party CENTRAL: Spaz FARSIDE: Blue's Jam (All Welcome) RIVIERA: Aurora 25	BS: The Mick Taylor Band BFH: The Chas White Band w/ Rush Hour CENTRAL: Plan B w/ Mad Mad Nomad FARSIDE: The Source RIVIERA: Aurora SQUARE ON YESLER: Nora Michaels 26	BS: Dub Squad BFH: Hank Ballard & the Midnighters w/The Chas White Bnd CENTRAL: Tough Momma FARSIDE: Phaze With Visitors RIVIERA: Aurora SWAN CAFE: Rumors of the Big Wave USB&G: The Squirrels 27	BS: Doug Hamblin BFH: Hank Ballard & The Midnighters w/The Chas White Bnd CENTRAL: Tough Momma FARSIDE: Phaze with Visitors RIVIERA: Aurora SWAN CAFE: Rumors of the Big Wave USB&G: Crop Dusters 28
BS: Christine Lavin & The Bitchin Babes Tour RIVIERA: Apocrypha w/ Teacher's Pett & Rakkett 29	BS: Christine Lavin & The Bitchin Babes Tour RIVIERA: Roc Kandy 30	BS: Ranch Romance BFH: Budda's Beef CENTRAL: Silk Worm w/ Quigry Stick RIVIERA: Roc Kandy 31		Ballard Firehouse (BFH) Backstage (BS) Central Tavern Meakers Lake City Concert Hall (LCCH) Univ. Sports Bar & Grill (USBG) New World Restaurant (NWR&L) Riviera Pier 70 New Orleans Cafe Farside Tavern Leslie's The Swan Cafe		

Fire Choir - Feature, City Heat

Seattle is a finicky city. We know when we like something and aren't slow to tell you if we don't. In this grunge metropolis we like it mega dirty in the clubs or crystal clean on the charts.

Seattle is a finicky city. We know when we like something and aren't slow to tell you if we don't. In this grunge metropolis we like it mega dirty in the clubs or crystal clean on the charts. So what's a melodic metal unit do if they're not Queensryche or Heart? Work hard, that's what. Fire Choir has worked hard for the full twenty or so months they've been together and come to this conclusion about Seattle's grunge loving club crowd, "We're real fickle here. But one thing I can say about Seattle; if it's true, if it's intense if it's sincere and has conviction, it's gonna happen and people are going to love it. That's what's happened with us in Seattle. It's been very exciting because knowing that Seattle's like that I wasn't expecting this response. I was expecting to get categorized and put on a shelf, but it wasn't like that at all." says native bassist Richard Gibson.

This group of seasoned individuals came together as the stronger parts of two bands. After hearing the woes of this band weak in vocals, an influential New Yorker put them together with a guitarist and vocalist from down south who were suffering from a weak rhythm section. So Scott Heard from Arkansas and Jeff Adams of Memphis arrived in Seattle with two weeks on the clock to see what they could come up with. Anxieties ran high but Gibson, along with guitarist Kelly Gray and drummer Scott Corothers felt an immediate connection with the Southerners and that connection showed up in the original collaborations. However, the companies they had been working with stifled the band's ability by having them work on the material of other writers. After big promises of contracts and a couple of fruitless cross-country jaunts the band decided that they'd been stroked enough and would use their own material and disassociate themselves from the production company. True, the company had gotten them together, and out to New York for a month of recording, but having to survive on $5 per day (the subway cost $2, leaving $3 for food) and sleep in a showerless warehouse in Manhattan's red light district did seem to tax their patience.

FIRE CHOIR

"We're real fickle here. But one thing I can say about Seattle; if it's true, if it's intense if it's sincere and has conviction, it's gonna happen!"

Hell in Manhattan was just one item in a seemingly endless array of complications. For example a story from their last trip to NYC. Gibson, who from past experiences greatly dislikes planes, decides to make the journey by train and so the band sets off on the three day trek. In Haver, Montana Gibson spots an IGA and confirming a twenty minute layover, he makes a dash, finds a huge line, says 'No way' and returns to the train as it's pulling out. Within seven minutes, he's chartered a plane to be flown by a 60+ dentist in 50 m.p.h. cross winds to the next stop in Malta. At the Malta air strip he's picked up by the local sheriff who speeds him to the train station where he again boards the train to an ovation from the passengers (Gibson's recounting is far more humorous than space allows me.).

That particular trip to New York didn't yield what they'd hoped for, but did provide invaluable experience. And like the Haver grocery run fiasco, I believe everything will work out for these guys. Through their own persistence and hard work they'll eventually get what they want, a recording contract. Judging from the four song demo I heard, they've definitely got the talent necessary (as, I'm sure, anyone who's seen them live will agree). The only thing they seem to be lacking is the major league egos. But certainly there's enough of those already. Speaking for the Choir boys, Gibson relates, "This is something all of us feel, is that attitudes are completely counter-productive, across the board. They stifle your creativity. You're sinking to their (people with attitudes) level if that's where they're at, so they can judge you and pull you into their world because you (also) have an attitude. It's really silly. Instead of putting all this thought into your whole image or whatever, it's you are who you are, and just be who you are."

by Michael Browning

11 CITY HEAT

So what's a melodic metal unit do if they're not Queensryche or Heart?

Work hard, *that's what.*

Fire Choir has worked hard for the full twenty or so months they've been together and come to this conclusion about Seattle's grunge loving club crowd,

> *"We're real fickle here. But one thing I can say about Seattle; if it's true, if it's intense, if it's sincere and has conviction, it's gonna happen and people are going to love it! That's what's happened with us in Seattle. It's been very exciting because knowing that Seattle's like that I wasn't expecting this response. I was expecting to get categorized and put on a shelf, but it wasn't like that at all,"*

says native bassist, Richard Gibson.

This group of seasoned individuals came together as the stronger parts of two bands. After hearing the woes of this band weak in vocals, an influential New Yorker put them together with a guitarist and vocalist from down south who were suffering from a weak rhythm section.

So Scott Heard from Arkansas and Jeff Adams of Memphis arrived in Seattle with two weeks on the clock to see what they could come up with.

Anxieties ran high but Gibson, along with guitarist Kelly Gray [who later played guitar for Queensryche, produced Candlebox's multi-platinum debut and some other excellent shit around town] and drummer Scott Corothers felt an immediate connection with the Southerners and that connection showed up in the original collaborations.

However, the management companies they had been working with stifled the band's ability by having them work on the material of other writers. After big promises of contracts and a couple of fruitless cross-country jaunts the band decided that they'd been stroked enough and would use their own material and disassociate themselves from the production company.

True, the company had gotten them together, and out to New York for a month of recording, but having to survive on $5 per day (the subway cost $2, leaving $3 for food) and sleep in a shower-less warehouse in Manhattan's red fight district did seem to tax their patience.

Hell in Manhattan was just one item in a seemingly endless array of complications. For example, a story from their last trip to NYC: Gibson, who from past experiences greatly dislikes planes, decides to make the journey by train and so the band sets off on the three-day trek.

In Haver, Montana, Gibson spots an IGA and confirming a twenty-minute layover, he makes a dash, finds a huge line, says "no way" and returns to the train as it's pulling out. Within seven minutes, he's chartered a plane to be flown by a 60+ dentist, in 50+ mph cross winds to the next stop in Malta.

At the Malta airstrip he's picked up by the local sheriff who speeds him to the train station where he again boards the train, to an ovation from the other passengers (altho Gibson's recounting is far more humorous & lengthy than space allows me).

That particular trip to New York didn't yield what they'd hoped for, but did provide invaluable, experience. And like the Haver grocery run fiasco, I believe everything will work out for these guys.

Through their own persistence and hard work they'll eventually get what they want; a recording contract. Judging from the four-song demo I heard, they've definitely got the talent necessary (as, I'm sure, anyone who's seen them live will agree).

The only thing they seem to be lacking is the major league egos. But certainly, there are enough of those already.

Speaking for the Choir boys, Gibson relates,

> *"This is something all of us feel, is that attitudes are completely counter-productive, across the board. They stifle your creativity. You're sinking to their [people with attitudes] level if that's where they're at so they can judge you and pull you into their world because you (also) have an attitude. It's really silly. Instead of putting all this thought into your whole image or whatever, it's you are who you are, and just be who you are."*

Tape Reviews — Hot Flashes

Bitter End
Harsh Realities
Metal Blade Records

Harsh Realities does not sound like a debut album.

With intelligent and political lyrics "Just say no to Ronnie's wife / Just say yes to real life," thrashing guitars, and a driving beat Bitter End just ought to make a lot of head's turn throughout the metal world. If not, then their truly is no justice in this world. With Randy "super-producer" Burns at the helm in the studio (and playing a wee bit o' guitar on the side) the band's mature sound pounds out. The album contains songs from their previous demos along with a few new ones. The "old" tunes like *Meet Your Maker* and *Save Us* benefit from the re-recording, as well as the addition of ex-Mad Hatter axeman Russ Stefanovich. Matt Fox's vocals sound stronger than ever as well. Great debut gentlemen.**JL**

Sedated Souls
On A Sunday Afternoon
Naked Records

A nifty little 4 song release from Sedated Souls. All four songs, *You Take Me Away, Me Without You, I Feel For You,* and *Where Will I Find Myself* have the Sedated ones grinding it out. Yes, this is a short review. Yes, I like this tape. Still, the live Souls is the best Souls.**JL**

GWAR
Scumdogs of the Universe
Metal Blade Records

Somebody had to do it I guess. These guys have more than just gone over the top. With names like Beefcake the Mighty and song titles like *Love Surgery* and *Sick of You* its awfully hard to take these guys seriously. But, if you can wade through all the crap and the language its obvious that there is some talent there.**JL**

Bruce Dickinson
Tattooed Millionaire
Columbia Records

I like Bruce Dickinson. I liked his singing when he was with Samson, and of course his Maiden days have made listening to music euphoric for me. This is even better. *Tattooed Millionaire* is an incredible piece of artistic excellence. From the opening cut, *Son of a Gun* to the final chords of *No Lies*, this record grabs you by the balls and doesn't let go. It has the heavy sound you would expect, but he has found the right choruses that will have you singing to yourself at work. (Check out *Dive, Dive, Dive* and you'll know what I mean.) Shell out the ten bucks for this record, you won't be disappointed.**RL**

Flotsam and Jetsam
When the Storm Comes Down
MCA Records

NO POSERS ALLOWED! There should be a sticker on this record to warn pseudo-wimps rocker fans from having their little hair-sprayed brains blown out. This is power. Arizona's own Flotsam have proven themselves worthy of mention with the big boys of power thrash metal. *When the Storm Comes Down* is their third and best album to date. The musicianship is crisp and concise, and while the singing of front-man Eric A. K. gets on your nerves at times, he is still listenable. *October Thorns* is the heaviest (and in my opinion) the best song on the record. Flotsam and Jetsam, remember the name.**RL**

Paisley Sin
It's Not Just A Hobby...It's a Hassle

Listening to Z-Rock the other day, I was somewhat surprised to hear *The Secret* on their station. Then it occurred to me that the song rocks plenty for that format. Which brought me back to why was I surprised? I've had this tape for about a year now and I just finally realized how versatile Paisley is. From the denying *Ain't Nothin'* to the starry night feel of *Tribute* to the funky, tongue in cheek *This is Life*, back to the heavy *Out & Down*. This bass driven collection of tunes runs the gamut, and is a good reference point but nothing compared to the live Sin. However, it is a must for Seattle aficionados. Looking forward to their next release.**MB**

Breda

Breda, formerly Jinxx from Seattle, has a demo showing their mainstream pop-metal expertise. Very radio / MTV accessible. Having a namesake monecker is not all these guys have in common with the likes of Winger and Dokken. Except for the whining on Suicide Love, its a very nice collection of tunes any pre-pubescent girl would swoon over.**MB**

Paisley Sin - Vinyl, Tape & Laser, Hot Flashes, City Heat

Paisley Sin

It's Not Just A Hobby...It's a Hassle

Self-Released Tape

Listening to Z-Rock the other day, I was somewhat surprised to hear The Secret on their station. Then it occurred to me that the song rocks plenty for that format.

Which brought me back to, "why was I surprised?"

I've had this tape for about a year now and I just finally realized how versatile Paisley is.

From the denying *Ain't Nothin'* to the starry night feel of *Tribute* to the funky, tongue in cheek This Is The Life, back to the heavy *Out & Down*.

This bass-driven collection of tunes runs the musical gamut and is a good reference point; but nothing compared to the live 'Sin. However, it is a must for Seattle aficionados.

There's simply *No Way Out*.

Looking forward to their next release!

Breda – Vinyl, Tape & Laser, Hot Flashes, City Heat

Breda

Breda

Demo Tape

Breda, formerly Jinxx from Seattle, has a new demo showing their mainstream pop-metal expertise.

Very radio/MTV accessible. Having a namesake moniker is not all these guys have in common with the likes of Winger and Dokken.

Except for the incessant whining on *Suicidal Love*, it's a very nice collection of tunes any pre-pubescent metal girl would swoon over.

BONUS TRACKS: To have your own listen to Breda's 5-Song Demo tape, surf over and visit me at michaeledwardbrowning.com/breda-5-song-demo-1990

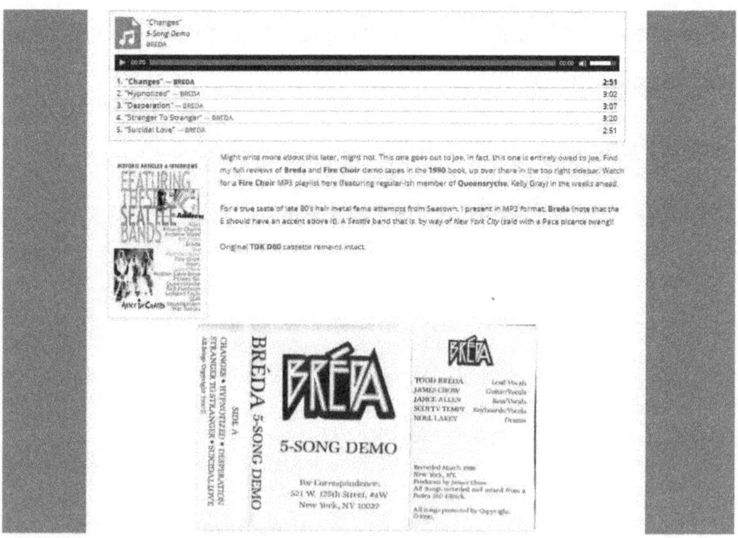

War Babies/SGM/Red Platinum – Show Reviews, Hot Flashes, City Heat

Heavy weekend.

Saturday the 16th and another deadly Central triple bill, notable Californians still in town from the previous night's peek at Chains on their home turf (not to mention the glimpse of Soundgarden's new bassist during their opening stint). They, along with somebody's mothers, added to an already widely diverse crowd.

The flyer said nine so sometime after ten began the "funkin' heavy sounds" of Red Platinum, which sounded far less funkin' than in days past. Could've been a phase. From where I sat, this night's set seemed pretty darn straightforward R & R.

Next, SGM played for us a rockin' set in which their new vocalist made good on their established material. It'll be interesting to see what new stuff they'll come up with together.

Then, sometime after midnight, War Babies hit the lights. Never having seen this band perform, I expected something of similar caliber to the two superb Seattle acts that preceded it.

You could say *that's what I bargained for.*

Needless to say, I got more.

From the first song they grabbed you much harder.

Brad Sinsel sounded great and I could even decipher a large amount of the lyrics. In short, they simply showed the cutting edge between signed and unsigned bands (just like Alice In Chains did the night before).

So goes another evening of world-class nightlife in Seattle's terminally trendy Pioneer Square.

Still, the only way to capture the essence of a truly tasty Central triple bill *is to be there.*

Hot Flashes

Show Reviews

WAR BABIES RED PLATINUM SGM

Heavy weekend. Saturday the 16th and another deadly Central triple bill, notable Californians still in town from the previous night's peek at Chains on their home turf (Not to mention the glimpse of Soundgarden's new bassist during their opening stint). They, along with somebody's mothers, added to an already widely diverse crowd. The flyer said nine so sometime after ten began the "funkin' heavy" sounds of Red Platinum, which sounded far less funkin' than in days past. Could've been a phase. This night's set seemed pretty darn straight forward R & R.

Next, SGM played for us a rockin' set in which their new vocalist made good on their established material. It'll be interesting to see what new stuff they'll come up with.

Then, sometime after midnight, War Babies hit the lights. Never having seen this band perform, I expected something of similar caliber to the two superb Seattle acts that preceded it. You could say that's what I bargained for. Needless to say, I got more.

From the first song they grabbed you much harder. Brad Sinsel sounded great and I could even decipher a large amount of the lyrics. In short, they simply showed the cutting edge between signed and unsigned bands (Just like Alice In Chains did the night before). So goes another evening of world class night life in the terminally trendy Pioneer Square. Still, the only way to capture the essence of a truly tasty Central triple bill is to be there."

by Michael Browning

IN CONCERT

Sinead O'Connor CONT FROM PAGE 16

anger reflected in her past work was still there but its now a healthier one; filled with passion, raw and untouched by the trappings of money and fame. If anything, Sinead seems a little older and wiser, equipped with a tongue-in-cheek sense of humor.

"Nothing Compares 2 U" brought the house down (I would have preferred hearing "Troy"). She dedicated "Last Day of Our Acquaintance" to all the females in the audience which got a loud response.

With success still a novelty to her, Sinead seemed overwhelmed by the audience's response. People were giving her flowers and she received a long standing ovation.

At one point she exclaimed happily, "You all must be mad!" She performed a Scottish ballad for her encore that brought a lull over the mesmerized audience. The crowd was so energized by her performance, people didn't want the show to end.

One of the things I admire most about Sinead is her ability to take the listener on an emotional rollercoaster. Her voice can lift you up so high and as quickly bring you to your knees as she wails, barely whispers and sings in defiance. Her music comes straight from the heart and is a welcome change from our highly commercialized world (I don't think you'll ever see her doing a Pepsi commercial.)

Sinead O'Connor is one artist who sounds better live than on vinyl and this show was one of the most powerful I've seen in a long while!

A.R. Stewart

22

HEY DUDE
ROCKWEAR
GO BEYOND THE ORDINARY...
Step into a new look at HEY DUDE!
T-SHIRTS
APPAREL
LEATHERS
HATS
JEWELRY
Look for our new store later this summer in Lynnwood!
(206) 784-0333 • 208 N 85th (1/2 block west of Greenwood Ave.)

1990
JFMAMJJASOND

LOCAL DIRT

By J. Hollywood

LOCAL DIRT/AUGUST

Joseph Lee Wood has been signed to a magnagement contract with the LA based Gottfried Management Agency. Gottfried also manages other major artists and has secured major label contracts for his clients in the past...We wish him the best! Z Rock AM 1590 is the sponsoring station for the 1990 Ill Will Games, August 4th at 7:00 in the Paramount Theater. Five hard rockin bands will perform and are bound to hurt some feelings. Some of the events include synchronized shredding, freestyle fopping and moshing for medals. ZRock is also broadcasting the Sounds of Seattle Summer Concert Series for the Mural Amphitheater each Saturday from 1-3pm. As you must know by ZROCK plays more local music than any other station and lots of bands like to show their appreciation,take San Prova for instance... They were playing a set at the KISW sponsored Mural stage for the Bite of Seattle when they decided to thank ZRock for the airplay, a very honorable gesture to say the least For some reason KISW didn't appreciate it. (.give credit where credit is due)

D.A.D. (Dollars Against Drugs) is holding it's 1st Annual Music Festival taking place Sept. 1st (Labor Day Weekend) at Cheney Stadium. if it sells out, they'll add a second show Sept. 2nd . Ticket prices are $12.50 advance and $15.00 day of show. Call ticketmaster for tickets.

Former Gypsy Rose members Rick Hoeye, Tony De Lisio, Duane Bakke , Dave Decker have finally decided on a name for their Rockin Quartet...Introducing "FANTASIA".

Applications for the Seattle Arts Commision's Individual Artists Programare now available at the S.A.C. office or call 6847171 for an application, deadline is Sept . 7 1990.

Fifth Angel has officially disbanded due to lack of labelsupport.

Last but not least Queensryche vocalist Geoff Tate tied the knot last month.

Thanks for your many letters and phone calls and if its loca and its dirtits for me J . Hollywood care of City Heat . Remember stay clean. Its the right thing to do.

CITY HEAT
An Aird Hooker Publication

Executive Publisher
Matthew Aird

Publisher
Robert E. Barr

Editor in Chief
Jeff Lageson

Associate Editor
Michael Browning

Account Executive
Stephen Watts

Contributing Writers
Katie McMillan
Jimmy St. Bitchin
Michelle Klossner
Andrea Long
David Sterling
Wendy Cook
Ron Lageson
Linnea Freed
Kristen Bordelon
J. Hollywood
Stephen Watts
Shay McGraw

Fashion Editor
A.R. Stuart

Photography
Charlie Hoselton
Karen Mason

Promotional Director
Kristen Bordelon

Graphic artist
Glen Mulvey

Concert Desk
Rita O'Harran

Distribution Manager
Ted Treichler

Computer Consultants
Doug Kammerer
Dan Stinson

CITY HEAT is published monthly at 929 SW 152nd St. Seattle, WA 98166. CITY HEAT accepts no responsibility for unsolicited materials. Subscriptions are available for $12/year U.S., $15/year first class or foreign. All inquiries please phone 206.242.3952

To our readers,

If you think that the Iranian government in their condemnation of Salman Rushdie or the Chinese government in their crackdown of protesters are the last bastions of repression left in our changing world, think again. That ugly "C" word (I refuse to say it because it disgusts me) has crept back into America and **2 Live Crew** aren't the only ones who will be feeling the heat if nothing is done. Another moral crusade against all of the arts (like the NEA), including music (arrests for purchasing albums and trials for **Judas Priest** lyrics), is being waged. You've read about it and you know about it so I won't patronize you with too many of the details. Let's just say that these people know what's RIGHT for us and apparently we don't. Fortunately, Seattle is a place where people care enough to speak up and stop it. I like to think people that pick up our magazine and other magazines of our genre give a damn. It's up to us, the music fans and fans of the arts to say, "No more!" Censorship (I went and said it anyway) is not what this country is about. If it was I wouldn't be able to write this editorial and we sure as hell wouldn't be able to print an independent magazine like we do.

Jeff Lageson,
Editor

CITY HEAT

MAGAZINE

JUNE 1990 • ISSUE 25

SOUNDGARDEN

COVER PHOTO KAREN MASON

3 CITY HEAT

The Seattle Sound 1990

To our readers,

If you think that the Iranian government in their condemnation of Salman Rushdie or the Chinese government in their crackdown of protesters are the last bastions of repression left in our changing world think again.

That ugly C word (I refuse to say it because it disgusts me) has crept back into America and 2 Live Crew aren't the only ones who will be feeling the heat if nothing is done. Another moral crusade against all of the arts (like the NEA) including music arrests for purchasing albums and trials for Judas Priest lyrics is being waged.

You've read about it and you know about it so I won't patronize you with too many of the details. Let's just say that these people know what's right for us and apparently we don't. Fortunately, Seattle is a place where people care enough to speak up and stop it. I like to think people that pick up our magazine and other magazines of our genre give a damn.

It's up to us, the music fans and fans of the arts to say, no more!

Censorship (I went and said it anyway) is not what this country is about. If it was, I wouldn't be able to write this editorial and we sure as hell wouldn't be able to print an independent magazine like we do.

Jeff Lageson

Editor

Soundgarden – Cover Story, City Heat

Soundgarden. Yeah, City Heat's got 'em!

Had to travel for it tho.

You think these guys would make it easy for Seattle's Music Magazine by granting an interview in Seattle?

No way!

So we motored down to Portland for their show with Alice In Chains at the Melody Lane Ballroom on July 25th. Okay, truth is we were stoked for the road trip and the killer double bill!

Getting dinner and a photo shoot behind them, we sat down with Kim, Chris and Ben to get the exclusive poop.

What's that?

Ben who, you say?

On their records, you know Hiro Yamamoto was playing bass. Then after the release of Louder Than Love you heard about Jason Everman dropping six in Nirvana to play four in Soundgarden.

Now, who's this Ben chap of which we speak?

Briefly, 21-year-old Ben Shepherd has lived and played on Bainbridge Island for the past 18 years. Some of you relics out there may remember him from the days of Gorilla Gardens and The Metropolis when he was in, what he termed, a melodic punk rock band called March Of Crimes. Laying low, he's since sang, played and wrote for a band (who shall remain nameless) that played a very few shows in island towns before its swift demise.

Then from out of his relative obscurity, he is suddenly an integral cog in the critically acclaimed machine that is Soundgarden. We asked Ben to tell us the whole story of his transformation into Soundgarden's *politically correct* bassist.

> *Ben Shepherd: "Well, I've known Kim for a while, so he hunted me down and asked me to try out."*
>
> *City Heat: "Then what?"*
>
> *Ben Shepherd: "Then they, ah.........they fucked up (laughter all around)."*
>
> *City Heat: "Like how?"*
>
> *Ben Shepherd: "They took the wrong bass player."*
>
> *Chris Cornell: "Actually I had a dream. Ben, did I tell you that? I had a dream I was in a room with your brother, apologizing to him for not choosing you in the first place. [Again addressing me] That was after we'd already chosen him."*

After Louder Than Love came out they held auditions for bass players. When Hiro decided to travel a different path, it left the band in a lurch with not-a-lot of time to spend deliberating over a replacement.

> *Ben Shepherd: "I practiced or jammed with them a couple of times, I didn't even know their songs worth a crap tho at all. But it was totally fun jamming with them. I hadn't jammed with anyone for a while and it was flattering as fuck."*

> *City Heat: "Then what happened? You came in, jammed about a week...."*

> *Ben Shepherd: "Not even a week, twice. Then Jason knew the songs better and they were in a really awkward bind at that time. They had the record out and needed to tour immediately, so they had to make a quick choice. So they chose Jason and the chemistry didn't work."*

By the end of the tour they'd made up their minds to give the job to Ben.

> *Chris Cornell: "We made the decision to play with Ben simultaneously with deciding that Jason wasn't the right guy."*

Although both players had auditioned at the same time last year, member replacement is seldom easy and far from an exact science.

> *Chris Cornell: "You can't predict from a few meetings exactly what someone's gonna be like and how they're going to interact with the band. Mainly musically, but in most ways, we just didn't click. It wasn't anything necessarily 'wrong' with Jason. Band chemistry is really fragile so you can't just make a choice and be one hundred percent correct."*

SOUNDGARDEN
Photos By Karen Mason
4

Soundgarden. Yeah! City Heat's got 'em. Had to travel for it tho. You think these guys would make it easy for Seattle's Music Magazine by giving an interview in Seattle? No way! So we motored down to Portland for their show with Alice in Chains at the Melody Lane Ballroom on July 25th.

Getting dinner and a photo shoot behind them, we sat down with Kim, Chris and Ben to get the exclusive poop. What's that? Ben who, you say? On their records you know Hiro Yamamoto was playing bass. Then after the release of **Louder Than Love** you heard about Jason Everman dropping six in Nirvana to play four in Soundgarden. Now, who's this Ben chap of which we speak?

Briefly, 21 year old Ben Shepherd has lived and played on Bainbridge Island for the past 18 years. Some of you relics out there may remember him from the days of Gorilla Gardens and the Metropolis when he was in, what he termed, a melodic punk rock band called March of Crimes. Laying low, he's since sang, played and wrote for a band (who shall remain nameless) that played a very few shows in island towns before its swift demise. Then, from out of his relative obscurity, he is suddenly an integral cog in the critically acclaimed machine that is Soundgarden. We asked Ben to tell us the whole story of his transformation into SG's 'politically correct' bassist.

Ben: "Well, I've known Kim for awhile, so he hunted me down and asked me to try out."

CH: "Then what?"

Ben: "Then they ah..........they fucked up." (laughter)

CH"Like how?"

Ben: "They took the wrong bass player."

Chris: "Actually I had a dream, Ben. Did I tell you that? had a dream that I was in a room with your brother, apologizing to him for not choosing you in the firstplace. That was after we'd already chosen him."

After the album came out they held auditions for bass players. When Hiro decided to travel a different path it left them in a lurch with not a lot of time to spend deliberating over a replacement.

Ben: "I practiced or jammed with them a couple of times, I didn't even know their songs worth a crap tho' at all. But it was totally fun jamming with them. I hadn't jammed with anyone for a while and it was flattering as fuck."

CH: "Then what happened? You came in, jammed about a week..."

Ben: "Not even a week, twice. Then Jason knew the songs better and they were in a really awkward bind at that time. They had the record out and they needed to tour immediately, so they had to make a quick choice. So they chose Jason and the chemistry didn't work."

At the end of the tour they'd made up their minds to give the job to Ben.

Chris: "We made the decision to play with Ben simultaneously with deciding that Jason wasn't the right guy."

Although both players had auditioned at the same time last year, member replacement is seldom easy and far from an exact science.

Chris: "You can't predict from a few meetings exactly what someone's gonna be like and how they're going to interact with the band. Mainly musically, but in most ways we just didn't click. It wasn't anything necessarily wrong with Jason. Band chemistry is really fragile and you can't just make a choice and be 100% correct."

CH: "So they got home and Kim called you up. What did he say to you, 'You're on the team?'"

Ben: "Actually Chris asked me. We were all looking at his little dog, hanging out at Chris' place and he said, 'Well, we were wondering what you'd think about playing with us.' I just looked at my shoes real quick, 'Fuck Yeah!'"

So they had a few days to practice and after playing a couple opening numbers for Alice at the Lake City Concert Hall were whisked off to Europe. Their first date there was at a festival in Roskilde, Denmark. Chris: "His first actual show with us was in front of about 5000 people."

Karen: "Was that a rush...first time going out?"

Ben: "Well, it was a rush knowing my bass was plugged in to a direct recording thing. That tripped me out 'cause they could hear every little sound."

Chris: "We were being recorded live for broadcast by some radio station over there."

After playing another festival and a few more dates they're back in the U.S. and working up new material together. The band as a whole seems to gel well and all are contributing to the new songs. They've got a song on the soundtrack for an upcoming movie and for those fortunate (intelligent?) enough to be members of Sub Pop's Single of the Month Club, a tasty surprise.

The 7-inch Featuring H.I.V. Baby and produced by their soundman, Stuart Hallerman, will be available only to those elite peoples. But that's not to say you may never find the tunes on a future full length. Cornell likens Shepherd's contribution (H.I.V. Baby) to a 90's feeling *"My Generation"*.

CH "What's on the the B side?"

Kim: *Room a Thousand Years Wide.*

Chris: "Yeah, *H.I.V. Baby* and A Room a Thousand Years wide are the names of the songs."

CH: "And did you play on both tracks?"

Ben: "Yeah."

Chris: "Actually We were deciding between three songs that were his, but we have trouble with that kind of thing. If somebody writes for a move or a single or something, a lot of times the songs will end up better than we'd expected and we want to save it for a record. So we kept juggling all these songs and couldn't decide what to use."

Next up is another (another? Yes another) U.S. leg of their Louder Than Love tour. After the tour is finally over, they'll be thinking about a new album which will be recorded either here in Seattle, Vancouver B.C. or San Francisco. (Just about anywhere but L.A. which they all agree is 'completely uninspiring').ꝏ

By Michael Browning
& Karen Mason

5

> *City Heat: "So they got home and Kim called you up?" What did he say to you, 'you're on the team'?"*

> *Ben Shepherd: "Actually Chris asked me. We were all looking at his little dog, hanging out at Chris' place and he said, 'Well, we were wondering what you'd think about playing with us?' I just looked at my shoes real quick, 'Fuck yeah!'"*

So they had a few days to practice and, after playing a couple opening numbers for Alice at the Lake City Concert Hall, were whisked off to Europe. The opening date of that tour happened to be the festival in Roskilde, Denmark.

> *Chris Cornell: "His first actual show with us was in front of about 5,000 people."*

> *Karen Mason: "Was that a rush, first time going out?"*

> *Ben Shepherd: "Well it was definitely a rush knowing my bass was plugged into a direct recording thing. That tripped me out 'cause they could hear every little sound."*

> *Chris Cornell: "We were being recorded for broadcast by some radio station over there."*

After playing another big festival and a few more club dates, they're back stateside and working up new material together. The band as a whole seems to gel well and all are contributing to the new songs. They've got a song [*Hands All Over*] on the soundtrack for an upcoming Michael Keaton movie

[Pacific Heights] and for those fortunate (intelligent?) enough to be members of Sub Pop's Single of the Month Club, a tasty surprise.

The seven-inch featuring *H.I.V. Baby* (produced by their sound man, Stuart Hallerman of Avast) will be available only to those elite peoples. But that's not to say you may never find the tunes on a future full-length. Cornell likens Shepherd's contribution (*H.I.V. Baby*) to a 90's feeling *My Generation*.

> *City Heat: "What's on the flip side?"*
>
> *Kim Thayil: "Room A Thousand Years Wide."*
>
> *City Heat: "So you wrote H.I.V. Baby and play on both tracks?"*
>
> *Ben Shepherd: "Yeah."*
>
> *Chris Cornell: "Actually we were deciding between three songs that were his, but we have trouble with that kind of thing. If somebody writes for a movie or a single or something, a lot of times the songs will end up better than we'd expected, and we want to save it for a record. So, we kept juggling all these songs and couldn't decide what to use."*

Next up is another (another? yes, another) U.S. leg supporting their Louder Than Love tour.

Once the tour is finally over, they'll be thinking about a new album which will be recorded either here in Seattle, Vancouver, B.C., or San Francisco.

Just about anywhere BUT Los Angeles [they had recorded Louder Than Love at the historic and fabled A&M Studios in Hollywood].

Which, they all agree and inform me, is 'completely uninspiring'.

Karen's Melody Ballroom stage pre-gig photo shoot spawned a shot that ultimately got used for the cover of, what I believe was, the last and final Soundgarden release for Sub Pop.

August 1990

Sunday	Monday	Tuesday	Wednesday	Thursday	Friday	Saturday
			1 BF San Prova Rocketts; Central Kristen Barry; Capping Day; Green Pajamas; Farside Leslie Byrd Trio; Riv Roc Kandy; Spinakers Young Fresh Fel ows; Meekers Boy Toy	**2** BF: Rangehoods; Heebie jeebies; Central: Group Therapy; Straylin' Streets; Far Side: Catalyst; USBG: Young Ghandie; Riv: Roc Kandy; BS:Diffy Bishop	**3** Central: Junior Cadallac; Farside: Edison Jones; USBG: Dogma Cypher; Liars Club; BS: Asleep at the Wheel	**4** Central: Razorbacks; Farside: Hit Men; BS: Lara lavi; Riv: Roc Kandy; Paramount: Bitter End; Dead Conspiracy; Sunshine; Talks Cheap; Six Gun Sal
5 BF: Sound & Fury; Broken Statues; BS: Tracy Moore album relesase party; Riv: LA Stad, Diamond Back, Neon Rain	**6** Farside: Tara's Love Child; East & West; Riv: Systems X; Meekers:Chain Reaction; BS: Boiled in lead	**7** Farside: Food Giant; Grey Fields Bobby; Crash Course; Central: Jesters of Chaos; Plug Uglies; BF: Nightshade; Dig City; Meekers: She died; Jangle town; bathtub Gin	**8** Farside: Street Romeo; Hard Margaret; Central: Bent Peter Rabbit; Sleep Capsule; BS: John Doe; Kimm Rogers; BF: Tairnan Gani; System 7; Meekers: Chain	**9** Farside: Final Nationl; Liquid Rainbow; Eternal Daze; Central: Silkworm; Other Peoples Children; Orphans Rea; USBG: Hard Rain; Sunshine; BF: Duffy Bishop	**10** Farside: Savey Brown & a Rock and Roll Band; Central: Flotsam & Jetsam w/ Prong; USBG: Green Pajamas; Capping Day; Gooch & the drifter; BS: Rumors of the Big Wave	**11** Farside: Savey Brown; Silent Affaif; USBG: Capping day; Medicine Show; Central: Royal Court o' China; My Sisters; Machine: Rhino Humpers; BS: Little Ceaser
12 Riv: Invade; Six Gun Sal: Jett City; Central: Doc Corbin Dart; Napalm Beach; BF: Delanies Midnight Caravan; Splinter party	**13** Farside: Mystery Train; Poverty Rockers; Asphalt Jam; Riv: Chain Reaction; Meekers:CO Ed	**14** Farside: Philocity; San Prova; Meekers: Unearth; Condemned No Avail	**15** Farside: Reckless X; Young Brains; Ramblers; Central: Gut Flower; Big Brown; House Homeland; BF: Canaan Elizabeth; East & West	**16** Farside: The Brittns; USBG: Jangletown; Acid Cats; Slime Circus; Central: Tough Mama; Wide Spread Pannic; BF: Edison Jones; Meekers: Co Ed; Swan Cafe: Modern Fabric; Laura Love;	**17** USBG: The Defenders; Backstage: The Tony Rice Unit; Farside: The Brittns; Riv.: Chain Reaction; Meekers: Co Ed; Electric Boys	**18** USBG: The Defenders; Backstage: The Tony Rice Unit; Farside: The Brittns; Riv.: Chain Reaction; Meekers: Co Ed; BF: Pat Travers Band; Catsltyst
19 Riv: Passion Fatal; Whisky Fixx; Tantera; BF: The Dumpil; Face to Face	**20** Farside: System 7; Meekers: The Fax	**21** Farside: Skankin Pickle; Meekers: Big City; Philocity; Jupiter	**22** Meekers: The Fax; Riv: Boy Toy	**23** Meekers: The Fax; Riv: Boy Toy; USBG: Heebee Jeebees	**24** Meekers: The Fax; Riv: Boy Toy; BS: Jerry Reed(From Smoky and the Bandit)	**25** Meekers: The Fax; Riv: Boy Toy; Central: L-7; Sunshine; Yummy Fur
26 Riv: Rakkett; Circus; Rockun' Dawgs; BS: Rory Block	**27** Riv: Aurora; Meekers: Roc Kandy	**28** Riv: Aurora; Meekers:Hall Of Flame; Wild Dogs; Machine	**29** Meekers: Roc Kandy; Riv: Aurora	**30** Meekers: Roc Kandy; Riv: Aurora; BF: Savatage ;Spread Eagle ;Trouble; Swan Cafe: Lokal Vision; BS: Duffy Bishop; Hard Rain	**31** Meekers: Roc Kancy; Riv: Aurora; BS: Tough Mama ; Zero	

Advertise In CITY HEAT

Everything NEON

CUSTOM MADE NEON DESIGNS

AURORA

Come see **AURORA** performing from their debut album **ON THE EDGE** to be released on CD and Cassette this month!

Call the **HOTLINE** at 781-8010 for details on where you can purchase this **HOT NEW RELEASE** and get their up to date performing schedule.

Aug. 27-Sept. 1 will be their last week in town for 9 WEEKS so come and see Aurora at the Riviera in Lynnwood for their send-off party.

FANTAZIA

August 6th Club Soda (B.C.)
w/ Son of Man

August 13th Pier 70
w/ Rakkett; 007

August 22nd Parkers
w/ Invader; Von Dutch

Sept. 2nd The Riviera
w/ Night Shade; Vicious Rumors

Sept. 16th The Riviera
w/ Tony MacAlpine; Teachers Pett

October 3rd Parkers
w/ Greg Howe; Sin City

Send $6.00 for tapes
$10.00 for T-Shirts
(+ $1 for postage)
To: FANTASIA
P.O. Box 4547
Kent, Wa 98032

For info call Brad Butler Promotions 526-8749

CITY HEAT 6

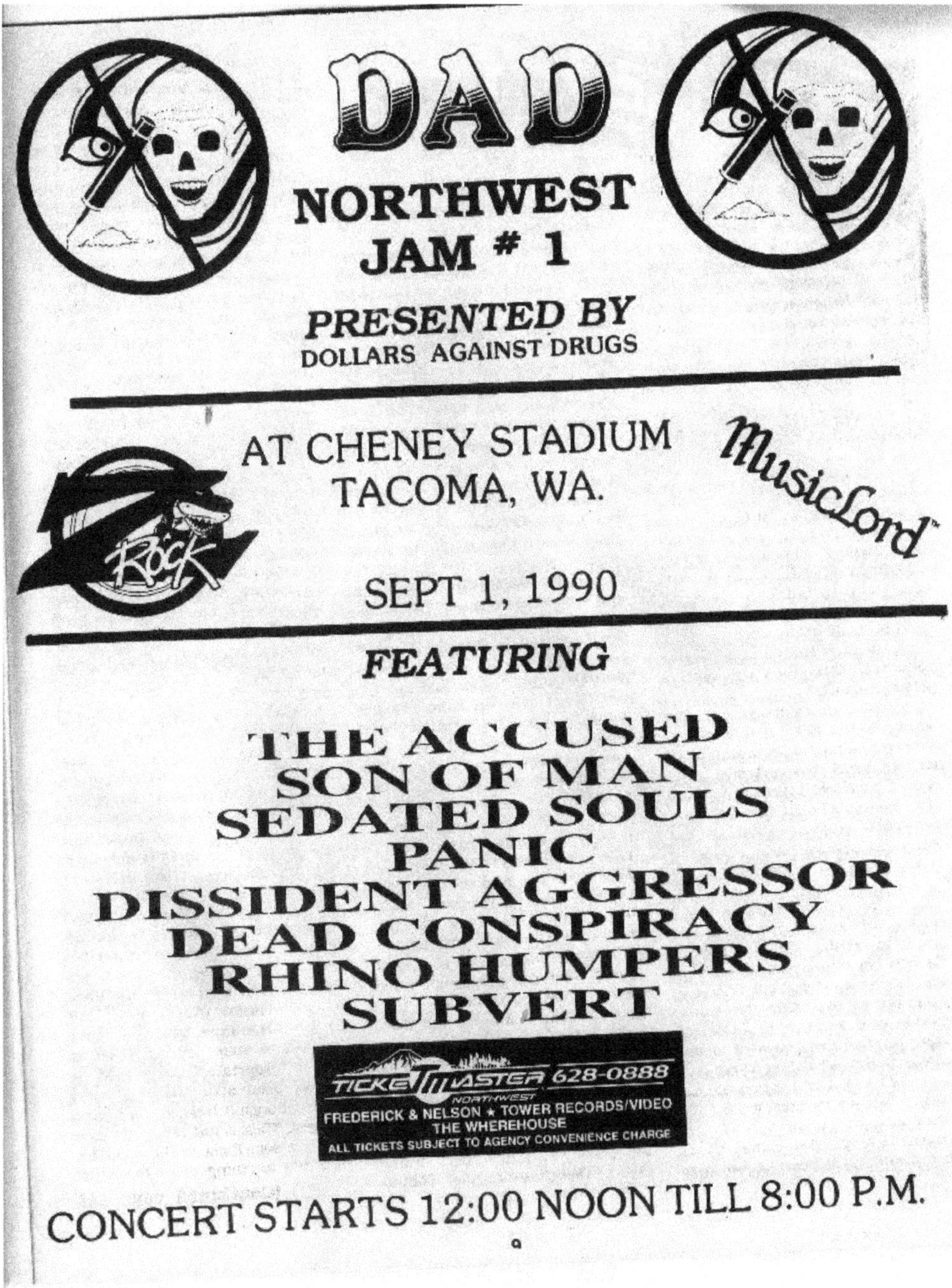
DAD
NORTHWEST
JAM # 1
PRESENTED BY
DOLLARS AGAINST DRUGS
AT CHENEY STADIUM
TACOMA, WA.
MusicLord
ROCK
SEPT 1, 1990
FEATURING
THE ACCUSED
SON OF MAN
SEDATED SOULS
PANIC
DISSIDENT AGGRESSOR
DEAD CONSPIRACY
RHINO HUMPERS
SUBVERT
TICKETMASTER 628-0888
NORTHWEST
FREDERICK & NELSON ★ TOWER RECORDS/VIDEO
THE WHEREHOUSE
ALL TICKETS SUBJECT TO AGENCY CONVENIENCE CHARGE
CONCERT STARTS 12:00 NOON TILL 8:00 P.M.

city fashion

ARENA '90

Saturday, July 21, 1990, marked a special night in Seattle. Perhaps you were there, and if not, make sure you are next year. Seattle celebrated its First Annual Multimedia Fashion Show ("ARENA") featuring local designers and stores.

Backed by the vision and drive of Jason Harler, ARENA is "designed to promote and support Northwest independent fashion designers." Jason feels "the arts are under attack these days, in more ways than one. To support these artists, designers and craftspeople is what I'm doing with projects like ARENA." His goal is to "help creative minds succeed."

Complete with crotch-grabbing, flesh-flashing, vogueing, cross-dressing and an almost anything goes attitude in the air, the designers strutted their stuff before a large, appreciative crowd.

So what's going on in Seattle couture? Skin! And lots of it!

What does this breast fest mean? Liberation? Provocation? Could it be we are growing up and realizing the human body is a work of art — not a possession or object? Or maybe it was the night to get funky and shed our second skin — who knows? It was refreshing to see both men and women doing it.

Fast Forward: opened the show with beaded bustiers that got everyone's attention, followed by body conscious garb in stretch cotton and lycra, versatile styles that can be worn around the clock. Fast Forward carries only local designers - hats, clothing, objects d'art, jewelry and shoes, to name a few. It really is showcase of Seattle's creative talent - stop in and visit Jason there!

Betsey Johnson:, new to Seattle, showed her whimsical style that has made her a fashion icon to the youth movement. Betsey's hot on the plaid binge with a Victorian influence dominating her fall line. Petticoats (a' la Little House on the Prairie), split skirts, ruffles and flowers are big here. Mixed with skull emblems, crushed velvet and crucifixes, Betsey brings together innocence with street styles,making a fashion statement with contradiction. She blends the light side of our personality with the dark to create a balance in style.

Fantasy UnLtd.: got the audience revved up as the models paraded inleather apparatus. Chaps with butt cut out, busties, biker jackets & thigh high boots, etc. — a sheer delight for you hard core cow fans. These fashions aren't for the faint of heart, ya gotta have an attitude (a few whips and chains would be good also). Sequined mini dresses that sculpt the body in bright crayon colors lit the runway as the models bumped and grinded. Fantasy managed to raise a few eyebrows as well as our blood pressure.

The Cramp "Change Your Attitude" was their anthem for the show as Brian Norton, designer, gave us a look at the future of fashion. Gold and silver lame' are translated to the 90s with a twist. Biker shorts are given a new look when done in sequins, topped with a matching baseball cap - very mod. On the polar end, Brian ref lects on the Golden Age of Hollywood . Garbo and Dietrich, glamour defined, with their cool and sophisticated manner is seen in his clothes . A svelte Jacket com-

Fashion by Basic

CITY HEAT 16

bined with a sheer ankle-dusting skirt whispers class.

Basic: An alternative to the fashion norm, Basic flirted with our sexual boundaries sending male models down the runway decked out in bustiers, bloomers and dresses. A real gender bender feel reigned supreme as the frocked models boogied to "That's the Way (Uh, Uh) I Like It", a fashion and disco inferno ignited! The favorite short subject of the 60s, hot-pants, are resurrected and worn this time around by men at Basic. So guys if you got it, flaunt it ! The Mother Earth motif is celebrated with SAVE THE EARTH tees . The women' s foundation industry may never be the same — guys can now cross their heart if they so desire.

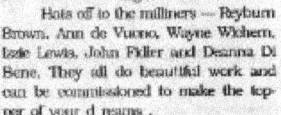

Fashion by Zoe

Grimalkin: Accompanied by a haunting melody, three Grimalkin muses floated down the runway, sprinkling rose petals, dressed in pastel silk and lace. Their clothing possesses a celestial quality that is subdued yet powerful. "Archaic designs for the curious minds," Grimalkin offers a cerebral and historical viewpoint to fashion. In my opinion, theirs is a talent to watch.

The Designers: **Nomad**, designer Andrew Burkhardt produces elegant separates in warm, sun drenched colors. A minimalist, Nomad focuses on the 60s hipness showing A-line styles, sarong skirts and lots of chiffon. **Carrie Omegna** ,"fun designs for women;" concentrates on velvet, pleated silk, and fringe. Great for p.m. wear. **Paul Dunn for Munroe.** His philosophy is to bring "imaginative decadence" to fashion transcends the usual with sculpted jackets, leather pieced vests and lycra separates. **Holly Elizabeth Rice** has a serious lace fetish. H.E.R. specializes in hand dyed lycra, cotton and lace combos. Mini dresses, sexy midriffs and bolero jackets all hug the body and softly define curves. **Max Montell** has vintage overtones with a Bardot emphasis . A jacket and pant lace ensemble (minus undergarments) caught my eye. Bell bottom bottoms, pagoda sleeves and a flirty peplum was a real stunner. **Zoe** has a refreshing tongue-in-cheek humor . Clothing for the bold ones, she designs for those "who prefer flamboyance over practicality". She toys with our fashionability with her quirky sense of style. **Bradley Reed** a 60s influenced line with long bloomer pants, satin minis and tye dye. **Rebecca** focuses on sweet, drop waist dresses in vintage fabrics and trimmings. **Lunatix** kept in their usual form with cool separates in all colors that emphasize the anatomy. All of these designers can be found in the above stores and they do custom designing.

Hats off to the milliners — Reyburn Brown, Ann de Vuono, Wayne Wichern, Izzie Lewis, John Fidler and Deanna Di Bene. They all do beautiful work and can be commissioned to make the topper of your d reams .

This article is just a small taste of what is going in Seattle's design community. Curious? Check it out!!!

A.R. Stewart

City Heat thanks Jason for all his hard work that made ARENA possible and looks forward to next year's show.

17 CITY HEAT

IT'S HAPPENING! OUR
GRAND
OPENING
IN LYNNWOOD
THIS AUGUST, WE'LL HAVE AN EXCITING NEW PLACE FOR YOU TO EXPLORE!
HEY DUDE ROCKWEAR OFFERS A NEW WAY TO EXPRESS YOURSELF WITH THE LATEST FASHIONS!
HEY DUDE
ROCKWEAR
(206) 784-0333

1990
JFMAMJJASOND

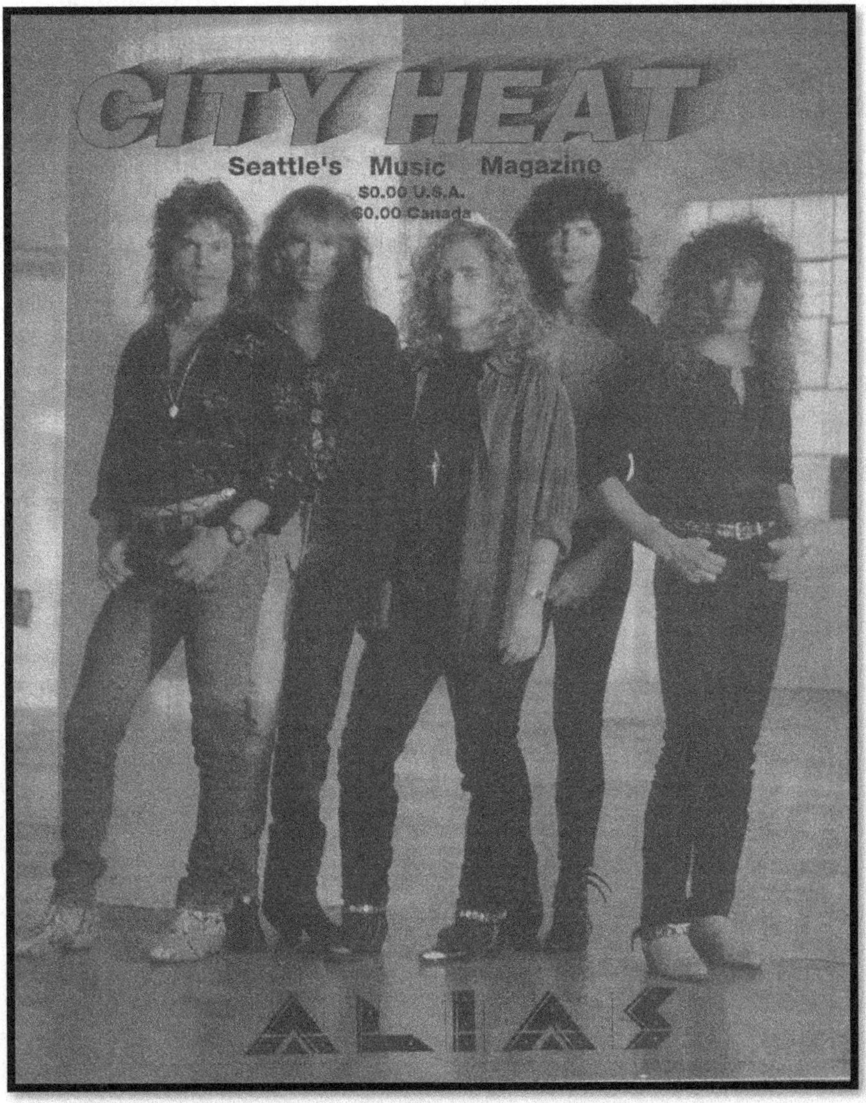

Alias - Cover Story, City Heat

You've definitely *heard* them on the radio, but it's not unusual if you haven't *heard of* them. Or, should I say, registered the name of this new 'supergroup'.

For simplicity sake, you could say that half the members from each of the bands Heart and Sheriff made this whole. But there's more to it than that.

Alias is the name for the current configuration of these seasoned chart veterans. You may have seen them treating home town crowds at the Backstage or Meekers or Pier 70 last month, but now founding Heart members Michael DeRosier (drums) Roger Fisher (guitar) and Steve Fossen (bass) along with Freddy Curci (vocals) and Steve DeMarchi (guitar) from the now defunct Sheriff are honing their show in Canadian clubs.

Before they left, City Heat arranged a pow-wow consisting of two Steves, two Mikes - and the occasional Karen.

City Heat: I was wondering how it felt to play a stage like Pier 70 after filling coliseums in the past?

Fossen: Great! You see, once you're a musician, you play where the stage is. And the way we look, or the way I look at it anyway, you're playing to one person at a time.

DeRosier: In fact when we left [Heart] a lot of the big bands back then were all going 'God it sure would be cool to play clubs again!' That was one of the last shows we did together, a club down in L.A. wasn't it?

Fossen: Yeah, The Whiskey.

City Heat: Touchy subject I could imagine, but was that an amicable parting?

Fossen: It was pretty much like a marriage, everyone was kind of just going... (yawns)... you know. Ugh. This isn't fun anymore.

City Heat: What's been going on since?

DeRosier: Orion the Hunter was a band I was in with Barry Goudreau, guitarist from Boston. And I was with Richard Marx for about 14 months or so.

ALIAS

By MICHAEL BROWNING

You've heard them, but it's not unusual if you haven't heard of them. For simplicity sake, you could say that half the members from each of the bands Heart and Sheriff made this whole. But there's more to it than that. Alias is the name for the current configuration of these seasoned chart veterans. You may have seen them treating home town crowds at the Backstage or Meekers or Pier 70 last month, but now founding Heart members Michael Derosier (drums) Roger Fisher (guitar) and Steve Fossen (bass) along with Freddy Curchi (vocals) and Steve DeMarchi (guitar) from the now defunct Sheriff are honing their show in Canadian clubs. Before they left, City Heat arranged a pow-wow consisting of two Steves, two Mikes and an occasional Karen.

CH: I was wondering how it felt to play a stage like Pier 70 after filling coliseums in the past?

FOSSEN: Great! You see, once you're a musician, you play where the stage is. And the way we look, or the way I look at it anyway, you're playing to one person at a time.

DEROSIER: In fact when we left (Heart) a lot of the big bands back then were all going 'God it sure would be cool to play clubs again.' That was one of the last shows we did together, a club down in L.A. wasn't it?

FOSSEN: Yeah, the Whiskey.

CH: Touchy subject I could imagine, but was that an amicable parting?

FOSSEN: It was pretty much like a marriage, everyone was kind of just going... (yawns) ... you know. Ugh. This isn't fun anymore.

CH: What's been going on since?

DEROSIER: Orion the Hunter was a band I was in with Barry Goodrow, guitartist from Boston. And I was with Richard Marx for about 14 months or so.

FOSSEN: I was in a Seattle-Tacoma group called Stripes for the first four years out of Heart and the past three years I've been kind of retired.

CH: Are you guys working jobs or just ...

FOSSEN: No, collecting royalties.

CH: Where do you guys make your home? Is it different for all of you?

FOSSEN: Mike, Roger and I live in Seattle.

DEMARCHI: Freddy and I are from Toronto originally, but American residents now. It's kind of a bi-coastal thing almost, North American.

FOSSEN: Our management company is based out of Los Angeles and I think if the band really hits it off big we'll probably move to Los Angeles.

DEROSIER: Not me. It will never happen. I'd never move down there.

CH: You'd just go on tour and keep your house here.

DEROSIER: Oh yeah, even though the traffic is a nightmare around here, I would never move down there. It just sucks. It's awful.

DEMARCHI: Steve and I would live there, split the difference and rehearse in San Francisco.

However, Los Angeles is the city that fostered this formation. Since the split of Sheriff in '85, Curchi and DeMarchi had been working as couriers by day and writing material by night. They bought a 16 track for the basement and recorded nearly twenty songs. Then a funny thing happened. A song that Sheriff had released in 1982 made an amazing return and went all the way to Billboard's top spot. "When I'm With You" gave the Canadians the renewed public interest that led to a development deal from EMI. They were in California working up new stuff when they crossed paths with session expert Mike DeRosier.

DEMARCHI: Ran into him down there, tossed around some ideas. That was about a year ago July.

CH: Then Mike brought Steve and Roger into the project?

FOSSEN: Mike had their tape and he said 'Hey, listen to this tape' and we grooved on it.

DEROSIER: Yeah, we all keep in touch anyway. Throughout the years we like to keep track, see what each other is doing and stuff. It was kind of an obvious choice really.

FOSSEN: We just listened to the music and appreciated the musicianship and songwriting and decided, 'let's give it a whirl.' Because...they did have a record contract.

CH: So now you've got a tour through Canada and the east coast headlining clubs, right?

DEMARCHI: 'Til September 29th. We start tomorrow.

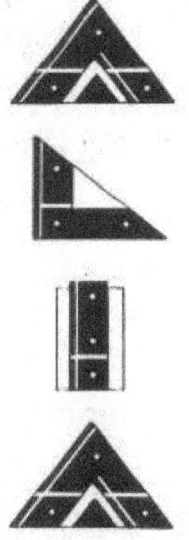

(The photographer butts in.)

MS. MASON: Is it just you or is there someone else?

FOSSEN: Just us.

DEROSIER: We might take Ann & Nancy with us as opener. No. This is really just to get tight. It's going to take a while for us to really just flow as a band on stage.

CH: Who came up with the name?

DEMARCHI: We had a ton of names and once we got together with Mike, Steve and Roger we just thought 'they used to be in Heart, we used to be in Sheriff and there it is!' We were going to call the band Use To Be, but it didn't have the same vibes.

DEMARCHI: But the first single was Haunted Heart.

CH: How's it doing?

DEMARCHI: Last Friday it was number 14 on Dial MTV.

CH: Any plans for the next single yet?

DEMARCHI: Oh yeah, it's coming out August 27.

DEROSIER: The video is already done.

(It's Nosy again.)

CH: On that note, I did notice a major badge-type emblem on the album cover.

DEMARCHI: Yeah, that's true, *alias* Sheriff.

FOSSEN: But it didn't have a heart.

CH: You didn't have the heart to put a heart on there.

MS. MASON: And what's the song?

DEMARCHI: More Than Words Can Say.

CH: Lots of mellow songs on this tape. It seems almost like youguys feel more comfortable or your stronger material is on the ballads. How do you feel about that?

DEROSIER:

Well, I'd never be able to survive in a band that was just to the floor all the time. Heart was real cool for me that way because you had a chance in the set to kind of relax a little bit and there was some place to go where you could kinda mellow out, play something nice and slow, and then shred again. And its the same thing with this band, for me anyway. A thrash band where you're sweatin' away, woods flyin' off the drums, strings are bustin' and guys are scrubbin' chords all night, that wouldn't be any fun for me.

CH: So you like ...

DEROSIER: I like ballads, yeah.

CH: And a balance?

DEROSIER: Yes, it's got to be balanced.

DEMARCHI: Freddy has such a great voice that ballads are ...

CH: A natch?

DEMARCHI: Yeah, it's a natural way for us to go.

It's a pretty safe bet as to the way Alias is going. Up the charts just like they've done before. Under a different name.

As the evening was winding down we wandered onto subjects political and Mr. Fossen, being the avid CITY HEAT reader he is, had this commentary on last month's To Our Readers: "I was reading that about censorship and I totally agree. I think these people have to get out of other people's lives. If they want censorship for their family in their life, that's fine, but don't censor other people's lives and what they want to see and want to do and want to hear. The main difference between Republicans and Democrats is that Democrats are willing to leave things up to the intelligence of the person to make a decision for themselves. But I've even heard President Bush say this, that without the freedom of choice you don't have freedom. I mean freedom is the freedom of choice. If they're going to tell us that we're the most free nation on earth, then we ought to be the most free nation on earth and they shouldn't limit freedom, limit choices.

Fossen: I was in a Seattle-Tacoma group called Stripes for the first four years out of Heart and the past three years I've been kind of retired.

City Heat: Are you guys working jobs or just...

Fossen: No, collecting royalties.

City Heat: Where do you guys make your home? Is it different for all of you?

Fossen: Mike, Roger and I live in Seattle.

DeMarchi: Freddy and I are from Toronto originally, but American residents now. It's kind of a bi-coastal thing almost. North American.

Fossen: Our management company is based out of Los Angeles and I think if the band really hits it off big we'll probably move to Los Angeles.

DeRosier: Not me. It will never happen. I'd never move down there.

City Heat: You'd just go on tour and keep your house here.

DeRosier: Oh yeah, even though the traffic is a nightmare around here, I would never move down there. It just sucks. It's awful.

DeMarchi: Steve and I would live there, split the difference and rehearse in San Francisco.

However, Los Angeles is the city that fostered this formation.

Since the split of Sheriff in '85, Curci and DeMarchi had been working as couriers by day and writing material by night. They bought a 16 track for the basement and recorded nearly twenty songs.

Then a funny thing happened. Like, weirdly funny.

A song that Sheriff had released in 1982 made an amazing return and went all the way to Billboard's top spot!

When I'm With You (for which Curci holds the Guinness World Record of Longest Note Held in a pop song, 30 seconds on the ending note) gave the Canadians the renewed public interest that led to a development deal from EMI.

They were in California working up new stuff when they crossed paths with session expert Mike DeRosier.

DeMarchi: Ran into him down there, tossed around some ideas. That was about a year ago, July.

City Heat: Then Mike brought Steve and Roger into the project?

Fossen: Mike had their tape and he said 'Hey, listen to this tape' and we grooved on it.

DeRosier: Yeah, we all keep in touch anyway. Throughout the years we like to keep track, see what each other is doing and stuff. It was kind of an obvious choice really.

Fossen: We just listened to the music and appreciated the musicianship and songwriting and decided, 'let's give it a whirl' because...they did have a record contract.

City Heat: So now you've got a tour through Canada and the east coast headlining clubs, right?

DeMarchi: 'Til September 29th. We start tomorrow.

(The photographer butts in.)

Ms. Mason: Is it just you or is there someone else?

Fossen: Just us.

DeRosier: We might take Ann & Nancy with us as opener. No. This is really just to get tight. It's going to take a while for us to really just flow as a band on stage.

City Heat: Who came up with the name?

DeMarchi: We had a ton of names and once we got together with Mike, Steve and Roger we just thought, 'they used to be in Heart, we used to be in Sheriff and there it is!' We were going to call the band <u>Use To Be</u>, but it didn't have the same vibe.

City Heat: On that note, I did notice a major badge-type emblem on the album cover.

DeMarchi: Yeah, that's true, alias Sheriff.

Fossen: But it didn't have a heart.

City Heat: You didn't have the heart to put a heart on there.

DeMarchi: But the first single was Haunted Heart.

City Heat: How's it doing?

DeMarchi: Last Friday it was number 14 on Dial MTV.

City Heat: Any plans for the next single yet?

DeMarchi: Oh yeah, it's coming out August 27.

DeRosier: The video is already done.

(It's Nosy again. Thanks, Karen, who would've guessed?)

Ms. Mason: And what's the song?

DeMarchi: More Than Words Can Say.

City Heat: Lots of mellow songs on this tape. It seems almost like you guys feel more comfortable or your stronger material is on the ballads. How do you feel about that?

DeRosier: Well, I'd never be able to survive in a band that was just to the floor all the time. Heart was real cool for me that way because you had a chance in the set to kind of relax a little bit and there was some place to go where you could kinda mellow out, play something nice and slow, and then shred again. And it's the same thing with this band, for me anyway. A thrash band where you're sweatin' away, woods flyin' off the drums, strings are bustin' and guys are scrubbin' chords all night, that wouldn't be any fun for me.

City Heat: So you like...

DeRosier: I like ballads, yeah.

City Heat: And a balance?

DeRosier: Yes, it's got to be balanced.

DeMarchi: Freddy has such a great voice that ballads are...

City Heat: A natch?

DeMarchi: Yeah, it's a natural way for us to go.

It's a pretty safe bet as to the direction this band is headed.

Up the charts, just like they've all done before, under a different name.

A pseudonym. An…

As the evening was winding down we wandered onto subjects political and Mr. Fossen, being the avid City Heat reader he is, had this commentary on last month's To Our Readers:

> *"I was reading [in City Heat] about censorship and I totally agree, I think these people have to get out of other people's lives. If they want censorship for their family in their life, that's fine, but don't censor other people's lives and what they want to see and want to do and want to hear. The main difference between Republicans and Democrats is that Democrats are willing to leave things up to the intelligence of the person to [decide] for themselves. But I've even heard President Bush say this, that without the freedom of choice you don't have freedom. I mean freedom is the freedom of choice. If they're going to tell us that we're the most free nation on earth, then we ought to and they shouldn't limit freedom, limit choices."*

That last line's the truth, no matter what label you want to put on it.

CITY HEAT

An Aird Hooker publication

Executive Publisher
Matthew Aird

Publisher
Robert E. Barr

Editor in Chief
Michael Browning

Associate Editor
Claude Flowers

Account Executive
Angela Metcalf

Contributing Writers
Katie McMillan
Jimmy St. Bitchin
Michelle Klossner
Andrea Long
David Sterling
Wendy Cook
Jana Skilingstead
Linnea Freed
Kristen Bordelon
J. Hollywoods
Kellee Francis
Shay McGraw

Fashion Editor
A.R. Stuart

Photography
Charlie Hoselton
Karen Mason

Graphic artist
Glen Mulvey

Concert Desk
Rita O'Harran

Distribution Manager
Ted Treichler

Computer Consultants
Doug Kammerer
Dan Stinson

CITY HEAT is published monthly at 929 SW 152nd St. Seattle, WA 98166. CITY HEAT accepts no responsibility for unsolicited materials. Subscriptions are available for $12/year U.S., $15/year first class or foreign. All inquiries please phone 206.242.3952

To our readers:

there are several issues of vital interest to artists and lovers of music alike that are currently up for public debate. Our population percentage has strong opinions that should be heard. Your opinions should be heard. Register to vote and when it's time, register your vote.

CITY HEAT MAGAZINE

September 1990 · ISSUE 26

Features

Departments

3 *CITY HEAT*

ALIAS

By MICHAEL BROWNING

You've heard them, but it's not unusual if you haven't heard of them. For simplicity sake, you could say that half the members from each of the bands Heart and Sheriff made this whole. But there's more to it than that. Alias is the name for the current configuration of these seasoned chart veterans. You may have seen them treating home town crowds at the Backstage or Meekers or Pier 70 last month, but now founding Heart members Michael Derosier (drums) Roger Fisher (guitar) and Steve Fossen (bass) along with Freddy Curchi (vocals) and Steve DeMarchi (guitar) from the now defunct Sheriff are honing their show in Canadian clubs. Before they left, City Heat arranged a pow-wow consisting of two Steves, two Mikes and an occasional Karen.

CH: I was wondering how it felt to play a stage like Pier 70 after filling coliseums in the past?

FOSSEN: Great! You see, once you're a musician, you play where the stage is. And the way we look, or the way I look at it anyway, you're playing to one person at a time.

DEROSIER: In fact when we left (Heart) a lot of the big bands back then were all going 'God it sure would be cool to play clubs again.' That was one of the last shows we did together, a club down in L.A. wasn't it?

FOSSEN: Yeah, the Whiskey.

CH: Touchy subject I could imagine, but was that an amicable parting?

FOSSEN: It was pretty much like a marriage, everyone was kind of just going ... (yawns) ... you know. Ugh. This isn't fun anymore.

CH: What's been going on since?

DEROSIER: Orion the Hunter was a band I was in with Barry Goodrow, guitarist from Boston. And I was with Richard Marx for about 14 months or so.

FOSSEN: I was in a Seattle-Tacoma group called Stripes for the first four years out of Heart and the past three years I've been kind of retired.

CH: Are you guys working jobs or just ...

FOSSEN: No, collecting royalties.

CH: Where do you guys make your home? Is it different for all of you?

FOSSEN: Mike, Roger and I live in Seattle.

DEMARCHI: Freddy and I are from Toronto originally, but American residents now. It's kind of a bi-coastal thing almost. North American.

FOSSEN: Our management company is based out of Los Angeles and I think if the band really hits it off big we'll probably move to Los Angeles.

DEROSIER: Not me. It will never happen. I'd never move down there.

CH: You'd just go on tour and keep your house here.

DEROSIER: Oh yeah, even though the traffic is a nightmare around here, I would never move down there. It just sucks. It's awful.

DEMARCHI: Steve and I would live there, split the difference and rehearse in San Francisco.

However, Los Angeles is the city that fostered this formation. Since the split of Sheriff in '85, Curchi and DeMarchi had been working as couriers by day and writing material by night. They bought a 16 track for the basement and recorded nearly twenty songs. Then a funny thing happened. A song that Sheriff had released in 1982 made an amazing return and went all the way to Billboard's top spot. "When I'm With You" gave the Canadians the renewed public interest that led to a development deal from EMI. They were in California working up new stuff when they crossed paths with session expert Mike DeRosier.

DEMARCHI: Ran into him down there, tossed around some ideas. That was about a year ago July.

CH: Then Mike brought Steve and Roger into the project?

FOSSEN: Mike had their tape and he said 'Hey, listen to this tape' and we grooved on it.

DEROSIER: Yeah, we all keep in touch anyway. Throughout the years we like to keep track, see what each other is doing and stuff. It was kind of an obvious choice really.

FOSSEN: We just listened to the music and appreciated the musicianship and songwriting and decided, 'let's give it a whirl.' Because...they <u>did</u> have a record contract.

CH: So now you've got a tour through Canada and the east coast headlining clubs, right?

DEMARCHI: 'Til September 29th. We start tomorrow.

(The photographer butts in.)

MS. MASON: Is it just you or is there someone else?

FOSSEN: Just us.

DEROSIER: We might take Ann & Nancy with us as opener. No. This is really just to get tight. It's going to

CITY HEAT 4

take a while for us to really just flow as a band on stage.

CH: Who came up with the name?

DEMARCHI: We had a ton of names and once we got together with Mike, Steve and Roger we just thought 'they used to be in Heart, we used to be in Sheriff and there it is!' We were going to call the band Use To Be, but it didn't have the same vibes.

DEMARCHI: But the first single was Haunted Heart.

CH: How's it doing?

DEMARCHI: Last Friday it was number 14 on Dial MTV.

CH: Any plans for the next single yet?

DEMARCHI: Oh yeah, it's coming out August 27.

DEROSIER: The video is already done.

(It's Nosy again.)

CH: On that note, I did notice a major badge-type emblem on the album cover.

DEMARCHI: Yeah, that's true, *alias* Sheriff.

FOSSEN: But it didn't have a heart.

CH: You didn't have the heart to put a heart on there.

MS. MASON: And what's the song?

DEMARCHI: More Than Words Can Say.

CH: Lots of mellow songs on this tape. It seems almost like youguys feel more comfortable or your stronger material is on the ballads. How do you feel about that?

DEROSIER:

Well, I'd never be able to survive in a band that was just to the floor all the time. Heart was real cool for me that way because you had a chance in the set to kind of relax a little bit and there was some place to go where you could kinda mellow out, play something nice and slow, and then shred again. And its the same thing with this band, for me anyway. A thrash band where you're sweatin' away, woods flyin' off the drums, strings are bustin' and guys are scrubbin' chords all night, that wouldn't be any fun for me.

CH: So you like ....

DEROSIER: I like ballads, yeah.

CH: And a balance?

DEROSIER: Yes, it's got to be balanced.

DEMARCHI: Freddy has such a great voice that ballads are ...

CH: A natch?

DEMARCHI: Yeah, it's a natural way for us to go.

It's a pretty safe bet as to the way Alias is going. Up the charts just like they've done before. Under a different name.

As the evening was winding down we wandered onto subjects political and Mr. Fossen, being the avid CITY HEAT reader he is, had this commentary on last month's To Our Readers: "I was reading that about censorship and I totally agree, I think these people have to get out of other people's lives. If they want censorship for their family in their life, that's fine, but don't censor other people's lives and what they want to see and want to do and want to hear. The main difference between Republicans and Democrats is that Democrats are willing to leave things up to the intelligence of the person to make a decision for themselves. But I've even heard President Bush say this, that without the freedom of choice you don't have freedom. I mean freedom is the freedom of choice. If they're going to tell us that we're the most free nation on earth, then we ought to be the most free nation on earth and they shouldn't limit freedom, limit choices.

5 *CITY HEAT*

SUBSCRIBE TO CITY HEAT

Everything NEON

"If you can draw it - we can bend it"

CUSTOM MADE NEON DESIGNS

ARCHITECTURAL / COMMERCIAL / RESIDENTIAL SIGNAGE / ARTWORK
1020 1st Avenue South Seattle, WA 98104 206/322-2065

LEATHERS

Largest Supply Leather Inventory on the West Coast

Name Brand U.S Made Cycle Jackets
Retail $179.95 Sale $129.95

Biker Jackets, Plain or Fringe
Retail $189.95 Sale $149.95

BENT BIKE

18327 Highway 99 Lynnwood 776-9157

4337 Auburn Wy N. Auburn 854-5605

AURORA

Auroras debut album

"on the edge"

ON SALE NOW

at a store near you

FIRE SALE

PA EQUIPMENT!

LIGHTING GEAR!

NO REASONABLE OFFER REFUSED!

The owner has singled out certain pieces of used gear.
Now he has his marshmallows ready.
We've got 30 days to sell it!

BUY IT OR WE BURN IT!

Full Scale DIMENSIONS
audio and lighting

16241 CLEVELAND ST • REDMOND • 883-4037

Hurry in and take advantage of some HOT deals! Anything left after September 29th is TOAST!

VISA

CITY HEAT 6

HAIR-RAISING.
Alice in Chains
Alice in Chains
FACELIFT
Including:
We Die Young
Sea Of Sorrow
It Ain't Like That
Real Thing
Man In The Box

When they played the Spud Goodman Show last April, Bothell's resident funk band the Hungry Crocodiles used a prop of Lionel Ritchie which vomited a froth of shaving cream. They originally planned for it to breathe fire, but resisted the idea for fear of setting the studio alight.

"Lionel gets brought out on special occasions," said Hungry Crocodiles vocalist Mike H. (the band keep their last names a secret). Gimmicks like this, hyperactive stage antics, and a bouncy bass and drum pulse all make, as Mike says, "Seeing us on a really good night a real one-on-one thing. We like to come across really tight onstage."

Onstage and off, Mike speaks forcefully and confidently. He's got the self-assurance to make his cocky homeboy image believable in concert. In person, however, he seems unrealisticly distant, cool, and businesslike. He's either a closet introvert or an obsessed James Dean fan.

Mike was born in Pittsburg, but relocated to Boulder, Colorado at age 4. Kiss songs were the background music of his childhood; they apparently inspired him to play bass, sing, and enter Hollywood's Musician's Institute of Technology. It was at M.I.T. that he first encountered bass guitarist Stuart ("Stool-D"), and guitarist Richard ("Rik-E-Lik"), two Bothell natives who were also at the college. Mike said, "I met these guys

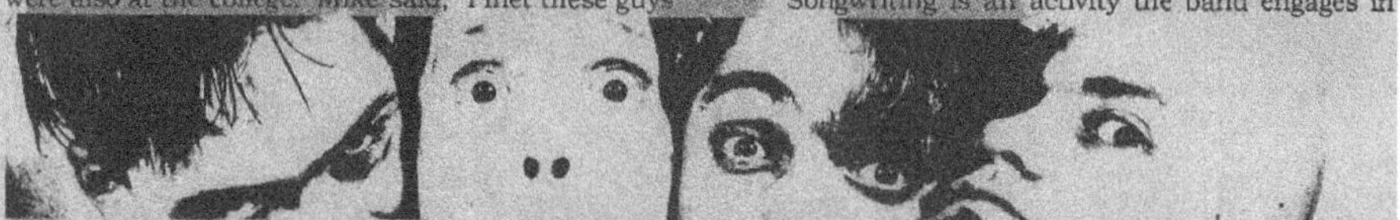

pretty much by accident. A friend and I heard them talking about a party and asked, 'Where's the party?' Stew looked at us like we were the biggest dicks in the world. Rick was a lot more easy to talk to."

In time, Stew became nicer to Mike, and invited him to join the Huh, a group which featured Stew's girlfriend on drums. Mike started by just sitting in with them, but became their permanent bassist. He left the Huh in mid 1986 to help his ailing mother-in-law, but got back in touch with Stew and Rick the following autumn. Both had dropped out of school and returned to Washington, where they were in a band with a drummer named Terry ("T-Bar"). Mike himself had formed an early version of the Hungry Crocodiles, but left when he learned his college buddies needed a singer. "They wanted someone with my agression," he said. After sending demotapes back and forth in the mail, Mike decided that he had found a band he could work with. He and his wife moved to the Evergreen State and dubbed the quartet the Hungry Crocodiles.

The Hungry Crocodiles sound is in the vein of the Beastie Boys, Faith No More, and the Red Hot Chilli Peppers: raw-knuckled rock music with a brawny rhythm that's as good for M.C. Hammer-style foot shuffling as it is for slamdancing; a nonracial, nonpartisan cadence welcoming listeners to have fun. When performed live, it's invigiorating. The band's recorded work, however, is lifeless. "Lucky Love Chain" backed with "No Hitter" and "Stich In Time," their first single, seems very contrived. Only the use of green-with-spots "Crocodile skin vinyl" for minting the record is memorable. If the music had been as fresh and witty as the graphic design, it would have been a stunning debut.

To date, the Hungry Crocodiles' best studio work is "Funky Drummer": a lyrical tribute yo the band's own rhythmatist laid over a James Brown backbeat. A sample:

"Well our funky drummer has got 2 sticks
He's got 2 strong arms to boss the mix
He's got the big sweet feet to keep the street beat...
Funky-ass drummer ain't got no hair
We don't care."
(c)1990 Knucklebone Sounds

Should they ever decide to release cover versions of other people's material, the Hungry Crocoodiles' live takes of "Fame" and "Immigrant Song" would make a knockout one-two punch. They put Bowie's own remake "Fame 1990" to shame and are so adept at capturing the momentum of the original "Immigrant song" that one can imagine Viking longships speeding from the band's ampa at 100 knots.

Songwriting is an activity the band engages in behind studio walls. They record live onto digital audiotape, only offering themselves the luxury of overdubs when background vocals are required. Mike said, "All of our songs are written off of jams. The lyrics are a stream of consciousness." At one point they were working on an LP, the often-delayed 12 Gauge Soul, but abandoned the project because of the money involved. "It got really super-super expensive," Mike admitted. "We decided that the best thing to do would be to release the single."

Besides their commitments to the Hungry Crocodiles, all four bandmembers have day jobs and side activities to keep them busy. Along with the Hungry Crocodiles alter ego the Wack Beat Posse (Mike says, "T-Bar is the main rapper. I'm called Clynt Eastwould. It's a funny, funny, funky affair."), Terry "does some jamming," Stew plays with other bands, and Mike has contributed his vocal skills to at least one other endeavor.

"I did a guest rap on a friend's video project for school. It was a commercial for Bagball. Do you know what that is? It's a minty antiseptic ointment that you put on cow teats." His friend got an 'A'.

By Claude Flowers

FOR THOSE WHO REALLY LIKE TO ROCK!
TOO COOL
BITCHIN'
Z ROCK
ROCKIN'
BAKIN'
AM 1590
ROCKS HARDER!
MAJOR
TOO OUTRAGEOUS FOR FM!
CRUCIAL
HOT
HIP
ROCK.
BE ROCKED.
OR STEP ASIDE!
Z ROCK
Z ROCK
BLAZIN'
AM 1590
9
CITY HEAT

RON HERRING

POLYESTER

When I met with Ron Herring at his modest beach house in Seattle, I was also introduced to some interesting aspects of the music industry. Herring, a seasoned guitarist, vocalist, and trumpet player of 26 years, has been working as a lounge entertainer or "single", since 1981. I've seen Herring perform on more than one occasion over the last three years, and his R&B styled covers have as much integrity as his original C&W tunes. Herring often plays in **local cocktail** lounges where the stages are small and dimly lit, and the drinks are inexpensive. As a matter of record, I've never heard Ron play a Manilow song, and I have never seen him come to work in a polyester leisure wear suit.

"As a single, the average guy can make between 20 and 40 grand a year." Herring said in his direct, gravelly tone of voice. "Depending on how good you are, and how long you've been working as a single, the average guy can work up to 12 months out of the year." (2-7 days a week)

During the interview I asked Herring what is it about lounge entertainers that seems to make them the root of every bad-music cliche, and Herring said honestly, "Because alot of guys are schmucks, I mean alot of singles are just real phony. And alot of them get into this business....I guess....because they just couldn't hack it in bands. But there are alot of guys that were in bands that are really good musicians. Some of the best musicians I've known are doing singles now. Some of my friends didn't understand what I'm trying to do up there until they saw me work."

From 1970 until 1980 Herring was involved with a rock/show band called Burgundy Express. Herring recalled, "We eventually became an 8 piece horn band, we had four full-time horns, I doubled on trumpet and valve trombone, and our bass player doubled on flugle horn, sometimes we'd have six horns going. We did alot of Chicago and Blood, Sweat and Tears' stuff. We had been together only about two weeks in Sacremento when we got a call to play the Hawaiian Islands. We spent the next six years on the road in the Islands, playing resorts and clubs for up to 9 months at a time before going to the next gig. A couple of our extra gigs were opening for Nancy Wilson in Honolulu, and going on tour with Burt Bacharach to Japan as his opening act. Now that was really outstanding because he had us come back on stage to sing on the finale that was in the show."

When Herring talked about the positive and negative sides of being a single, he replied frankly. "The drunks can get on your nerves if you let it get to you, and there are always the people who expect you to be a human juke box, and to know every song written since 1884. I like being my own boss, and playing the kind of music I like. I like playing everything, I like Country and Western, I like Rock which I've always played. I especially like Rhythm and Blues, which I really love. I've always wanted to be a musician, ever since I was a kid, that's all I've ever wanted to do was to play music. And this way I can earn a living doing what I love most. I decided to get into being a single when my wife and I were tired of being on the road all the time. I could read the writing on the wall, which is basically if you want to make any kind of money in a band you have to be on the road all the time. After 11 years we wanted to settle down."

Near the end of our conversation Herring said contentedly, "I'm really very fortunate that I don't have to keep a day job in order to play music. We're not getting rich but we're not hurting either. I've got more work than I can handle, and my wife doesn't have to work, she can stay home and raise our little girl. I give thanks for that everyday, because God takes such exquisite care of us, and that's what gives me the tolerance to put up with the drunks everynight."

By Katie Mcmillan

For booking information contact King/Vac productions @ (206) 778 -1553

CITY HEAT 10

THE CROPDUSTERS

"Handle it from the angle of a continuum. The band has become derailed."

Joey Kline was talking over the phone one Friday afternoon from University Coffee, Inc., the shop he owns and operates in Seattle. He's a warm, friendly, very stable individual whose latest band, the Cropdusters, was in the process of breaking up. "It was an experiment," he concludes, "we couldn't work out the personalities."

Kline formed the Cropdusters six months ago when he needed musicians to play on his second solo LP, the unreleased Derailed. A former member of Prudence Dredge, multiple N.A.M.A. winner, guitarist for the Squirrels and actor in Mark Nichols' studio musical "Little Boy Goes To Hell," he had chosen fellow Squirrel/Prudence Dredger Craig Ferguson to play bass, Scott Sutherland of Chemistry Set and Brian Kenney of Best Kissers In the World on guitars, and Andy Davenhall of Pure Joy on drums. The Derailed sessions proved fruitful, and the quintet took their music to local stages. Davenhall was stolen away by the Purdins after just one show, and replaced by Mark Guenther of the Cowboys.

When they settled into this lineup, the bandmembers started doing interviews and promoting the group more vigorously. During one question& answer session, the suggestion was offered that the Cropdusters' hard-to-define sound was, in fact, country. The band seemed visibly disturbed at this. "I wouldn't classify us as a country band," Scott remarked slowly. His trepidation at being hit with the C & W brand seemed legitimate. After all, the form is dominated by cartoonish bimbos and buckaroos who pander to the tastes of a largely closeminded audience. Those who don't submit to the customs of music city are run out of Nashville- witness the resistance to k.d. lang. The Cropdusters loved the sound and sincerity of good country songs, but had no use for the showbiz phoniness of country figureheads.

When asked who they do like, the five Cropdusters replied in round-robin style: "the Byrds," "Desert Rose Band," "Grand Funk Railroad," "John Hiatt." Mark summed it up neatly: "Honest rock."

"Not Ricky Skaggs," Craig quipped.

Their repetoire of twenty-odd songs included covers like "Running Down A Dream," "Brown Sugar," and catchy originals like "Tin Whistle and a Wooden Drum," all bathed in a three-vocal, three-guitar rainbow of sound. Joey was the main singer, with Craig and Scott giving him background vox whenever needed. "Scott has lungs that go beyond Ted Nugent," Mark said. Scott smiled.

Craig finished the conversation by divulging the origins of the "Cropdusters" tag: "Our mentor and guiding light Jimmy Silva came up with the name." That an English band was already using it didn't seem to bother him. "We figured we'd use it until somebody gave us trouble," he said.

Trouble never came from the outside, it came from within. Despite a symbiotic musical partnership, the people in the band had incompatible personalities. Brian quit and joined the Picketts; Joey calls him, "the Cropduster I am least likely to work with again." Scott also parted company with the group, and Joey's comment that, "I might work with Scott again, but not in the same band as Mark and vice-versa," gives some hint as to the fractures which split them up. The extant band still had a live commitment to fill- a slot opening for the Fabulous Thunderbirds- and they achieved this with the help of Jon Auer and Ken Stringfellow of the Posies. Joey insisted that it was, "a one-shot deal. One night only. The Posies are really busy."

The three remaining Cropdusters might work together in the future, but probably not until late 1990 or early 1991. Joey and Craig will be promoting the Squirrels CD What Gives? in the fall, and it is doubtful that they will have time to dedicate to more than the one band. Mark will reportedly continue as the Cropdusters' drummer when and if the band reforms. A parting statement from Joey makes a reunion seem likely:

"I'm going to keep writing and working on solo stuff. When Derailed comes out, I might get a band together..."

By C. Flowers

11

CITY HEAT

Photo SHOT IN THE DARK

September 1990

Sunday	Monday	Tuesday	Wednesday	Thursday	Friday	Saturday
						B.F. Curtis Salgado & The Stilettos Coca (SHOWCASE) HammerBox Suicide Bride Medicine Show New World Kry B.S. Tough Mama & Zero RCP Duffy Bishop & Rhythm Dogs Lox Sam Smith & Project 3 Crystal Star Chris Lunn Meekers Roc Kandy 1
Flag Plaza (BUMPERSHOOT) The Walkabouts 6:15-7:15 New World Kingsfoil RCP Duffy Bishop & Rhythm Dogs Chandells Pink Slip Meekers Roc Kandy 2	Meekers Roc Kandy Coliseum (BUMPERSHOOT) 7:30 -8:30 The Posies New World TBA 3	6.F. Blatent Disregard, Vicious, Regress, Maelstrom NEw World Coed Chandells The Fact Meekers Roc Kandy 4	Meekers Roc Kandy BF: Broken Statue New Melody Tav : Like Rain, Pounding Serfs, & Guests New World : Coed Lox: Euphoria Chandells : The Fact Drift On inn : The Flame Parkers : Metal Madness 9:00 5	BF: Luther Tucker New World Coed BS: Del Ray & The Blues Gators, The Nyetz & modern Fabric The Square : Silkworm & Tina Chop Chandells: The Fact Drift On Inn: The Flame Meekers Roc Kandy 6	BF: Duffy Bishop & Rhythm Dogs New World: Coed BS: The Subdudes The Square: Joey Klien Lox: Freddie & the Screamers Chandells: The Fact Safari Rest: Bill Brown & Kingbees Crystal Star: Philip & Teresa Morgan Drift On Inn: The Flame 7 Z-ROCK PRESENTS - KISS	BF: Duffy Bishop & Rhythm Dogs Central: Medicine Show New World: Coed BS: Kelly Willis & Radio Ranch Lox: Freddie & the Screamers Chandells: The Fact Safari Rest: Bill Brown & Kingbees Drift On Inn: The Flame Mural Amph: (THE SOUNDS OF SEATTLE CONCERT) 8
Mural Amph: Capping Day New World: Coed Eastlake Zoo: Duffy Bishop & Rhythm Dogs Meekers Roc Kandy 9	New World: Diamond Back Meekers Roc Kandy 10	BF: Road kill, Aggressor, Lethal Dose New World: Fax BS: Pinetop Perkins, Little Mike & The Tornados Meekers Roc Kandy 11	New Melody Tav: Jim Erwin & Sean Denton New World: Fax BS: Zacary Richard Lox: Sam Smith & Project 3 Parkers: Metal Madness 9:00 Meekers: Roc Kandy Drift On Inn: The Flame 12	The Off Ramp: Walkabouts & The Buckets New World: Fax Moore Theater: Duffy Bishop Silver Spoon: David Malhoney Drift On Inn: The Flame Meekers: Roc Kandy 13	BF: Big Wave KCMU: Ships Of Fools, Capping Day New World: Fax BS: MC 900 Foot Jesus & Consolidadet Parkers: Duffy Bishop & Rhthyrn Dogs Lox: The Brittns Drift On Inn: The Flame 14	BF: Big Wave PLU: The Posies & Hammerbox New World: Fax BS: Backstage Benifit Parkers: Duffy Bishop & The Rhythm Dogs Lox: The Brittns Crystal Star: Master Thomas Slye Drift On Inn: The Flame 15
New World: Fax BS: Backstage Benifit 16	New World: TBA 17	BF: Legacy Central: Suicide Bride, Bathtub Gin, Sedated Souls New World: Roc Kandy Z-ROCK - PRESENTS -DIO - LOVE HATE - COLD SWEAT AT THE PARAMOUNT 18	New Melody Tav: Bonnie Hammond & Laura Weller Also Joey Klien & Dave Hillis & Capping Day New World: Roc Kandy 19	New World: Roc Kandy BF: Shakey Jake & Dicks Delux BS: David Baerwald The Square: Somebodys Daughter & The Picketts Owl Cafe: Duffy Bishop & Rhthym Dogs Drift On Inn: Dick Kent Band 20	BF: C.J. Chenier & the Red Hot Louisana Band New World: Roc Kandy BS: John Bayley & the Morning Star Band Bucks in Bellingham: Duffy Bishop & the Rhthyn Dogs Lox: Bochinche (ETHNIC) Swallow Tavern: Freddie James Rocken 88 21 Drift On Inn: Dick Kent Band	BF: C.J. Chenier & the Red Hot Louisana Band Central: The Walkabouts, The Picketts, Paisley Sins USB: Suicide Bride & SGM New World: Roc Kandy BS: Electric Bonsai Band Bucks in Bellingham: Duffy Bishop & Rhthym Dogs Lox: Bochinche (ETHNIC) 22 Swallow Taver
New World: Roc Kandy Z - ROCK WELCOMES BAD CO. DAMN YANKEES (IN THE ARENA) 23	New World: TBA 24	New World: Chain Reaction BS: John Hammond 25	New Melody Tav: Somebodys Daughter, Silkworm, Epiffanie New World: Chain Reaction BS: Wild Rose Lox: Stingrays Drift On Inn: Dick Kent Band Parkers: Metal Madness 9:00 26	New World: Chain Reaction BS: Lucie Blue Tremblay The Square: Mad Mad Nomad, Like Rain Drift On Inn: Dick Kent Band 27	New World: Chain Reaction BF: Duffy Bishop & Rhthym Dogs BS: Crazy Eights & Bop Harvey Lox: The Look Swallow Tavern: Freddie James Rockin 88 Crystal Star: Sockey Blue Grass Band Drift On Inn: Dick Kent Band 28	New World: Chain Reaction BF: Duffy Bishop & Rhthym Dogs BS: Crazy Eights & Bop Harvey Lox: The Look Swallow Tavern: Freddie James Rockin 88 Crystal Star: Rick Ruskin Drift On Inn: Dick Kent Band 29
New World: Chain Reaction Mural Amph: 2:00 P.M. Duffy Bishop & Rhhnym Dogs 30						

JETT CITY

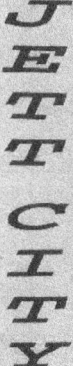

PHOTO: SHOT IN THE DARK

"You are dying your hair."

"Not tonight."

"Yes, you are."

"Uh, well..."

"Then I'm not playing."

No, it's not a masochistic beauty salon, it's **Jett City;** drummer **Lance Lemming**, bassist **Jeff Waibel**, and vocalist **Mark Ash** badgering guitarist **Doug Price** into coloring his hair purple, the rest of them having already drenched theirs in it. But for this band (well, most of them) it's no big deal, they do this kind of stuff all the time.

"We went through a string of about two months where every show we looked different," Jeff explained. "We would wear.. really obscure things.. just to be weird. We wore boxer shorts one night.. and we'd have pizza delivered on stage..."

"..Wear bathrobes...pass out flowers, pass out leis; we did a Hawaiian show...We were going through this thing where people were trying to classify us," Lance elaborates, "and we figured the best way around that was to be different every time..."

What influenced this appreciation of originality do you suppose? Listen to their music, you should be able to guess.

"Hanoi Rocks," Jeff stresses, "that's the Number one influence; beyond that.. a lot of stuff that's not so heavy... Adam and the Ants.. the Electric Angels... But it all basically revolves around Hanoi Rocks."

They've taken a few cues musically as well. "I think we're... middle of the road rock n' roll, like Hanoi, it's not really wimpy, and it's not heavy, either. It's just fun rock n' roll... something you can sing along with and have fun."

These guys remember that rock is entertainment, and you don't need to make a life changing social statement to be entertaining.

"Some of our songs are about absolutely nothing, our first big Z rock hit was called "Bangkok Baby"... It was a popular riff that Doug and I wrote.. and then we just started slapping words together.... We liked the word 'Bangkok', obviously got that from Hanoi, so we wrote songs that didn't really mean anything, the words just sounded cool."

That's not to say they don't ever show a serious side; "Our old stuff always meant a lot.. Every time you watched him [Mark] sing, you thought he was just gonna have an emotional breakdown on stage!"

Lance contrasts Mark's current antics; "Now when we watch him sing it looks like he's going to hyperventilate! "

"And have sex on the floor!" Jeff adds. Well, almost;

"I've been known for baring myself on stage," Mark grins, "Got arrested for it."

"And there's a 'no crack' law in this room," Lance mentions.

Excuse me?

"You can't do this " Mark demonstrates a B.A. about a foot and a half from my face, "or you'll get arrested."

Oh.

Pause.

"Lance, your hair is purple."

"Yours is gonna look like that in a few hours!"

"It just came out more purple because it was lighter."

"I'll dye it black."

"We don't have black dye."

"You're gonna do it *before the show tonight!*"

Despite the fun and games, they're a dedicated bunch, especially live; they give it their all.

"Yeah, we're very active," Jeff admits. "We work our asses off... I mean, live, we can't even walk [after a show]. I passed out once after we got off the stage.". These guys aren't sitting home storing up energy for these shows, either, they're active on the scene as well; "Yeah, we will throw in that we tied for the most times played at Lake City [Concert Hall, since closed down.]. Us and Sedated Souls hold the record to this day," Lance states proudly. "We played there seven times.... piece of history," he adds.

Speaking of history, um.. didn't there used to be **five** of you?

"We did just lose a member," Jeff explains, "Mike Ruggerio, who was our other guitar player. We're still great friends with Mike. He left because he's... going back to school out of state in September... There was no fight, and no 'it wasn't working out', and he wasn't pissed at us. It was really cool. Anyways...we thought we might as well clear it up."

"We're going back into the studio before the end of summer," Jeff informs, "and we'll have a quality tape, probably for sale around here. It'll be like a 4 or 5 song tape, different versions [of our songs] that are quality recordings" Someone in the room is discussing the possibility of dying Doug's hair in the toilet if he holds out much longer. Jeff continues,"We want to put horns

CITY HEAT 14

on our tape [also]. We're auditioning horn players. We're gonna try to put together a horn section: Trumpet, trombone, saxophone, whatever works... also a good piano player."

Well, it appears this visit must draw to a close, as the band is already loading their gear for that night's show. So do the guys have anything to add?

"Put down we're having a party next weekend. Let's give Doug's parents' address!"

"You can lie about us, we don't care!"

"Say Mark only has seven inches instead of ten."

"I always wear Snoopy bandaids!" Mark interjects.

What?!

"You said if I had anything to add   Oh yeah!!! We all dyed our hair purple because, uh, why?"

"Because we felt like it?!"

"Because they were out of the other colors?!"

"Because we wanted to force Doug to do something he didn't want to do?!!"

"Well, Lance has forced Doug to do a lot of things..."

I think I better be leaving this conversation now. I think it was Doug who had the best line of the day while eyeing Jeff's hair outside:

"Man, you look like a Slurpee!"

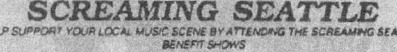

city fashion
Chop Suey

Well, another summer is coming to an end - back to school, time to throw your cutoffs to the bottom of the closet and kiss the sun goodbye for another 9 months. Sounds depressing? Naw, 'cuz the temperature change means you can now break out the leather!

Aah... just the sound of the word conjures up sweet memories. My first leather traveled around Europe with me, just looking at it takes me to another place. And there's nothing like the sound of leather scrunching or the feel of a jacket that is broken into perfection.

Leather is also the fashion chameleon. It can evoke many moods and emotions. From the hard core biker jacket that screams of defiance to the sexy, supple leather that begs to be touched it truly is a versatile piece of hide.

Now is the ideal time to invest in a new jacket for those cold winter months ahead. There are many different roads you may take when purchasing this fashion staple. You can go to your friendly local mall and buy one right off the rack or go the second hand route, but don't be misled. Often used leather is more expensive than new!Secondhand is the perfect choice for some, but you may end up with a jacket that is already thrashed and miss out on the fun of doing it yourself. So be choosy and get the most for your $.

Located at Chop Suey (next to Basic on Capitol Hill), WFO Leather (biker terminology which translates to Wide Fucking Open) is owned by John Ishii: bike lover, heavy metal afficiando and world traveler. John got started in the business about 10 years ago when he became the owner of Chop Suey. His desire to expand into different areas of business led to WFO's birth about 2 years ago. His ultimate goal is to,"create my own line and not buy from the middleman." This means lower prices for the consumers.

WFO offers several basic styles of tannery: the basic bicycle model ($142),fringe jacket ($189),vest ($109),and women's crop ($139). The fringe and crop styles come in black, white, red and pink. Most of their business is from mail orders from the south and east coast, but walk-ins are more than welcome. Right now WFO is having a special:biker jackets for $95, a true bargain.

WFO also carries jackets exclusive to them designed by local artist John Fidler, so if you're looking for something unique, you check out John's work. A really cool mid-length leather can be yours for a mere $300. A good price considering the workmanship and quality of leather. John's motto: "I'll meet or beat anybody's deal in the city."

Drop in to Chop Suey- you can peruse the leather, shop for vintage or just chat about bikes and bands (Sky Cries Mary and War Babies are local faves of John's).

And remember: a good leather never goes out of style!

A.R. Stewart

BACH TO SCHOOL
Music to your eyes . . .
Shop the 2nd floor !
Leather, Spikes, Vinyl, and More . . .
Where else can you find the fun stuff?
The Mozart Jacket
FANTASY Unlimited
WE'RE AT FIRST & PIKE

club scene

THE NEW WORLD

The New World. The name brings to mind images of a foreign land, not yet discovered by people. Well, if your the adventurous type, or even if your not, you should head down to 1417 NW 85th ST. in Ballard and discover The New World, that is, The New World Restaurant and Lounge.

If you remember the days of the China Chef, The New World will pleasantly surprise you. The club still features the best in live music, but more on that later.

The improvements that have been made at the club are easily recognizable. The atmosphere alone is a lively, upbeat, and friendly one. The clientele' is diverse, bringing executives, blue-collar workers, and rock-n-rollers together, yet still maintaining the feeling that everybody knows everyone else.

The bar is fully stocked so that you can order just about any drink imaginable, as well as a variety of beer and wine. If your looking for a non-alcoholic beer, you can find that too!

As far as live music goes, The New World has got it all. Tuesday through Sunday you can dance to your favorite Top-40 songs featuring the best in local Top-40 bands including Aurora, The Fax, New London and Joseph Lee Wood. Monday nights come alive with the Z Rock sponsored World Rock Monday. Local musicians assemble onstage to jam to all the old rock standards, such as, Led Zeppelin, Aerosmith, and Black Sabbath.

When asked the reason for starting World Rock Monday, manager Steve Benzin told us,"We wanted to do something different, as well as provide support to the local musicians." The New World is currently setting the trend as the only club in town offering an arena for local musicians to play together in an impromptu setting. Just the right combination of musicians on drums, guitar bass and vocals and you could have an exciting new band happening. World Rock Monday's also feature one showcase band headlining the evening. Recent World Rock Monday headliners have included Jagged Dagger and Son of Man.

Steve and The New World are very much involved in supporting the local music scene. If your a musician and a friend if Steve's, you'll probably receive a break on the cover charge. Steve also employs musicians and fellow rock-n-rollers. Everyone from the doorman to the waitresses are involved in the local music scene, helping to create that great rock-n-roll atmosphere found at The New World.

All the booking for the club is done by Steve himself, and although The New World is termed a Top-40 club, Steve promises more national acts to come, and he hopes to generate an interest in more original bands.

The New World has a large stage with a roomy dance floor accented by a great light and sound system. In the corner by the bar you'll find pinball games and dart boards to keep you occupied. Besides the games and entertainment, The New World is also a full Chinese restaurant serving lunch and dinner from 11a.m.-1a.m.

Cover charges at The New World are some of the lowest in town for a club with live entertainment. World Rock Monday is$2, but come early and stay for the show and you're in for free. Weekdays (including Sundays) are just $1. Weekends are $4, but come early and your price is only $1, how's that for cost efficient entertainment?

If you'd like to find out who's playing so that you can plan ahead, just call The New World's 24 hour entertainment hotline at 784-4686 and you'll get the rundown for the current week's musical lineup.

So what's the *best* reason to go to The New World? The excellent service, of course! The waitresses and bartenders are friendly, prompt, and willing to take the time to help with any special request you might have.

So now you know why The New World is rapidly becoming the place to be, and be seen. There is a ton of free parking, so get off your couch and check out The New World.

By Kellee Francis

17 CITY HEAT

WE'RE HERE!
HEY DUDE
ROCKWEAR
AND
RocKutz
WELCOME YOU TO OUR
GRAND OPENING BASH!
ALL AGES!
LIVE MUSIC!
DISCOUNTS!
DOOR PRIZES!
MUSICIANS! Bring a photo of your band to Hey Dude! We'll display it on our wall, and you'll receive 20% off merchandise!
HEY DUDE NOW OPEN 7 DAYS A WEEK 10am - 10pm
Sunday, September 30
Call for Details
RUB ELBOWS WITH ROCK CELEBS!
$3.00 HAIRCUTS
PROCEEDS TO BENEFIT S. SNOHOMISH COUNTY BOYS & GIRLS CLUB
3614 -196th, Lynnwood • 670-2640

The 10th Annual 100% OFF
ANNIVERSARY Sale
Discount Sale Prices on a Huge selection of Gear! Plus Three Special Events
with much more than the regular American Music Anniversary Sale Prices!
Grand Prize Give Aways!
Here's Just a Few of the Grand Prizes:
Gibson Les Paul Guitar
Yamaha Pacifica Guitar
Yamaha SY77 Synth
Fender P-Bass
Peavey Bandit Amps
Teac CD Players
CALL FOR INFORMATION
Seattle Special Sale
Sat. Sept 29th, 11-6pm
TENT SALE featuring Rental Returns, Used Equipment, Discontinued Models, and Demo Units at Super Low Prices
Southcenter Special Sale
Sat. Oct. 20th, 11-6pm
TRUCK SALE featuring Rental Returns, Used Equipment, Discontinued Models, and Demo Units at Super Low Prices
Bellevue Special Sale
Sat. Nov. 10th, 11-6pm
TRUCK SALE featuring Rental Returns, Used Equipment, Discontinued Models, and Demo Units at Super Low Prices
PLUS Free Door Prizes
Sony Walkman, Pickups, Headphones, Mics, Cables Proco Cords, Strings, T-Shirts, Starflight Case, Paradise Rack and much more given away as Door Prizes, seperate from the Grand Prize Drawings.
PLUS HOT PRO SEMINARS!
Billy Sheehan 9/17 Yamaha
Day appearance at all stores
Danny Hofer 9/25 Yamaha
Day Appearance at All Stores
Plus an Evening clinic
Blues Saraceno 10/2
Ibanez/TASCAM
Day Appearance at All Stores
Plus an Evening clinic
Fred Newell 10/6 Gibson
Day appearance at All Stores
Plus an Evening clinic
Vinnie Colaiuta 10/27
Zildjian/Yamaha
Coming in October
Greg Howe Fender
Bellevue • 641-5005 • 14340 NE 20th
Seattle • 633-1774 • 4450 Fremont Ave. N.
Southcenter • 575-1970 • 17185 S'center Pkwy.
AMERICAN MUSIC
19
CITY HEAT

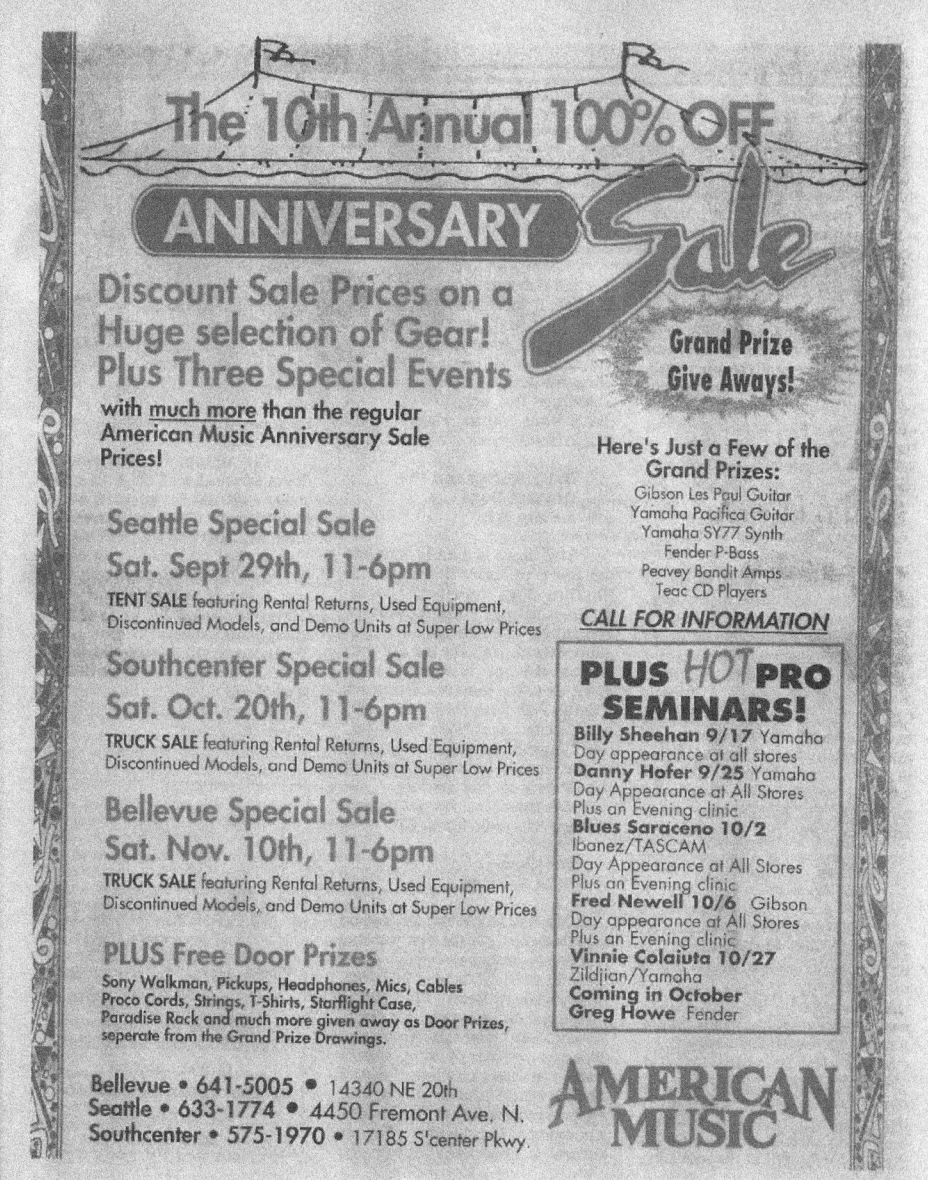

Hot Flashes

Tape Reviews

Hard Rain
Fire In My Loins
Half Rabbit Music

Okay, I know what you're thinking: Cheesy title, probably full of male chauvinist three minute screams about sex and beer. But actually, this is good stuff; there's talent in here, and diversity, too. Lots of different styles pop up, especially with "Salsa Boogie": a cool little ditty whose only flaw is a monotonous drum line. There are a few weak spots: at times the vocals are too distanced from the music, but there are enough cool effects and amusing surprises (check out the intro to "Chasing The Moon") to keep you on your toes. I'd recommend it, despite the title. **JS**

Heir Apparent
4 Song E.P.

This crunchy style of metal might edge into thrash territory, and if you're not psyched for it, it's instant headache music. But if you like a hard-edged scream against conformity and the daily trudgemill of life, you'll dig into this. "Sweet City Child", with its tense strains would make a good atmosphere song in concert, and cries for a video set in a dark, candle lit room. This isn't stuff I'd crush skulls to get my hands on, but I might not toss it out, either. **JS**

Jetboy
MCA Records

Take Jetboy's first album, Feel The Shake, add a little more blues, more gravelly vocals, and a touch more maturity, and you might get this. It's not bad; the soaring choruses reappear on tracks like "Stomp It Down To The Bricks" and "Trouble Comes." My personal favorite, "Bullfrog Pond", throws in a sly bass and a 'birds & banjos' intro that must be a throwback to bassist Sam Yaffa's Hanoi Rocks days. It's good-not as good as I would have expected from them(some lyrical variety wouldn't hurt), but it's cool;just summertime rock n' roll. **JS**

Anthrax
Got The Time
Island Records

I'm not completely sure about this one. It sounds like an Anthrax song, but was written by Joe Jackson(?!). Somehow I can't picture this: are we talking about the same Joe Jackson? You could have fooled me! But hey, it rocks, and that's what counts, right?! Can't wait to hear the rest of the album!**JS**

Duffy Bishop and the Rhythm Dogs
4 Song E.P.

This demo is a lively companion piece to Duffy Bishop & the Rhythm Dogs' excellent but restrained debut LP On A Journey. Pouring on the blues thicker than paint, "My House"- the apex of their current live set- is offered in full glory, as is the sunset soundtrack "Gonna Play With Fire," the sultry witchdoctor chant "Take Me Down," and "Vagabond," a touching study of homelessness resurrected from the LP for a second reading.

Get this tape. It's dangerous, it's sexy, it's rock 'n'roll. **CF**

Steelheart
MCA Records

The bastardized Wings logo on the album cover is the first warning that Steelheart has no original ideas. "Love Ain't Easy" begins like "Sgt. Pepper's Lonely Heart's Club Band," then chugs into a riff so similar to "Crazy Train" that Ozzy Osbourne deserves royalties or an apology or both. "Sheila" is what "I Drink Alone" would sound like if Led Zeppelin covered it on a bad night. A competent band which offers no surprises, no sense of discovery, Steelheart disappoints **CF**

Alice in Chains
We Die Young/Face-Lift
Columbia Records

This review combines both new releases from Seattle's Alice In Chains. We Die Young, one of this summer's hardest to find items is a solid little three song EP that did exactly what it was supposed to do, get people listening to 'Chains before the full length album came out to crerate some added interest in the band. The only song not actually on the album, Killing Yourself, I first heard on Z-Rock and is a good ,solid rocker.

The album, Facelift, doesn't disappoint either, filled with many songs the band has cranked out to its loyal fans. From the start, its a solid, full length debut, with We Die Young , Sea of Sorrow, and Bleed the Freak highlighting side one. Side two, however (assuming it's not a CD you're listening to) does not disappoint either. It Ain't Like That(also on the EP) starts out the side and along with Sunshine and Real Thing highlight the side. The band seems justifiably optimistic about this release.

IN CONCERT

PHOTO: KAREN MASON

(With Deborah Harry, Tom Tom Club, and Jerry Harrison)

While being strung through the Paramount like a flailing fish by a human trawler, I pondered the tour's name but was only to find myself at a loss. I know all of these band's had originated in New York, but "Escape from New York, why *Escape* from New York?", I thought. "Did these bands actually escape from the city of New York? Or did their security guards recently escape from New York's maximum security corrections facility?" I realized that either choice would have been appropriate when the massive, not-quite fully evolved creature with eyes of fire grappled my arm through a sea of people and violently yanked me down to the lower level of the Paramount ("violently" being the milder of applicable adjectives), which at the time seemed like a crocodile dragging its prey down to the murky depths for one last death roll. And as I was to discover later- at the same time this monstrosity (let's call him "Grape Ape") was ridding me of the tape in my microcassette recorder, another of his primordial counterparts were simultaneously extracting the film from our photographer's camera. Totally uncool! If you're familiar with the arcade boxing game "Knockout", you've seen a video interpretation of the killing machine of whom I speak. "Bald Bull" they call him. He's a fierce, snarling black man of about 300 pounds, with biceps for miles. I mean, this guy makes Mr. T look like Michael Jackson. So I felt like saying "drop your gold chains, that ridiculous haircut and pedal your pansy ass home pal!"—I didn't.

Although an avid and severely dedicated fan of the Ramones, I found it nearly impossible to give the Ramones (or anyone else on the bill) a shred of favorable mention. Hell, I only caught ten minutes of the Ramones before Grape Ape threw me around like a Samsonite suitcase! But after coming to terms with myself, I realized that the bands played as little a part in the atrocious nature of their hired help as does Iraqi dictator Saddam Hussein stand a chance at winning this year's Humanitarian award. In support of their 13th album and the appropriately entitled "Escape from New York" tour, the Ramones show that they're here to stay And stay they will! Singer Joey, guitarist Johnny, bassist Marky, and drummer C.J. Ramone blew the sold-out Paramount Theater apart with a barrage of tunes from their chest of well-stocked ammo. like rapid machine gun fire, the Ramones assaulted the audience with round after round of heavy artillery. The average song weighing in at a mere two minutes, stripped of extraneous guitar solos and the other delusions consistent with today's other Yngwie-esque performers. Clad in black leather jackets and thrift store quality blue jeans, the Ramones played to an overly-varied crowd, breaking down the barriers between age groups.

The Ramones may not be the most handsome fellas ever to rush the stage but that's no reason to confiscate an entire roll of film. We're just doing our job! The Ramones don't try to pretend their pretty boys. And if you're a true Ramones fan, you like 'em because they're ugly. Loud, obnoxious, and UGLY! And from what I heard, the Ramones sounded great live. And everyone wag totally getting into them. So what's up with Grape Ape man-handling me, and seizing my tape?! It certainly wouldn't even be of mediocre bootleg quality. Who knows, maybe it was just an in-between meal snack for my overgrown aggressor.

Oh well, hearing my personal favorite "I Wanna Be Sedated", and escaping from the Paramount unscathed made the whole ordeal worthwhile. The Ramones are the Timex of punk rock. If the earth were to be the subject of nuclear war, there would be only two things left cockroaches, and The Ramones. Unfortunately, their bouncers are more than likely oblivious to nuclear attack as well. They'll be back though, and perhaps by then the zoo will have recaptured Grape Ape and the remainder of its primate section.

by Shay McGraw

The Royal Court of China

On Saturday, August 11th, the Tennessee-based group, The Royal Court of China, played to one of the hottest and sweatiest crowds the Central Tavern has ever held between its four walls. The melodic, hard-hitting act was one of four in that night's line-up, including My Sister's Machine, The Rhino Humpers, and Shedied.

The Royal Court lived up to what some are calling one of the hottest live groups around as best they could, battling the conditions of "The Central Sauna". It was hot, sweaty, loud, and energetic, nothing short of what they'd promised to deliver. Seattle made guitarist, Brian Jennings, a former Seattlite, feel at home for the night, and responded to the entire group with a lot of enthusiasm. The other 75% of Royal Court are Joe Blanton, vocals/guitar, Drew Cornutt, bass, and Chris Mckow (they called him "Fuzz"- I didn't ask why...), on drums. Seattle was just one of many stops on the band's club tour; they named only Boise and Butte as yet untouched.

The Royal Court of China was formed back in 1986, in Nashville of all places, adding to the list of hard rock acts you wouldn't expect to cross the Mason-Dixon line, let alone putting down the

pedal to the steel. With a self-titled debut album and their latest release ("Geared and Primed" on A&M records) behind them, you can expect to hear and see a lot more of these guys. They'll be starring in a soon-to-be-released movie titled "The Monster Tour", which is as Joe says, "basically rock-n-roll high school, but we're monsters."

OK...

The group did have a lot of good things to say about Seattle bands, referring in particular to the lyrical writing that has been the strong point of many local bands. They also pointed out that although they, too, concentrate on writing good lyrics, that they don't want to be compared to any certain group of bands, and they really don't want to be categorized. They summed it up best themselves. "We don't want to copy somebody else, although we wouldn't say we're doing anything particularly original, except for our stage show. In most bands, everybody's too damn lazy to go out and give it their all. It's usually just one guy in the band, like Steven Tyler of Aerosmith. But there are four guys in this band who go balls-out, nonstop. If people want a band with some real energy, then we're the band for them. That's the magic to our music."

By Michele Klossner
& Andrea Long

21 *CITY HEAT*

SHOT IN THE DARK
Music Photography
PHOTOGRAPHY
MARCO RADWICK
SHOT IN THE DARK
Seattle Trade Center • 2601 Elliott Avenue Studio 5114 • Seattle 98121 • 206.441.5532
CITY HEAT
22

Bitchin's Corner

Hello again everybody I can't believe how lucky I am. I just got back from an all-expense-paid vacation to kuwait. It worked out great because I had to drop off a couple bundles of CITY HEATS there anyway. Not to be cool or anything but they liked me so much that they weren't gonna let me leave the country! until I started telling them my best jokes. Then there I was headed back to the U.S. of A just like that.

On one of my layovers in Houston Texas I had a couple of hours to kill. so I see this country and western bar in the distance. So I said to myself, it's time to partake in a couple of tall cool ones! So I walked into this HICK!!! bar and all the dudes were wearing those pointed boots and cowboy hats and they see this long haired dude walk in. So they all looked at me with that look like "GET A ROPE"!! and again I'm thinking to myself, it's nice to be well hung but this is ridiculous!! I just said if you people start messing with me today will be the last day of the rest of your life. Needless to say, chairs were flying everywhere. I was getting beat like a red headed step child. Sure, I ended up in the hospital but you should see the other guys!! I hope they don't wake up on the wrong side of the bedpan, and try to finish me off. If they do I won't take the law into my own hands I'll take then to court. My lawyers, Duey, Cheetum and Howe always take care of me. So keep watching the peoples court, I'll probably on right after the case of "using scruffy as a sponge" that's the case where a guy used his neighbors poodle to wash his truck.

It's that time again to take another excellent trip to Bitchin's Kitchen. This months Top Ramen recipe is "Ramen goulash"

2 PKGS. Top Ramen
2 cans of cream of mushroom soup 1 can of chicken noodle soup
1 bag of Fiesta blend veggies (must be Fiesta) because they RULE!!

Then if you want to you can add and undetermined amount of brown rice. Season to perfection There you have it a tasty treat for all to enjoy...And believe it or not this one is edible!!

Well it looks like i'm running out of time and money so until next time, if you have any questions, comments or recipes write to:
"ASK BITCHIN"
c/o City Heat
929 S.W. 152nd.
Seattle Wa. 98166

DON'T MISS IT
SEATTLE music
6th Anniversary Sale
Saturday September 8th • 10 a.m. to 6 p.m.
Everything in stock is on sale for the biggest event in SEATTLE MUSIC history!
Strats from $199.00
Les Pauls from $399.00
Sure SM-58 mics from $99.00
Tubular guitar stands $9.00
All floor effects 40% off
There is a limited supply of items on sale for this
ONE DAY EXTRAVAGANZA
We are also giving away a $1000.00 gift certificate on the day of the sale
SIGN UP NOW TO WIN!!!
Enter every time you come into the store from now till September 8, 1990
Seattle Music 1st & Seneca
622-1134 nation wide 1-800-422-7730

1990
JFMAMJJASOND

Dio & Love/Hate – In Concert: In Depth, Hot Flashes, City Heat

Last time Love/Hate was in town they played Meeker's Landing on a Tuesday night. Playing at no cost to the fan on a Z-Rock sponsored tour, they played after two local hopefuls and tore it out on the small stage.

At that time, Skid (Love/Hate's bass player) was heard to comment:

> *"It's just been a dream come true, it really has. You know, we spent our whole life fantasizing about what it would be like to be travelling around the country in a big rock and roll tour bus, and it's just exceeded all of our expectations."*

Three months later they returned to play the Paramount (on a Tuesday night no less) sandwiched between headliner Dio and new metal contenders Cold Sweat.

They grabbed the focus of the audience immediately with their die-hard Z-Rocker and title track from their gold debut, *Blackout In The Red Room*, then held it captive throughout the set (which had twenty or so minutes trimmed since last time, leaving *Wasted in America* the only new song remaining on this evening's set list).

We tasted the harder side with the likes of *Tumbleweed*, *Fuel To Run*, *Rock Queen*, and *One More Round*, then the lighter and nearly sensitive *She's An*

Angel. They ended the show with a strobe-lit extravaganza, *Why Do You Think They Call It Dope?* (their current MTV rotator).

Love/Hate will be back in the Emerald City soon, this time taking another step up playing the Coliseum with AC/DC. Heck, they may even move here they like it so much. I asked the man out front, Jizzy Pearl, about his favorite tour stops;

> *"Well I like it up here if it wouldn't fuckin' rain so much! I dig the Oregon/Washington vibe of the greenery and just the cleanliness. L.A.'s a bit dirty sometimes."*

Yes, Jizzo, we understandably echo your sentiments.

Now on to the headliner, Dio!

Unfortunately, his diminutive head was about all I saw of Ronnie James Dio.

From the moment the lights dimmed and the screen on stage lit up, the packed Paramount crowd was scrambling for higher ground as though a flood had come coursing through the building. They maintained the arm rests as a floor thru the entire set and for those less emphatic or more polite, tough shit!

Anyway, the screen kicked it off with a weird sequence culminating in a suited woman reading a list of crimes to which Ronnie James (obviously) plead guilty. They then took off with *Wild One* from his new album.

The theatrical staging was that of a carcass rotting in a post nuclear wasteland. Situated amongst the weathered ribs were two stories of power. Keys and skins held ground upstairs with all chords (vocal and fretted) down under.

ripping our heads off and bellowing Nordic warchants for *Immigrant Song*, but during *In the Mood* he made Seattle Center seem very small and his message, very personal. It was the evening's emotional high point.

Going to California, Nobody's Fault But Mine, Liar's Dance, The Way I Feel, Living Loving Maid, Ship of Fools... sixteen songs burned into the audience's collective consciousness until our brains were fried into dried, blackened husks and our faces carved into wide grins. The crowd was a sea of happy jack o' lanterns. The band was smiling, too.

Prior to dashing offstage after his last encore, Plant bid the crowd to,"be careful and... be happy." The unspoken reply: lighten up, Percy, we're in love with you. Robert Plant is God. Honest.

By Claude Flowers

Dio
Love / Hate

Last time **Love/Hate** was in town they played Meeker's Landing on a Tuesday night. Playing at no cost to the fan on a Z-Rock sponsored tour, they played after two local hopefuls and tore it out on the small stage. At the time, Skid (bass player) was heard to comment: "It's just been a dream come true, it really has. You know, we spent our whole life fantasizing about what it would be like to be travelling around the country in a big rock and roll tour bus, and it's just exceeded all of our expectations."

Three months later they returned to play the Paramount (on a Tuesday) sandwiched between headliner Dio and new contenders Cold Sweat. They grabbed the focus of the audience immediately with their die hard Z-Rocker, and title track from their gold debut, *Blackout In The Red Room*. Then held it captive throughout the set, which had twenty or so minutes trimmed since last time leaving *Wasted in America* the only new song remaining. We tasted the harder side with the likes of *Tumbleweed, Fuel To Run, Rock Queen*, and *One More Round*, then the lighter and nearly sensitive *She's an Angel*. They ended the show with a strobe lit extravaganza, *Why Do You Think They Call It Dope?*, their current MTV rotator. Love/Hate will be back in the Emerald City soon, this time taking another step up playing the Coliseum with AC/DC. Heck, they may even move here they like it so much. I asked the man out front, Jizzy Pearl, about his favorite tour stops, "Well I like it up here if it wouldn't fuckin rain so much! I dig the Oregon-Washington vibe of the greenery and just the cleanliness. L.A.'s a bit dirty sometimes." Yes, Jizzo, we echo your sentiments.

PHOTO: G. PATRICIA STOMM

Now on to the headliner, **Dio**. Unfortunately, his head was about all I saw of Dio. From the moment the lights dimmed and the screen on stage lit up, the packed Paramount crowd was scrambling for higher ground as though a flood had come coursing through the building. They maintained the arm rests as a floor through the entire set and for those less emphatic or more polite, tough shit. Anyway, the screen kicked it off with a weird sequence culminating in a suited woman reading a list of crimes to which Ronnie James (obviously) pleaded guilty. They then took off with *Wild One*, from his new album. The theatrical staging was that of a carcass on a post nuclear wasteland. Situated amongst the weathered ribs were two stories of power. Keys and skins upstairs with chords (vocal and fretted) down under. Although there were a lot of notable tunes missing, he still gave us a sizeable cross section of his career, from Rainbow through Black Sabbath up to his solo work. He played the ancient *Man On the Silver Mountain* to the merely old *Children Of The Sea* and *Heaven And Hell* up to the title track and *Hey Angel* from his new Lock Up The Wolves LP. Also in there were heavy favorites *Last In Line, Stand Up And Shout* as well as *Long Live Rock And Roll*. Being the metallic traditionalist he is, we can forgive his decision for the obligatory solos of his band. Especially since the keyboard piece was so nifty. Starting upstairs the ivory man ran down to meet a keyboard that had descended from the ceiling. He continued his solo as it swayed to and fro, then on the last resonating note it ascended back to the rafters where it erupted into a shower of sparks. In true Dio fashion no expense was spared and the night was filled with fires, flashpots and explosions.

They wound it down with his most notable, *Rainbow In The Dark*. After the show, our publisher asked Ronnie his feelings toward our fair city. "The crowds in Seattle are always the best," he exclaimed, "and tonight's was exceptional. The security thugs here, however, like the Gestapo, they were really pummeling some of those kids." This last bit, unfortunately, isn't really news to Paramount veterans. But, all told, it still was one of the best Tuesday nights in a long time

By Michael Browning
CITY HEAT

17

Although there *were* a lot of notable tunes missing, he still gave us a sizeable cross section of his career from Rainbow through Black Sabbath up to his solo work. He journeyed thru the ancient *Man On the Silver Mountain* to the merely old *Children Of The Sea* and *Heaven And Hell* up to the spanking newness of the title track and *Hey Angel* from his just-released Lock Up The Wolves LP. Also in there were heavy favorites *Last In Line*, *Stand Up And Shout* as well as *Long Live Rock And Roll*.

Being the metallic traditionalist he is, we can forgive his decision for the obligatory extended solos of his band. Especially since the keyboard piece was so nifty.

Starting upstairs the ivory man ran down to meet another keyboard that had descended from the ceiling. He continued his solo as it swayed to and fro. Then on the last resonating note it ascended back to the rafters where it erupted into a shower of sparks. In true Dio fashion, no theatrical expense was spared thus the night was filled with fires, flash pots and explosions.

They wound it down with his most notable, etched into the collective consciousness of the initial MTV generation, *Rainbow In The Dark*.

After the show, our publisher [Bob Barr] asked Ronnie his feelings toward our fair city.

> *"The crowds in Seattle are always the best," he exclaimed, "and tonight's was exceptional! The security thugs here, however, are like the Gestapo! They were really pummeling some of those kids."*

This last bit, unfortunately, isn't really news to Paramount show veterans. But, all told, it still was one of the best Tuesday nights I've had in a long time (three months, at least)!

1990

JFMAMJJASOND

LOCAL DIRT

By J. Hollywood

First off, I'd like to thank all the bands and musicians who sent promo pic's for the J. Hollywood "Wall of Shame"; they were all great and there's room for more if you haven't sent yours yet.

Eternal Daze has released their full length tape entitled **Escapade** and it's available by writing 7425 202nd SW, Lynnwood, WA 98036. Seattle based trio, The Crucible, just released their second EP entitled **Try**. It's available by calling (206) 641-1687. Capping Day's EP entitled **Post No Bills**, has just been released on CD by Popllama Records with Jon Auer of The Posies producing. Speaking of....The Posies left Oct. 21st to begin their tour to support the release of their **Dear 23** album. They'll return to Seattle in late December. Congrats to local band Like Rain for being named finalists in Musician Magazine's "Best Unsigned Bands Contest". They hope to release a CD in December.

Lox, Stock & Bagel Cafe & Bar is now featuring live entertainment in the U-District. Their November line-up includes The Brittins, The Look, In Effect, The Stingrays, Dix Deluxe (featuring Mark Shaffer) & Euphoria. Call 634-3144 for any information.

Attention Bands that are having trouble getting a show: The Nasty Girls Management and Promotion Company promises they can get you booked!! From Grunge Rock to Glamour Rock, and everything in between. They also offer a full spectrum of other promotional services. For more info call Mikki, Jazz, or Sebastian at (206)726-7976 or 228-0580. Side F-X will have their *Rock the House* music and video featured in an upcoming episode of the new **SUPERFORCE** T.V. show which airs Saturday, Nov. 24th on the FOX network nationally. Check your local listings. Also on the FOX Network this season: NASTY MIX rap artists will be featured on the nationally syndicated show Pump It Up.

Pistol Moon has returned as a four-piece with lots of new material and a slightly different sound. John has changed his focus from keyboards to all guitar duties, and bassist Troy Moss has been added to the lineup. Rick's still drumming, and Scott's still singing. They're playing the 27th at the Firehouse, then the 4th at Meeker's. Check 'em out!

Portland band, The Dharma Bums, headline a fall fund drive benefit concert at Green River Community College, Saturday, Nov. 10th, 8:00 p.m. Also on the bill are The Squirrels and Dreaming I Am. Karla Cruz's record release party has been scheduled for Nov. 19th at the Backstage in Ballard at 8:00 p.m.

Have a great Thanksgiving holiday and stay clean, you'll feel better.

CITY HEAT
An Aird Hooker publication

Executive Publisher
Matthew Aird

Publisher
Robert E. Barr

Editor
Michael Browning

Associate Editors
Claude Flowers
Shay McGraw

Editorial Consultant
Jeff Lageson

Account Executive
Angela Metcalf

Contributing Writers
Katie McMillan
Jimmy St. Bitchin
Michelle Klossner
Andrea Long
David Sterling
Jana Skillingstead
Linnea Freed
J. Hollywood
Kellee Francis
Nadia Felker

Fashion Editor
A.R. Stuart

Photography
Charlie Hoselton
Karen Mason

Art Director
Mark Cole

Concert Desk
Lori DeLano

Distribution Manager
Ted Treichler

Computer Consultants
Doug Kammerer

CITY HEAT is published monthly at 929 SW 152nd St. Seattle, WA 98166. CITY HEAT accepts no responsibility for unsolicited materials. Subscriptions are available for $12/year U.S., $15/year first class or foreign. All contents © 1990 Aird Hooker Publishing. All inquiries please phone 206.242.3952

CITY HEAT November 4

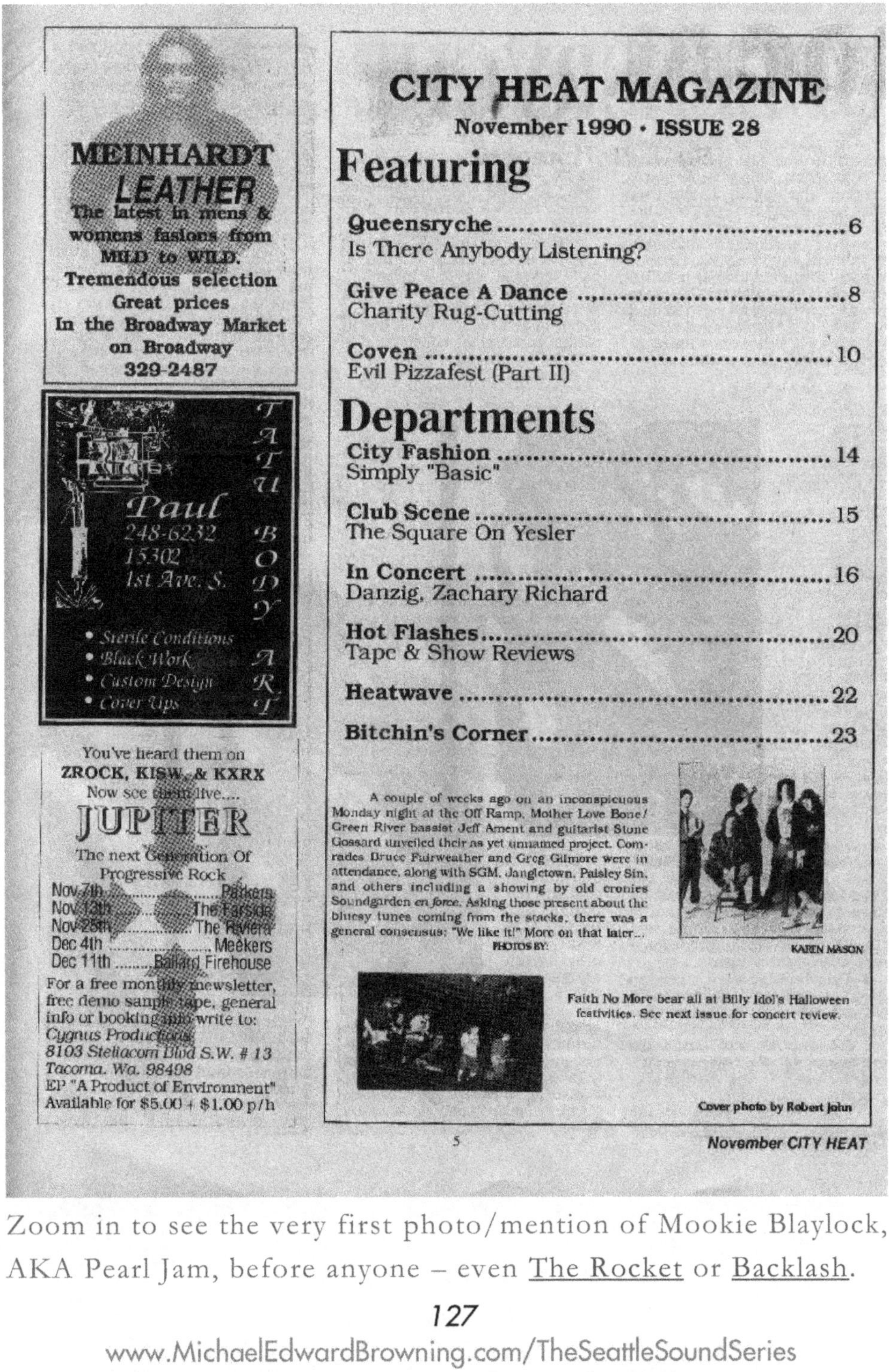

MEINHARDT *LEATHER*
The latest in mens & womens fasions from MILD to WILD.
Tremendous selection
Great prices
In the Broadway Market on Broadway
329-2487

TATU BODY ART
Paul
248-6232
15302
1st Ave. S.
• *Sterile Conditions*
• *Black Work*
• *Custom Design*
• *Cover Ups*

You've heard them on
ZROCK, KISW, & KXRX
Now see them live....
JUPITER
The next Generation Of Progressive Rock
Nov 7th .... Parkers
Nov 13th .... The Farside
Nov 25th .... The Riviera
Dec 4th .... Meekers
Dec 11th .... Ballard Firehouse
For a free monthly newsletter, free demo sample tape, general info or booking info write to:
Cygnus Productions
8103 Steliacom Blvd S.W. # 13
Tacoma. Wa. 98498
EP "A Product of Environment"
Available for $5.00 + $1.00 p/h

CITY HEAT MAGAZINE
November 1990 • ISSUE 28

Featuring

Departments

A couple of weeks ago on an inconspicuous Monday night at the Off Ramp, Mother Love Bone/ Green River bassist Jeff Ament and guitarist Stone Gossard unveiled their as yet unnamed project. Comrades Bruce Fairweather and Greg Gilmore were in attendance, along with SGM, Jangletown, Paisley Sin, and others including a showing by old cronies Soundgarden *en force*. Asking those present about the bluesy tunes coming from the stacks, there was a general consensus: "We like it!" More on that later...

PHOTOS BY: KAREN MASON

Faith No More bear all at Billy Idol's Halloween festivities. See next issue for concert review.

Cover photo by Robert John

5 November CITY HEAT

Zoom in to see the very first photo/mention of Mookie Blaylock, AKA Pearl Jam, before anyone – even The Rocket or Backlash.

QUEENSRŸCHE

At press time they'd just played the first date of the Empire tour in Belfast, Ireland (where local custom is to spit on bands they like). As you read this, they're either making their way down the English coast or somewhere between Scandinavia and Italy. On December 6th, they wind it down in Milan for a long Christmas break. Stage production and more video filming will keep them off the road 'til late February when they cross the other ocean for their Japanese fans

Between flying here and there for television appearances and video shoots, they've been home rehearsing for the lengthy tour. Also on the agenda are affairs of the heart as Scott gets engaged and Geoff gets married while Chris and Michael enjoy time with their families. (Yes, ladies, Eddie is still available!) Last October, City Heat talked with Chris and Geoff so this year in the interest of diversity we spoke to the other guitarist extraordinaire of this essential eastside outfit, Michael Wilton. A few nights before they shot the video for *Best I Can*, Michael took a moment from his hectic schedule to sit and talk about the year past and the year ahead. Not surprisingly, it was another rainy night.

CH: "So have most all of you guys been removed from the singles category now that Geoff's a married man?"

Wilton: "No. Scott and Eddie are still single (last week Scott's status changed.) The rhythm section is still pumping."

CH: "And you other three are all married Jet City women, of course?"

Wilton: "Yeah. If you're meaning like—did we marry any models from L.A. or New York? No. All of the women that we married are from Seattle."

CH: "Do you guys get a chance to go out in town much? You used to like the Vogue, any new haunts?"

Wilton: "I live out in Issaquah so I don't really get out there that much but Chris and Geoff live in Seattle and they are constantly going to restaurants that cater healthier food."

CH: "I don't suppose any of you ever entertains the notion of relocating, do you?"

Wilton: "No, because one thing about New York and L.A. is that there's so much competition and you find that all the bands are trying to copy what the other bands are doing because they are so desperate to get a record deal or get a hit or just get into the industry. So you find these bands chasing trends all the time. And with all the bands that are being signed up in Seattle it's amazing. It's like all the record companies are looking up here in Seattle for home grown talent. You know, it's different up here. If you don't have a huge club scene, for rock or metal bands, then there's really not that much going for them except to sit in the basement and write their own music."

CH: "How do you suppose this solitude or lack of venue affects the bands?"

Wilton: "They tend to be a bit more honest in their writing. They're not trying to sound like Poison. I think that's what the industry is looking for these days, bands that are a bit more true to their writing. They're not just trying to copy a Guns-N-Roses or a Slaughter or whatever. That's why bands like Alice in Chains and Soundgarden and Sanctuary are all getting good reviews and touring the world now. Everyone's going 'Fuck, what's going on up in Seattle?' I think it's just the environment up here. You know, there is no way I would move to New York. There's just no way. I mean, I can handle the rain. No problem."

They didn't have any problem getting noticed way up here initially either. First they put together their own 206 Records and independently released 3,000 units of their four song demo. They sold. After pressing an additional 15,000, they sold. At this point they'd done much of the work for the record companies and all that was left was for the top bidder to capitalize on the bands efforts. People call Seattle remote and isolated. Even with 3,000 miles and a continent between them, EMI Manhattan heard the call and came running. With no "real" performances under their collective belt, they sat an EMI rep in their West

CITY HEAT November

6

IN THEIR EMERALD EMPIRE

BY MICHAEL BROWNING

Seattle rehearsal room and after three songs of being "pinned to the wall" she said simply, "Okay, you're signed," and left.

Between here and there the road has been one of highs and lows. Heavenly expectations and grounding realities. True fans of the Ryche have never wavered in their support but the general public has only granted widespread acceptance with the last release, **Operation: Mindcrime**. After such high anticipation for the success of **The Warning** and **Rage For Order**, Mindcrime's belated astronomical sales caught them somewhat off guard. More than a year after its release, they suddenly had the notoriety they'd been waiting so long for. Fortunately, they're not ones to remain content. So we now have a new collection of songs from them dramatically different from the conceptual tracks that form Mindcrime. The title track was recorded right here at Triad.

Wilton: "I already had the music written for *Empire* and Geoff came in with this low voice for the chorus then he got an idea for lyrics. He wanted to kind of have that song like a connector between **Operation: Mindcrime** and **Empire**, so that it still had elements of Mindcrime."

CH: "*Resistance* kind of does that also. Those two seem like the bridge between the albums."

Wilton: "Yeah, it's funny. *Resistance* was written in the studio. That's something we never do. I just had this riff with a Stonesish vibe and I said, 'Geoff, this feels like an environmental song.' Then he wrote the lyrics in a day and we went into the studio and did a guide track. Scott listened to it and did his track in the same day. Scott has become a one take drummer. His stuff is instantaneous."

CH: "How is it that the song Empire was recorded at Triad while the rest of the album was done at Vancouver Studios?"

Wilton: "We went out to Redrock, Colorado to bring in an audience for filming a concert scene. Then they wanted to use one of our songs on the sound track for the movie (Ford Fairlane). We made a demo and sent four or five songs and they chose *Empire*. We went into Triad to record it and it turned out that they didn't want it because it was too heavy and too dark. They finally ended up using *Last Time in Paris*. Then when we recorded the album, we were thinking about rerecording *Empire* because we had use of all digital facilities and our engineer and everything. Then we started getting this positive feedback from everyone that had heard that demo at Triad and they said just leave it. The recordings are good and it's comparable, so we just remixed it."

"Well, I just think that the songs that we wrote on this album were directly opposite of what we did on Mindcrime because we didn't want to do a follow-up conceptual album. So we decided to go 180 degrees and just write these natural songs so we just wrote about ourselves, and some issues, and the world. That's about it."

—Michael Wilton

CH: "Is that the first you've worked with Tom Hall since the EP?"

Wilton: "We always do little one-off recording sessions and stuff at Triad with Tom. Whether it's doing demos or transferring stuff from tape to DAT or whatever. We still do a lot at Triad."

The tour is anticipated to last as long as two years. Their first time headlining, the set will be two hours long and contain Operation: Mindcrime in it's entirety. They won't be playing any American dates until March unless we get very lucky with another New Years Eve appearance like two years ago. Unfortunately, they declined to comment on that possibility. Keep your fingers crossed.

Empire is a fresh, viable direction for the thinking man's metal band as they embark on the massive appeal portion of their career. The next year will see their music and performances reaching millions of fans all over the globe. A few metalheads will say they sold out to commercialism. I couldn't disagree more. The raw vitality that has always been Queensryche is still there along with the intense growth they've experienced as musicians. From the very beginning that's been a major goal for the band—to better themselves as musicians and remain honest in their songwriting.

Wilton: "It's a natural progression and it shows a different side of us. You know, it's just a point in our career where we have actually become somewhat parallel with what society wants. They played stuff from Operation: Mindcrime on the radio and that was a very cynical record and I think that kind of broke the doors down a little bit."

CH: "Does the change have anything to do with your guys' new focus on family life?"

Wilton: "Well, I just think that the songs that we wrote on this album were directly opposite of what we did on Mindcrime because we didn't want to do a follow-up conceptual album. So we decided to go 180 degrees and just write these natural songs so we just wrote about ourselves, and some issues, and the world. That's about it."

November CITY HEAT

Queensryche - Cover Story, City Heat

Queensryche: In Their Emerald Empire

At press time they'd just played the first date of the Empire tour in Belfast, Ireland (where local custom is to spit on bands they like).

As you read this, they're either making their way down the English coast or somewhere between Scandinavia and Italy.

On December 6th, they wind it down in Milan for a long Christmas break. Stage production and more video filming will keep them off the road 'til late February when they cross the other ocean for their Japanese fans.

Between flying here and there for television appearances and video shoots, they've been home rehearsing for the lengthy tour.

Also on the agenda are affairs of the heart as Scott gets engaged and Geoff gets married while Chris and Michael enjoy time with their families.

(Yes, ladies, Eddie is still available!)

Last October, City Heat talked with Chris and Geoff so this year in the interest of diversity we spoke to the *other* guitarist extraordinaire of this essential eastside outfit, Michael Wilton.

A few nights before they shot the video for *Best I Can*, Michael took a moment from his hectic schedule to sit and talk about the year past and the year ahead.

Not surprisingly, it was another rainy night.

City Heat: "So have most all of you guys been removed from the singles category now that Geoff's a married man?"

Wilton: "No. Scott and Eddie are still single (last week Scott's status changed). The rhythm section is still pumping."

City Heat: "And you other three are all married Jet City women, of course?"

Wilton: "Yeah. If you're meaning like—did we marry any models from L. A. or New York? No. All of the women that we married are from Seattle."

City Heat: "Do you guys get a chance to go out in town much? You used to like the Vogue, any new haunts?"

Wilton: "I live out in Issaquah so I don't really get out there that much but Chris and Geoff live in Seattle and they are constantly going to restaurants that cater healthier food."

City Heat: "I don't suppose any of you ever entertains the notion of relocating, do you?"

Wilton: "No, because one thing about New York and L.A. is that there's competition and you find that all the bands are trying to copy what the other bands are doing because they are so desperate to get a record deal of get a hit or just get into the industry. So you find these bands chasing trends all the time. And with all the bands that are being signed up in

Seattle, it's amazing. It's like all the record companies are looking up here in Seattle for homegrown talent. You know, it's different up here. If you don't have a huge club scene, for rock or metal bands, then there's really not that much going for them except to sit in the basement and write their own music."

City Heat: "How do you suppose this solitude or lack of venue affects the bands?"

Wilton: "They tend to be a bit more honest in their writing. They're not trying to sound like Poison. I think that's what the industry is looking for these days, bands that are a bit more true to their writing. They're not just trying to copy a Guns-N-Roses or a Slaughter or whatever. That's why bands like Alice In Chains and Soundgarden and Sanctuary are all getting good reviews and touring the world now. Everyone's going, 'Fuck, what's going on up in Seattle?' I think it's just the environment up here. You know, there is no way I would move to New York. There's just no way. I mean, I can handle the rain. No problem."

They didn't have any problem getting noticed way up here initially either.

First they put together their own 206 Records [even tho there's a Chris on staff, it's not the current 206 Records] and independently released 3,000 units of their four-song demo [containing the operatic classics *Queen Of The Reich* and *Lady Wore Black*].

They sold.

After pressing an additional 15,000, they sold.

Oh my goodness, did they sell!

At this point they'd done much of the work for the record companies and all that was left was for the top bidder to capitalize on the band's efforts.

People call Seattle remote and isolated. Even with 3,000 miles and a full continent between them, EMI Manhattan heard the call and came running.

With no "real" performances under their collective belt, they sat an EMI rep in their West Seattle rehearsal room and after three songs of being "pinned to the wall" she said simply,

> *"Okay, you're signed,"*

and left.

Between here and there the road has been one of highs and lows, heavenly expectations and grounding realities. True fans of the 'Ryche have never wavered in their support but the general public has only granted widespread acceptance with the last release, Operation: Mindcrime.

After such high anticipation for the success of The Warning and Rage For Order, Mindcrime's belated astronomic sales caught them somewhat off guard.

More than a year after its release, they suddenly had the notoriety they'd been waiting so long for.

Fortunately, they're not ones to remain content.

So, we now have a new collection of songs from them dramatically different from the conceptual tracks that form Mindcrime. The title track was recorded right here at Triad Studios.

> *Wilton: "I already had the music written for Empire and Geoff came in with this low voice for the chorus then he got an idea for lyrics. He wanted to kind of have that song like a connector between Operation: Mindcrime and Empire, so that it still had elements of Mindcrime."*
>
> *City Heat: "Resistance kind of does that also. Those two seem like the bridge between the albums."*
>
> *Wilton: "Yeah, it's funny. Resistance was written in the studio. That's something we never do. I just had this riff with a Stonesish vibe and I said, 'Geoff, this feels like an environmental song.' Then he wrote the lyrics in a day and we went into the studio and did a guide track. Scott listened to it and did his track in the same day. Scott has become a one-take drummer. His stuff is instantaneous."*
>
> *City Heat: "How is it that the song Empire was recorded at Triad while the rest of the album was done at Vancouver Studios?"*
>
> *Wilton: "We went out to Red Rocks, Colorado to bring in an audience for filming a concert scene. Then they wanted to use one of our songs on the sound track for the movie (Ford*

Fairlane). We made a demo and sent four or five songs and they chose Empire. We went into Triad to record it and it turned out that they didn't want it because it was too heavy and too dark. They finally ended up using Last Time In Paris. Then we were thinking about re-recording Empire because we had use of all digital facilities and our engineer and everything. Then we started getting all this positive feedback from everyone that had heard that demo at Triad and they said just leave it. The recordings are good and it's comparable, so we just remixed it."

City Heat: "Is that the first you've worked with Tom Hall since the EP?"

Wilton: We always do little one-off recording sessions and stuff at Triad with Tom. Whether it's doing demos or transferring stuff from tape to DAT or whatever. We still do a lot at Triad."

The Empire tour is anticipated to last as long as two years. Their first time headlining, the set will be two hours long and contain Operation: Mindcrime in its entirety. Happy ticket holders.

They won't be playing any American dates until March unless we get very lucky with another New Year's Eve appearance like two years ago. Unfortunately, they declined to comment on that possibility. Keep your fingers crossed.

Empire is a fresh, viable direction for the thinking man's metal band as they embark on the massive appeal portion of their career. The next year will see their music and performances reaching millions of fans all over the globe.

A few metalheads will say they sold out to commercialism. I couldn't disagree more. The raw vitality that has always been Queensryche is still there, along with the intense growth they've experienced as musicians.

From the very beginning that's been a major goal for the band—to better themselves as musicians and remain honest in their songwriting.

> *Wilton: "It's a natural progression and it shows a different side of us. You know, it's just a point in our career where we have actually become somewhat parallel with what society wants. They played stuff from Operation: Mindcrime on the radio and that was a very cynical record and I think that kind of broke the doors down a little bit."*
>
> *City Heat: "Does the change have anything to do with your guys' new focus on family life?"*
>
> *Wilton: "Well, I just think that the songs that we wrote on this album were directly opposite of what we did on Mindcrime because we didn't want to do a follow-up conceptual album. We decided to go 180 degrees and just write these natural songs. So, we just wrote about ourselves, about some issues, and the world. That's about it!"*

Rainy City
Sports Bar & Grill
&
Guitarists bring your axe
CITY HEAT
Drummers bring your sticks
PRESENT
THE SUNDAY NIGHT HARD ROCK JAM
Bands:bring in any promo picture & get discounts on pitchers of brew.
FOR BOOKING INFO. CALL THE RAINY CITY AT 933-9500 OR CITY HEAT
NOVEMBER LINE-UP
Blues Thursdays
1st Little Bill & the Bluenotes
8th The Dick Powell Band
15th Kathy Hart & The Bluestars
29th Out of the Blue
Friday & Saturday
2nd & 3rd Freddie & The Screamers
9th & 10th Dix Delux
16th &17th Nightspell
23rd & 24th The Royals
30 & 31 Rudy & The Tube Shakers
2306 California Ave. S.W. West Seattle 933-9500
(take I-5 to West Seattle Freeway. Take the Admiral Wy exit up the hill to California Ave. Take a right and you are there!!!)

November 1990

Sunday	Monday	Tuesday	Wednesday	Thursday	Friday	Saturday
				1 The Square - Greta Goethe Group Riv - Chain Reaction FS: Street Ramao, Vodun, Red Alert Meekers: Fax	2 B.F. - Convertables Riv * * University: Bodhinche Central: Paisley Sin, Son of Man Love Brother 9 B.S.: Jumbalassy, Dub Squad FS: Canaan Elizabeth Meekers: Fax	3 B.F.: Convertables Riv: * * Jules Maes: Rambles & Room to Move University: * * Central: The Life B.S.: Roy Rogers, Delta Rhythm Kings FS: Paisley Sin, My Sisters Machine Meekers: Fax
4 B.F.: Sla Sun Sal - Suicide Blooze, Concrete Jungle Riv: Final Nation, Vodun, Melissa	5 Riv: Systems Ex New World: Rock Monday FS: 007, Dirty Cartoons Meekers: Fax	6 B.F.: Peace & Silence, Bam Bam & All Fall Down Riv: * * Central: First Thought New World: Aurora FS: Traffic Jam, Gloria Meekers: Petting Zoo, Fantazia, Rebel	7 B.F.: Eternal Daze & Phenomenal Essence Riv: * * Hollywood Underground: Bodhinche Central: Life Ring New World: * * BS: John Renbourn, Bert Jansch FS: Lady Jugs Aplenty, Naked, Prayer Muffin Meekers: Fax	8 The Square: Sam Smith B.F.: Variables & Liquid Rainbow Riv: * * University: Somerset Maughams, Machicks New World: * * BS: Steve Forbert FS: Food Giant, The Chasren Meekers: * *	9 B.F.: The Defenders Riv: * * University: Killing Fields, Mad Mad Nomad Central: Tailgators, Splinter Party New World: * * BS: Saffire Uppity Blues Women FS: Crash Course, The Source, Pistol Moon Meekers: * *	10 B.F.: Curtis Salgado & Stilettos Riv: * * Jules Maes: Interurban University: Cherry Poppin Daddies Sadhappy Central: * * New World: * * BS: Young Fresh Fellows, Monsetars, Eggplant FS: The Life, Lost Image, Agitated Native Meekers: * *
11 B.F.: Luther Johnson & The Magic Rockers Riv: Vicious Rumors, Rhino Buckett, Fantazia New World: * * BS: Patty Larkin	12 New World: Rock Mondy FS: Chaos, Stark Raven, The Crunch	13 B.F.: Israel Vibrations, Ficto Radios Central: Little Women New World: Aurora BS: Robin Holcomb FS: Jupiter, Vodun Meekers: Suicide Blooze, Love Brother 9, Rhino Humpers	14 B.F.: Big Top & Negative EArth Riv: Boy Toy Hollywood Underground: Latin Expression Central: Sunshine, The Wanted Sledge New World: * * BS: Seattle Comedy Competition Semi Finals FS: Mystery Train, Hard Margaret Meekers: Chain Reaction	15 The Square: The Prime Weirdz, The Lost Boys B.F.: Canaan Elizabeth & Tinderbox Riv: Boy Toy University: Like Rain, The Bold Brothers, GGOCH The Drifter Central: Sadhappy, Somebodys Daughter, Adnans Childhood New World: * * BS: Ginny Reilly FS: December	16 B.F.: Duffy Bishop & Rhythm Dogs Riv: * * University: The Life, Breathin Heathen Central: Sweaty Nipples New World: * * BS: Lemonheads, Love Battery, Delinquent Johns Meekers: * *	17 B.F.: Duffy Bishop & Rhythm Dogs Riv: * * Jules Maes: Mal Chicks University: The Tiny Hat Orchestra Central: Walkabouts, Jimi Talks, Terry Lee Hale New World: * * BS: Queen Ida, The Bontemps Meekers: * *
18 B.F.: Sabre & Dutrol Riv: Apocrypha, Invader, Rakkett New World: * * BS: Seattle Women's Ensemble Cabaret	19 Riv: Aurora BS: Karla Cruz Meekers: * *	20 B.F.: Rhino Humpers, Philosity, Prayer Muffin Riv: * * Meekers: Blade of Death, Rakkett, No Avail	21 BF: Sam Pierce Riv: * * Hollywood Underground: Bodhinche Central: KVI Presents Jr. Cadillac, Lilly Wild BS: Claudia Schmidt Meekers: Boy Toy	22 HAPPY THANKSGIVING FROM THE CITY HEAT STAFF!! Riv: * * Meekers: Closed	23 BF: Rumors of the Big Wave Riv: * * University: The Banjo Farmers Central: Red Platinum, My Sisters Machine, Son of Man, Hail Mary BS: Crazy Eights Meekers: * *	24 BF: Rumors of the Big Wave Riv: * * University: Buckets & The Weeds BS: Crazy Eights The Paramount Theater: The Nylons 5:00 p.m. Meekers: * *
25 Riv: Wyndh, Big City, Jupiter	26 Riv: Bad Actor Central: Nylon Docent, Kinetics, F-Holes, Splinter Party Meekers: * *	27 BF: Pistol Moon, Von Dutch Riv: * * Central: Variant Cause, Fastbacks, Hammerbox Meekers: Terrorist, Mad Hatter, My Remains	28 BF: Agitated Native, 007 Riv: * * Hollywood Underground: Latin Expression Central: Forced Entry, The Acousoc, Panic, Bitter End, Myra Mainz, Unearth Meekers: * *	29 The Square: Sam Weiss, Laura Love, Venus Envy, Chris Bingham BF: Vodun, A Rock & Roll Band University: All Acoustic Show Central: The Squirrels CD Release Party - Medicine Show - Moving Parts BS: Teresa Trull Meekers: Boy Toy	30 BF: Rangehoods Riv: * * BS: Greg Brown Meekers: * *	

"Word" by Patrick MacDonald – Tempo, Seattle Times

MUSIC
ROCK • POP • JAZZ • BLUES
FUTURE FILE

Word

A weekly column of news, opinion and information about rock 'n' roll.

Mould's lyrics on new album probe memories

by Patrick MacDonald
Times staff critic

Andrew Wood of Mother Love Bone is remembered in an interview in the December issue of Rip Magazine. Conducted by writer Michael Browning, the interview took place last March 15, one day before Wood was found unconscious from a heroin overdose. He died four days later when taken off life support systems.

Wood is open about his drug problems, saying, "I'm lucky to be sitting here. He talks about getting out of rehab and insists he is clean. "I was a druggy until I went into treatment," he says, "I'm not doing it anymore."

He's upbeat and positive about MLB's future.

rd, and is very
ust ask 'em),
show to the
8 p.m. Dec. 9.
s and Primus
7.50; 628-0888).

plays songs
iew album, "Re-
ınd past hits at 8
. 18 at the Taco-
e ($20; 628-0888).

Ida & the Bon
ydeco Band let
times roll at 8
. 17 at the Back-
3.50; 628-0888).

AY: Patrick Mac-
views "Rhythm of
," the new Paul
um, on the A&E
page.

MacDonald inter-
ıedian Jerry Sein-
his upcoming
ıe 5th Avenue The-

• **Andrew Wood** of **Mother Love Bone** is remembered in an interview in the December issue of **Rip Magazine.** Conducted by writer **Michael Browning,** the interview took place last March 15, one day before Wood was found unconscious from a heroin overdose. He died four days later when taken off life support systems. Wood is open about his drug problems, saying "I'm lucky to be sitting here." He talks about getting out of rehab and insists he is clean. "I was a druggy until I went into treatment," he says, "I'm not doing it anymore." He's upbeat and positive about MLB's future. A companion piece includes an interview with **Xana La Fuente,** Wood's girlfriend, who found him unconscious. "It's really cool and weird, 'cause he wrote so much religious stuff in the weeks prior to his death," she is quoted as saying. "All these songs about heaven and dying." Incidentally,

Robert Cray
"Final concert" contest

Bob Mould, formerly of Husker D
solo album, "Black Sheets of Rain

the same issue has articles on **Queensryche** and **Alice in Chains.**

• Speaking of **Alice in Chains,** the band has the honor of opening for one of the living legends of rock, **Iggy Pop,** Dec. 9 at the **Hollywood Palladium.** Unfortunately, the Ig will not be bringing his tour here because there is still an arrest warrant hanging over his head from a 1982 concert that got out of hand at the old **Eagles Auditorium.** Iggy knocked over some speaker cabinets that fell off the stage and hit a person in the audience, who sued.

• **Robert Cray** closes out his current tour with a concert **New Year's Eve** at the **Coliseum.** The great blues star – and former Seattleite – is teaming with **Fender,** the musical instrument com-

Andrew Wood
Remembered in Rip

The Seattle Times, Friday, November 2, 1990

A companion piece includes an interview with Xana La Fuente, Wood's girlfriend, who found him unconscious. "It's really cool and weird, 'cause he wrote so much religious stuff in the weeks prior to his death," she is quoted as saying. "All these songs about heaven and dying."

Incidentally, the same RIP issue also had articles on Seattle bands Queensryche *and* Alice In Chains [which Patrick *did not* note as also being written by Michael Browning].

Keep reading...to see both of the Mother Love Bone and Alice In Chains articles from RIP Magazine's December 1990 issue in the pages that immediately follow.

1990
JFMAMJJASOND

P L A Y L I S T

COVER PHOTOS:
Motley Crue: Neil Zlozower
Queensryche: Rick Gould/ICP
Judas Priest: Rick Gould/ICP

Something different, something new. Something fresh to sink your teeth into. Something familiar yet not. Isn't this what we are all looking for?

Unchain Alice, and that's precisely what you'll find. Although true to Seattle's trademark grunge style, Alice brands it with their own personality. Heavily influenced by other Emerald City stars like Soundgarden and Mother Love Bone, their music reflects the close-knit camaraderie between the bands working the Seattle scene. With the big family attitude of the bands there, it would mean there was something wrong if they didn't.

However, Alice's influences certainly aren't limited to locals only. Their Columbia debut, *Facelift*, expresses their interest in the Cult and vintage Judas Priest as well. It's a heavy, crunchy album rounded out by some slower tempos artfully produced by Dave Jerden. Thanks in part to him, Layne Staley's nasal-inflected vocals have matured into a strong, tough, street-wise sound, while Jerry Cantrell's guitar injects painful emotion into cuts like "Sea of Sorrow" and "Love/Hate/Love," then fills "Sunshine" and "We Die Young" with raw, boisterous energy. The pounding, grinding rhythms come via Sean Kinney's enthusiasm-filled drumming and Mike Starr's thick 'n' meaty bass. The sometimes morbid, always thoughtful lyrics focus less on sex than the world in general, as viewed from the perspective of youth specifically. Staley attributes much of the band's sound to the fact that they are all young and somewhat angry about the state of society. But this does not mean that they have no sense of humor. They try to deal with serious subjects in their music while retaining an irreverent attitude about themselves. They like to have fun.

As for the name, they just don't know. The stories range from Warrel Dane (Sanctuary's singer) once wanting to form a thrash band that wore dresses onstage, to a recent quote from Staley that starts with the band owning a cat named Alice and concludes unprintably. Its origination is generally credited to Staley, but I asked Kinney what it means. He said, "For some people it sounds like a girl's name, like Allison Chanes," then turns the question over to Cantrell. "What's it mean, Jerry?"

"Alice in Chains could very well have been Herbert In Chains—or Herbert In The Mud, for that matter. It actually means nothing." Then, as an afterthought, "Actually, it sounds like the title to a really good porno movie." To which Kinney adds, "We're hoping to make one." They will be touring the states in the months ahead, so remember: You're never too young for a *Facelift*. —*Michael Browning*

28 DECEMBER • RIP

Alice In Chains – Fresh Blood, RIP Magazine

Something different, something new.

Something fresh to sink your teeth into.

Something familiar, yet not.

Isn't this what we are all looking for?

Unchain Alice, and that's precisely what you'll find. Although true to Seattle's trademark grunge style, Alice brands it with their own personality. Heavily influenced by other Emerald City stars like Soundgarden and Mother Love Bone, their music reflects the close-knit camaraderie between the bands working the Seattle scene. With the big family attitude of the bands up there, it would mean there was something wrong if they didn't.

However, Alice's influences certainly aren't limited to locals only. Their Columbia debut, Facelift, expresses their interest in The Cult and vintage Judas Priest as well. It's a heavy, crunchy album rounded out by some slower tempos artfully produced by Dave Jerden.

Thanks in part to him, Layne Staley's nasal-inflected vocals have matured into a strong, tough, streetwise sound; while Jerry Cantrell's guitar injects painful emotion into cuts like *Sea Of Sorrow* and *Love/Hate/Love*, then fills *Sunshine* and *We Die Young* with raw, boisterous energy. The pounding rhythms come via Sean Kinney's enthusiasm-filled drumming fleshed out with Mike Starr's thick 'n' meaty bass licks.

The sometimes morbid, always thoughtful lyrics focus less on sex than the world in general, as viewed from the perspective of youth specifically. Staley attributes much of the band's sound to the fact that they are all young and somewhat angry about the state of our society.

But this does not mean that they have no sense of humor.

Quite the opposite! They try to deal with serious subjects in their music while retaining an irreverent attitude about themselves. They like to have fun.

As for the name, they just don't know. The stories range from Warrell Dane (Sanctuary and Nevermore's singer) once wanting to form a thrash band that wore dresses on stage, to a recent quote from Staley that starts with the band owning a cat named Alice and concludes unprintably.

Their name's origination is generally credited to Staley, so I asked the major prankster Kinney what it means.

> *"For some people it sounds like a girl's name, like Allison Chanes."*

Then he turns the question over to Cantrell,

> *"What's it mean, Jerry?"*

> *"Alice In Chains could very well have been Herbert In Chains or Herbert In The Mud, for that matter. It actually means nothing."*

Then, as an afterthought,

> *"Actually, it sounds like the title to a really good porno!"*

To which Kinney adds [in typical deadpan],

> *"We're hoping to make one."*

Alice will be touring the states in the months ahead, so remember:

You're never *too young* for a Facelift.

Mother Love Bone – Feature, RIP Magazine

Mother Love Bone Remembered - Andy Wood: The Last Interview

Some readers may consider the following interview depressing, exploitive, and even tasteless. We here at RIP feel it is an important and, yes, tragic piece of 1990's music history. To deny it to the fans of Mother Love Bone would be an injustice.

It was late '88 when the world first took notice of Seattle's Mother Love Bone, formed by members of two superb local acts, Green River and Malfunkshun. After an unexpected bidding war, MLB signed to PolyGram and released a five-song EP, Shine. They earned their first taste of nationwide attention after a very successful club tour with the Dogs D'Amour. It was the beginning of a very promising career.

On Thursday, March 15, 1990, writer Michael Browning and Mother Love Bone's talented and troubled songwriter/singer Andrew Wood conducted the following interview. Mother Love Bone were scheduled to be a part of a RIP-sponsored three-band tour, and their superb debut album, Apple, was ready to be released. It was agreed that the duo would speak again the following week at the Northwest Area Music Association conference, where Wood was scheduled to serve on the songwriter panel. That meeting would never occur.

Twenty-six hours later, about 10:30 p.m. Friday, Wood's fiancée, Xana, found Andy face down, unconscious, on their bed. After completing a month-long rehabilitation program and remaining clean for 116 days, Wood succumbed to the incredible cravings known only to heroin users. Paramedics rushed Wood to Harborview [Medical Center], where he was immediately hooked up to life-support systems. Wood had slipped into a

MOTHER LOVE BONE REMEMB

ANDY WOOD: THE LAST INTERVIEW

Some readers may consider the following interview depressing, exploitive, and even tasteless. We here at RIP feel it is an important and, yes, tragic piece of 1990's music history. To deny it to the fans of Mother Love Bone would be an injustice.

It was late '88 when the world first took notice of Seattle's Mother Love Bone, formed by members of two superb local acts, Green River and Malfunkshun. After an unexpected bidding war, MLB signed to PolyGram and released a five-song EP, Shine. They earned their first taste of nationwide attention after a very successful club tour with the Dogs D'Amour. It was the beginning of a very promising career.

On Thursday, March 15, 1990, writer Michael Browning and Mother Love Bone's talented and troubled songwriter/singer Andrew Wood conducted the following interview. Mother Love Bone were scheduled to be a part of a RIP-sponsored three-band tour, and their superb debut album, Apple, was ready to be released. It was agreed that the duo would speak again the following week at the Northwest Area Music Association conference, where Wood was scheduled to serve on the songwriters panel. That meeting would never occur.

Twenty-six hours later, about 10:30 p.m. Friday, Wood's fiancee, Xana, found Andy face down, unconscious, on their bed. After completing a month-long rehabilitation program and remaining clean for 116 days, Wood succumbed to the incredible cravings known only to heroin users. Paramedics rushed Wood to Harborview Hospital, where he was immediately hooked up to life-support systems. Wood had slipped into a coma. His family was informed that he had suffered considerable damage from lack of oxygen, and even if he recovered from the coma, he would very likely remain brain dead. On Monday, March 19th, when no improvement in Wood's condition was noted, he was taken off life support. Wood's heart slowly came to a stop as he lay in the arms of the woman he loved.

RIP: Mother Love Bone recorded *Shine* in five days, as compared to over three months for *Apple*. Is there a very noticeable difference?

ANDREW WOOD: Yes, definitely. There

By Michael Browning

40

ERED

coma. His family was informed that he had suffered considerable damage from lack of oxygen, and even if he recovered from the coma, he would very likely remain brain dead.

On Monday, March 19th, when no improvement in Wood's condition was noted, he was taken off life support. Wood's heart slowly came to a stop as he lay in the arms of the woman he loved.

> *RIP: Mother Love Bone recorded Shine in five days, as compared to over three months for Apple. Is there a very noticeable difference?*
>
> *Andrew Wood: Yes, definitely. There were some mixes that were sent to us, and we sent them back to be remixed; and there was still, like, four or five songs that still had to be remixed again. Now it's all settled and ready to be pressed. Apple is nearly an hour long. It may not even fit on one side of a cassette, so beware, kids, when taping at home [laughs].*
>
> *RIP: Did Mother Love Bone lose any of its grunge?*
>
> *Andrew Wood: I don't know. Did we have any grunge in the first place? I guess there's still a little grunge in the guitars from the Green River days. We didn't lose any of the grunge we needed, but we may be right in throwing some of the ugly grunge away. It's called stale grunge.*
>
> *RIP: Do you wish there was more funk in Mother Love Bone?*

Andrew Wood: I'm pretty content with the sound right now. I think I'm a bit more mellow than anybody else in the band. The whole set is pretty mid-tempo. We're not like a real "head swinging" type of band. When time off from Mother Love Bone allows, I might make a record, and my brother Kevin [who played with Andy in Malfunkshun] will be my guitar player.

RIP: Andy Wood goes solo?

Andrew Wood: No, it won't be called Andy Wood *or anything. It'll have some weird name, so it'll be kinda disguised.*

RIP: Let's talk about some of the songs on Apple.

Andrew Wood: Stardog Champion *is a kinda... fake, kinda patriotic rock anthem of sorts. That's gonna be the first single and video. When I wrote* Holy Roller, *I didn't even know what a holy roller was. I just thought it was a cool term. Actually, I was thinking of a* Paul McCartney *and* Wings *song,* Let Me Roll It. *I don't know why it made me think of holy rollers.* Captain Hi-Top *is just a total rock propaganda kinda thing. I kinda see* Heartshine *as our "Achilles' Last Stand" of the album. It's long and real powerful. I was kinda depressed about leaving* Malfunkshun *for a long time. Still am, kinda. I feel like, you know, I left them stranded. I've got a brother besides Kevin who, ah, is kinda insane in a way, and he makes the whole family worry about him, so* Heartshine *is a little about both of my brothers.*

RIP: Mr. Danny Boy *is obviously a slam on* Danny Thomas*.*

Andrew Wood: Yeah, I don't know why we decided to do such a mean thing to Danny.

RIP: But you did.

Andrew Wood: That's right. No offense to Marlo*. I still like her from* That Girl *[laughs].*

RIP: Come Bite the Apple*, is there any significance to that?*

Andrew Wood: That's a meaningful song. It's a Crown Of Thorns *type of song. The lyrics are personal, whereas some of the songs have absolutely nothing to do with me. Come Bite The Apple and* Crown Of Thorns *are probably mostly about me. It's kind of a synopsis of the whole past year. I'm lucky to be sitting here.*

RIP: Do you write all the lyrics?

Andrew Wood: Yeah. Nobody else has really brought any in. I think I'd find it hard to sing someone else's lyrics. I've got a guitar, but I've written most of my songs with keyboards as of late. I wrote Stargazer on guitar. I don't really consider myself a songwriter but, rather, a guy who makes up music. I don't know chords. I don't know notes. I can't even tell the guys in my band what I'm playing. I can't say, "Well, it's G-A-C-D," or whatever. They have to come and watch me and figure it out.

RIP: You taught yourself how to play guitar and keyboards?

Andrew Wood: Yeah, just kinda making up my own method of playing. That's been my whole thing. It seems as of late—I'm not going to name names or anything—but there seems to be some people who are real concerned about who their fans are, which doesn't make any sense to me, because they're all basically rock fans. We want them to be our fans. We don't want to draw any kind of lines.

RIP: Are those the only two instruments you play, guitar and keyboards?

Andrew Wood: I play wrinkle-neck trouser snake, guitar and keyboards...I also play Nintendo.

RIP: Do you ever worry about hitting writer's block?

were some mixes that were sent to us, and we sent them back to be remixed; and there was still, like, four or five songs that still had to be remixed again. Now it's all settled and ready to be pressed. *Apple* is nearly an hour long. It may not even fit on one side of a cassette, so beware, kids, when taping at home [laughs].

RIP: Did MLB lose any of its grunge?

A.W.: I don't know. Did we have any grunge in the first place? I guess there's still a little grunge in the guitars from the Green River days. We didn't lose any of the grunge we needed, but we may be right in throwing some of the ugly grunge away. It's called stale grunge.

RIP: Do you wish there was more funk in MLB?

A.W.: I'm pretty content with the sound right now. I think I'm a bit more mellow than anybody else in the band. The whole set is pretty mid-tempo. We're not like a real "head swinging" type of band. When time off from MLB allows, I might make a record, and my brother Kevin [who played with Andy in Malfunkshun] will be my guitar player.

RIP: Andy Wood goes solo?

A.W.: No, it won't be called "Andy Wood" or anything. It'll have some weird name, so it'll be kinda disguised.

RIP: Let's talk about some of the songs on *Apple*.

A.W.: "Stardog Champion" is a kinda... fake, kinda patriotic rock anthem of sorts. That's gonna be the first single and video. When I wrote "Holy Roller," I didn't even know what a holy roller was. I just thought it was a cool term. Actually, I was thinking of a Paul McCartney and Wings song, "Let Me Roll It." I don't know why it made me think of holy rollers. "Captain High-Top" is just a total rock propaganda kinda thing. I kinda see "Heartshine" as our "Achilles' Last Stand" of the album. It's long and real powerful. I was kinda depressed about leaving Malfunkshun for a long time. Still am, kinda. I feel like, you know, I left them stranded. I've got a brother besides Kevin who, ah, is kinda insane in a way, and he makes the whole family worry about him, so "Heartshine" is a little about both of my brothers.

RIP: "Mr. Danny Boy" is obviously a slam on Danny Thomas.

A.W.: Yeah, I don't know why we decided to do such a mean thing to Danny.

RIP: But you did.

A.W.: That's right. No offense to Marlo. I still like her from *That Girl* [laughs].

RIP: "Come Bite the Apple," is there any significance to that?

A.W.: That's a meaningful song. It's a "Crown of Thorns" type of song. The lyrics are personal, whereas some of the songs have absolutely nothing to do with me. "Apple" and "Crown of Thorns" are probably mostly about me. It's kind of a synopsis of the whole past year. I'm lucky to be sitting here.

RIP: Do you write all the lyrics?

A.W.: Yeah. Nobody else has really brought any in. I think I'd find it hard to sing someone else's lyrics. I've got a guitar, but I've written most of my songs with keyboards as of late. I wrote "Stargazer" on guitar. I don't really consider myself a songwriter but, rather, a guy who makes up music. I don't know chords. I don't know notes. I can't even tell the guys in my band what I'm playing. I can't say, "Well, it's G-A-C-D," or whatever. They have to come and watch me and figure it out.

RIP: You taught yourself how to play guitar and keyboards?

A.W.: Yeah, just kinda making up my own method of playing. That's been my whole thing. It seems as of late—I'm not going to name names or anything—but there seems to be some people who are real concerned about who their fans are, which doesn't make any sense to me, because they're all basically rock fans. We want them to be our fans. We don't want to draw any kind of lines.

RIP: Are those the only two instruments you play, guitar and keyboards?

A.W.: I play wrinkle-neck trouser snake, guitar and keyboards...I also play Nintendo.

RIP: Do you ever worry about hitting writer's block?

A.W.: I'm not too worried about it, though it definitely happens. Writer's block...I've never had that problem. When I have my keyboards around, I could definitely write a song a day. I've got so many old songs, I could go find an old one that I like if I

can't write a new one.

RIP: There are a lot of references to the group Queen in your lyrics.

A.W.: Queen's probably my favorite band. Queen, Kiss and Elton John. I'm kind of a hybrid of all those things that influenced me the most when I was growing up.

RIP: How old are you?

A.W.: 24.

RIP: You just got out of rehab.

A.W.: The old 28-day business. I have a weekly follow-up every Monday night.

RIP: Obviously you feel a lot better now that you're clean.

A.W.: Yeah. Still, though, it's a total struggle. When you first get out, you're on this pink cloud, and it's pretty easy. After a while things start getting more real, and you have to just stay straight a second at a time.

RIP: Do the other guys in MLB still get stoned?

A.W.: No! That's one lucky thing about this band. I was the druggy until I went in for treatment. We've got some people in the band that I don't doubt are alcoholics. The day Bruce quits drinking will be the day monkeys fly out of my butt, like on "Wayne's World." Luckily no one was into the drugs as much as I was, so I don't have to worry about them staying stoned, even though I'm not doing it anymore. Ever since I've known Stoney, and that's been years, he's never smoked pot.

RIP: Stoney?

A.W.: I know, with a name like Stoney. It's just his normal name: Stone. They all enjoy their beer. God, that's the thing: Back when I was taking all those drugs and everything, I thought the other guys were so damn boring. I thought, *What do these guys do for fun?*

RIP: Will this upcoming tour present any problems for you, like temptation?

A.W.: We all decided that on the upcoming tour there will be no alcohol at all on the bus. If they want to drink, they'll have to do it inside the clubs.

RIP: Is there any particular member of MLB that you seem to connect with the best?

A.W.: It's weird, 'cause it fluctuates. Sometimes I feel like me and Stoney are a team, partners in crime. And then me and Jeff have a lot of the same musical interests too. We're both kinda jocks in a way. I'm a video jock, whereas he's an actual jock. Then me and Greg are both Capricorns, so we get along well. Besides practicing five times a week, none of us spend that much time together.

RIP: Maybe it's better that way.

A.W.: Yeah. I mean, we'll be spending a lot of time together real soon.

RIP would like to extend it's deepest condolences to the family and friends of Andrew Wood. Since PolyGram and Mother Love Bone have decided to release the nothing short of superb Apple, *a bit of Andy Wood will live on forever.* •

Andrew Wood: I'm not too worried about it, though it definitely happens. Writer's block, I've never had that problem. When I have my keyboards around, I could definitely write a song a day. I've got so many old songs; I could go find an old one that I like if I can't write a new one.

RIP: There are a lot of references to the group Queen in your lyrics.

Andrew Wood: Queen's probably my favorite band. Queen, Kiss and Elton John. I'm kind of a hybrid of all those things that influenced me the most when I was growing up.

RIP: How old are you?

Andrew Wood: 24.

RIP: You just got out of rehab.

Andrew Wood: The old 28-day business. I have a weekly follow-up every Monday night.

RIP: Obviously you feel a lot better now that you're clean.

Andrew Wood: Yeah. Still, though, it's a total struggle. When you first get out, you're on this pink cloud, and it's pretty easy. After a while things start getting more real, and you have to just stay straight a second at a time.

RIP: Do the other guys still get stoned?

Andrew Wood: No! That's one lucky thing about this band. I was the druggy until I went in for treatment. We've got some people in the band that I don't doubt are alcoholics. The day Bruce quits drinking will be the day monkeys fly out of my butt, like on Wayne's World. Luckily no one was into the drugs as much as I was, so I don't have to worry about them staying stoned, even though I'm not doing it anymore. Ever since I've known Stoney, and that's been years, he's never smoked pot.

RIP: Stoney?

Andrew Wood: I know, with a name like Stoney. It's just his normal name: Stone. They all enjoy their beer. God, that's the thing! Back when I was taking all those drugs and everything, I thought the other guys were so damn boring. I thought, what do these guys do for fun?

RIP: Will this upcoming tour present any problems for you, like temptation?

Andrew Wood: We all decided that on the upcoming tour there will be no alcohol at all on the bus. If they want to drink, they'll have to do it inside the clubs.

RIP: Is there any particular member of MLB that you seem to connect with the best?

Andrew Wood: It's weird, 'cause it fluctuates. Sometimes I feel like me and Stoney are a team, partners in crime. And then me and Jeff have a lot of the same musical interests too. We're both kinda jocks in a way. I'm a video jock, whereas he's an actual jock. Then me and Greg are both Capricorns, so we get along well. Besides practicing five times a week, none of us spend that much time together.

RIP: Maybe it's better that way.

Andrew Wood: Yeah. I mean, we'll be spending a lot of time together real soon.

RIP would like to extend its deepest condolences to the family and friends of Andrew Wood. Since PolyGram and Mother Love Bone have decided to release the nothing short of superb Apple, a bit of Andy Wood will live on forever.

LAMENT FOR A STAR CHILD

"Crazy, crazy—I'm the boy who defies all."
"Stargazer"

Seattle's 1st Street is alive with people and music tonight. Just a short block or two stroll down this quaint, but bustling downtown drag, and you're overcome by the sights, sounds and smells of this mini-San Francisco's inner-pop-culture consciousness. From one club a drum machine strain blares, from another the divine whine of a jazz saxophone. But the beat that bellows biggest on 1st Street comes from the Central Tavern, *the* rock hangout in Seattle. Tonight, Mother Love Bone's bassist Jeff Ament is jamming with his local unsigned band, War Babies. Members of Alice In Chains, Queensryche and Metal Church chat with their buds out in front; there's a scraggly looking fellow selling hot dogs out of a trashcan lid; and leaning up against the brownstone building wall of the venue, surrounded by friends and hangers, is a tall, slender, curiously attractive girl with deep brown eyes and a lilting, yet firm demeanor. She smiles reservedly at those who share a moment of idle chatter, but you can't help but notice that she looks...lonely.

When Mother Love Bone's enigmatic and gifted vocalist died suddenly last March, Xana La Fuente was wearing his engagement ring. She'd spent the past four years connected to him physically, emotionally, spiritually and musically. In tragic irony, she was the one to discover his overdosed body.

"He was dead when I found him, and I didn't really realize it," she remembers. "I flipped him over and was shaking him. I looked at his arm and dialed 911. They told me to get him on his back and give him CPR. When they arrived, they pronounced him dead, made me sign this paper, and then told me to go to the hospital. When I got to the hospital, Andy was alive. He was alive for three days.

"He had an aneurysm in his brain that would have caused him to have a stroke eventually; so he did the drugs and probably had a stroke a few hours later, which knocked him out. They got his heart going again at the hospital, but his brain had swelled up from not breathing. They told me he could get worse, which he did. We had a meeting with the doctors on that Monday, and they said Andy's brain was dying, and it wasn't going to get any better. We had three hours to say goodbye to him.

"His whole family was at the hospital, like 20 people. They all went in and saw him. Then all of his friends went in and saw him. Then I went in and cut his hair off and kept it. I played some Queen for him—they were his favorite band. The doctors turned everything off, and I just held him really tight and listened to his heart until it stopped. It took like 15 minutes. God, it's so wild. I can't believe I went through that. When I think about it all, it freaks me out."

BY LONN M. FRIEND

Their relationship is reflected in the songs on *Apple*. "Crown of Thorns" was written about a nasty breakup between Andy and Xana over his on-and-off-again dabbling in heroin and alcohol. "This song is about a relationship ruined by drugs," she explains. "He wrote it about our near breakup, and how I tried to control him and the drugs—hence his allusion to being tied to the ceiling." According to Xana, "Andy was always ashamed of his addictions, choosing to lose himself in his music and poetry, bathing himself in concepts of real love and acceptance. 'Stardog Champion' was one of his 'anthem for survival' songs. It was an *up* time, and he really felt he was beating it. He had a choir, children from the San Francisco area (made up of foster and abused children), come in and sing backing vocals on this song.

"They were recording *Apple*, and he called me," she recalls. "He said to me, 'Xana, I know I need help when I get home. I know I need help, and you have to help me. I want you to help me.' "

"Stargazer, you call the shots/ stargazer, won't you kick with me."

No one knew Andy Wood like Xana did. She had helped him time and again struggle with his drug addiction. Amazingly, Andy had been clean 116 days prior to his overdose. Those around the Seattle drug scene claim that, on the weekend of Andy's death, three other individuals OD'd on the same bad heroin he had shot. They survived, and Andy didn't, it is surmised, because on that particular day, Andy was alone. The others weren't. There was no one there to help him this time—not even Xana.

There are numerous questions surrounding Andy Wood's death, but they're not worth elaborating. The most important fact remains that rock 'n' roll has lost a wonderful artist whose talent was never allowed to flourish. For those of us who didn't know Andy, we have but his one and only offering. Xana insists that Mother Love Bone will not continue without its founder, singer and inspirational leader. A dear Friend of Andy's and a central figure in the Seattle music scene, Soundgarden's manager Susan Silver, believes that Andy and Love Bone were destined for huge success. "No one will ever know what incredible talent was really there."

But Apple was not the culmination of Andy's musical legacy. "I have a box full of all his solo stuff," Xana says proudly. "It's mine. Hardly anybody else has copies of it. There's stuff there that the band has never even heard. It's really cool and weird, 'cause he wrote so much religious stuff in the weeks prior to his death. All these songs about heaven and dying. I loved him so much." •

DECEMBER • RIP

45

"Home," "Pussy Power" and "Baby Wants to Rock 'n' Roll"—with Slash and Duff in one marathon 11-hour session, the very first for the album.

Iggy says with a guffaw, "The record started by Duff coming into the studio and telling [producer] Don [Was, of Was (Not Was)], 'Hey, Don, I guess I'm gonna have to take off all the chains, eh? 'Cause they're gonna clink on the track.' He's holding a beer bottle. I started laughing. I thought, *This is gonna be fun*."

The band (joined tardily by Slash, who arrived, as is his custom, about four hours into the session) cut two numbers in short order in what sounds like it was a highly spontaneous and well-lubricated rev-up.

"By then we were all pretty merry, and they'd had to send out for another bottle," Iggy chuckles. "Don comes over and says, 'Listen, Ig, this is great, but these guys are pretty gone by now. I think they're drunk. We should just cool it for the night.' I said, '*No!* Don, I've done this before. Trust me, this is going to be really good.' So he said, 'Aw, all right.' "

And, maybe to everyone's surprise, the band wound up cutting "Baby Wants to Rock 'n' Roll" (rearranged on the spot by Slash) live in the studio in only two full takes.

The Iggy/Guns collaboration didn't end there, for Iggy, Slash and Duff wound up wowing a flabbergasted crowd with a four-song surprise set at the *Brick by Brick* album release party in L.A. in July. "I had a great time," Iggy says with obvious pleasure. "I needed that."

While Iggy can still make like the rock 'n' roll savage onstage, he admits that some of the songs on *Brick by Brick*—tough but reflective numbers like "Home" and "I Won't Crap Out"—are far removed from the gale-force blasts of the Stooges' early material. But he's proud of his new work.

"I thought, *Goddamn, I like a lot of the things I stand for, and I like a lot of the things that are going on in my head. I'm going to talk about them*," he explains. "I thought, *I have a home life, and if people don't like it, screw 'em*. There's a lot of very conservative attitudes on this record. A lot of it's saying, 'I want to live a quiet life.' The usual rock 'n' roll thing is, 'Oh, baby, I love your bushy wig,' but I've never really thought about that, not really."

In 1990, Iggy is looking beyond rock 'n' roll as a career. He took a featured role (cast against type as an uptight Middle American) in *Cry Baby*, a comedy by the bizarre Baltimore film director John Waters.

The pairing of director and player was near-ideal. Iggy says admiringly of Waters, "He's really witty and really together. In his sickness, he's really together. Sick individual. I remember when I first saw his films, I was down and out in L.A., and they were an absolute inspiration and joy to me. When Divine says, 'I sentence you to death for assholism,' and blows 'em all away, I saw no irony in that. I was like, 'Yeah, yeah, right on, death to the assholes.' I loved the colorful people living on the edge of life in his movies. It meant a lot to me."

Iggy has even hit the college lecture circuit. He was recently hired by the student bodies at the University of Wisconsin at Oshkosh, Rock Valley College in Illinois and Wright State in Ohio, to speak to classes there. "I talked about what I thought I've been doing with my life, and what I had to escape from in society to be able to do something creative. There was a lot of social comment in it, and then a lot of musical information. I played 'em a lot of cuts of my favorite stuff, and played some of my own songs."

But even in the groves of academe, Iggy couldn't escape his raunchy rock 'n' roll rep: "The content was very serious, but then at the end I would get questions like, 'Did you really shit on your windowsill, and why?' After this heartfelt two and a half hours, I got that. So I had to explain the artistic reasons why I had to shit on my windowsill."

But fear not—despite Iggy's recent forays into the movies and academia, he's not looking to jettison rock 'n' roll for a career in Hollywood or tenured professorship. As *Brick by Brick* shows, he's still one of rock's most vital and unpredictable performers, and he intends to stay that way.

Staring owlishly at me through his specs, the Ig says, "I do try to be as naked as I possibly can up there, and try to give what I got; and as long as people want to see it, I would like to do it." •

62 DECEMBER • RIP

CITY HEAT
Seattle's Music Magazine
Absolutely Free
HEART

Heart – Cover Story, City Heat

> *"Like Chief Seattle said, 'Everything is connected.' If you think that you can just be a consumer inside your own little world and not affect the world outside you, you're nuts. All the new people moving up who don't have environmental consciousness are acting like flood waters eroding the area. I'm not trying to be anti-California or new people at all. What we are trying to do is just educate everybody that we have a great area. When you move into the area, slow down, take a look around, recycle and change your way of thinking."*

Many other Washingtonians share the sentiments of the Wilson sisters and are actively involved in this education process. Even if you fancy yourself to be more of the 'inactive' type, you're helping out just by attending Heart's benefit concert on the 8th.

Since we all know who Heart are, I'll keep the history to a minimum.

Way back in the late 60' s. Ann Wilson was in love with a draft evader named Michael Fisher. His brother Roger and Steve Fossen had a band called The Army (Somewhat ironic, eh?). Ann joined and they called it Hocus Pocus. When they ran to Canada they re-named it Heart.

Nancy had been playing coffee houses in college and when she came in the line-up included Howard Leese and Michael DeRosier circa '75. Around the turn of the decade Ann, Nancy and Howard enlisted the talents of Mark Andes on bass and Denny Carmassi on drums, and that's been Heart ever since.

PHOTO: GREG GORMAN / 1990

"Like Chief Seattle said, 'Everything is connected.' If you think that you can just be a consumer inside your own little world and not affect the world outside you, you're nuts. All the new people moving up who don't have environmental consciousness are acting like flood waters eroding the area. I'm not trying to be anti-California or new people at all. What we are trying to do is just educate everybody that we have a great area. When you move into the area, slow down, take a look around, recycle and change your way of thinking."

Many other Washingtonians share the sentiments of the Wilson sisters and are actively involved in this education process. Even if you fancy yourself to be more of the 'inactive' type, you're helping out just by attending Heart's benefit concert on the 8th. Since we all know who Heart are, I'll keep the history to a minimum.

Way back in the late 60's, Ann Wilson was in love with a draft evader named Michael Fisher. His brother Roger and Steve Fossen had a band called The Army (Somewhat ironic, eh?). Ann joined and they called it Hocus Pocus. When they ran to Canada they re-named it Heart. Nancy had been playing coffee houses in college and when she came in the line-up included Howard Leese and Michael DeRosier circa '75. Around the turn of the decade Ann, Nancy and Howard enlisted the talents of Mark Andes on bass and Denny Carmassi on drums, and that's been Heart ever since.

CH: "Let's talk about the benefit. Who came up with the idea?"

Ann: "Actually we've been trying to do this for a few years. We got to thinking what could we possibly do for our area. We have been all over the world and we always come back to Seattle. There is something about it that is so different and so sweet, fresh, and special to us that we wanted to make a gesture and so we thought what we can do is just not blow through town like usual and take the money and run. How about if we give our services. Do what we do best. Make the money and turn around and put it back into the hands of the city, but for a certain purpose which is cleaning the water, cleaning the air, the wetlands especially. Puget Sound is only the front yard. The mountains and the forests are the backyards so what we're doing is trying to get the whole area, keeping it stable by putting all this money into various groups that know what to do with it. Nancy and I first came up with the idea about four years ago and tried to get it together in Seattle then and we couldn't even make anyone bat an eyelash then because it wasn't hip."

CH: "And probably the need hadn't been realized."

Ann: "Right. It was before the big influx of people from California and all that kind of stuff. And so now we just kept on pushing and we finally were able to get some business people around town to put in some money and get the whole thing moving and also our other sister Lynn is married to Ted Pankosky, who is the president of the Washington Environmental Council and so all of a sudden it is like a family thrust, you know. So it's also about now that it's

HEART

CITY HEAT December 4

sold out in the round and it's going to be quite an exciting night."

CH: "So who will this benefit and in what ways?"

Ann: "It's a push to make money for local environmental groups, especially the Washington Council and at the concert there is going to be literature galore specifying exactly where all the mo... [illegible] We plan to raise probably [illegible] 00 that night. Purely for the environment. If people are curious as to where it is going, they can read this from Nancy and I saying how people, what they do inside their own home. Not a big scary governmental finger shaking thing. Just like, tips that normal people can do in normal ways in their homes, to make a difference. It's just like a very middle class kind of idea. It's not aimed at anything except every man."

CH: "Almost at the grass roots level. OK, how about the show itself?"

Ann: "what people can expect to see, really is Heart at its peak, at it's stride in 1990. What began in the Moore Theatre way back in March is now like a big monster. We took the Moore for two weeks to get the show together and like rehearsed everything and get used to being on stage and stuff. So what you are going to see is the latest generation of lighting technology that is not technology any more. It's more like art. It's just like the colors we are using in the air right now are rich, thick jewel colors and it's almost like the music is only half of the beauty. It's something to see and it's something to hear. Nancy is back playing acoustic guitars along with electric guitars. We are doing a couple of songs that aren't even on a record."

CH: "Cool Covers? Or are they unreleased originals?"

Ann: "One of them is called 'You're the Voice', which we have released in Russia only so far. The rest I want to be a surprise. I don't want to wreck the whole thing."

CH: "After the benefit you only have a couple of stops left on the tour, right?"

Ann: "Then we are going to come home and be people and have Christmas with our families. After that, we're going to just be people for a while and then start writing songs. Nancy and I are going to write songs for the next Heart record..We're also very excited about doing a dual solo album. Only Anne and Nancy. I mean not to the break up of the band or anything but just two of us doing what we like to do that's not appropriate for Heart. Which is more acoustic stuff, more deeper lyrical content, bluesy stuff."

CH: "As though there were room for anymore, what else ya got going?"

Ann: "When we get back to Seattle after Christmas, we'll be way into that. We are going to build a world class studio in Seattle at last."

CH: "Now, will that be something that's in your homes or is it going to be available to local musicians that have money to rent it?"

Ann: It will be for everybody to use but it will be to our specifications. Seattle so far has been very backward when it comes to state of the art, up to the minute, recording studios. We are so sick of having to always go away to L.A. to record and living in that place down there. We feel like it actually infringes on our edges as musicians. So that's why we are making the studio in Seattle finally."

CH: "Best city ever."

Ann: ""Capital Hill is really an amazing area. It's full of artists and full of rock people. That's where I live when I'm not on the road. Our drummer lives in San Francisco and our bass player lives in L.A. but the core of the band Howard, Nancy and I still live in Seattle. People in Seattle have always coexisted with us and let us just be ourselves and not made our lives miserable. Like, there is always a few kids hanging around my gate but they are loving people, they are not nutso or wierdos, necessarily. It's where we were raised and where we intend to be with our families."

Speaking of families, you may have heard something a while back about Ann pursuing an adoption. Seems the rumor's true and she may be a mother as soon as February. Yet another good reason to make Seattle home. We're glad that they're proud of their home and we'd like to thank them for their efforts that will benefit everyone. We'd also like to wish Heart (and everyone else) a happy holiday season and a rippin' nineteen ninety-one.

CH: "How long do you see Heart going on? You've just renewed your Capitol contract for five more albums."

Ann: "That's impossible to say. Heart will exist as long as it's meaningful to do it. As long as it's appropriate. If it turns into a nightmare, we'll knock it on the head. But, if it keeps on being cool, then..."

CH: "Is that Nancy laughing in the background?"

Ann: "Yeah, Nancy's laughing. She thought that was a funny way to put it. Like Nancy says, 'we'll knock it on the head, we'll clean it, cook it and eat it.'"

CH: "Alright some fisher woman."

Ann: "Yeah, fisher woman, fisher folk. Fish wives. But anyway, so I think we've got a few more years left in us, you know?"

CH: "We agree"

BY MICHAEL BROWNING

5

December ***CITY HEAT***

CH: "Let's talk about the benefit. Who came up with the idea?

Ann: "Actually we've been trying to do this for a few years. We got to thinking what could we possibly do for our area. We have been all over the world and we always come back to Seattle. There is something about it that is so different and so sweet, fresh, and special to us that we wanted to make a gesture and so we thought what we can do is just not blow through town like usual and take the money and run. How about if we give our services. Do what we do best. Make the money and turn around and put it back into the hands of the city, but for a certain purpose which is cleaning the water, cleaning the air. the wetlands especially. Puget Sound is only the front yard. The mountains and the forests are the backyards so what we're doing is trying to get the whole area, keeping it stable by putting all this money into various groups that know what to do with it. Nancy and 1 first came up with the idea about four years ago and tried to get it together in Seattle then and we couldn't even make anyone bat an eyelash then because it wasn't hip."

CH: "And probably the need hadn't been realized."

Ann: "Right. It was before the big influx of people from California and all that kind of stuff. And so now we just kept on pushing and we finally were able to get some business people around town to put in some money and get the whole

December 8 1990
Seattle

Dear Friends

Thanks for being here tonight to celebrate our commitment to a liveable environment: By joining us, you show you care.

Our children and grandchildren depend on us to do our best now to save valuable resources for their future. We hope you'll practice these three "**R's**" at home. They'll really help.

REDUCE: Avoid wasteful products and packaging. No need to go without, just don't buy what you don't need.

REUSE: Use products till they drop! Repairing, borrowing, buying second-hand or renting are all great ways to cut down waste.

RECYCLE: Use a three bin system for your household trash; paper, cans, & glass. Check out curbside recycling in your neighborhood.

These are just a few basic ideas but use your imagination and discover more. Maybe you can't solve all the problems – but do what you can. You'll make a difference!

Thanks and Love, Ann & Nancy

Printed on recycled paper

thing moving and also our other sister Lynn is married to Ted Pankosky, who is the president of the Washington Environmental Council, and so all of a sudden it is like a family thrust, you know. So it's also about now that it's sold out in the round and it's going to be quite an exciting night."

CH: "So who will this benefit and in what ways?"

Ann: "It's a push to make money for local environmental groups, especially the Washington Council and at the concert there is going to be literature galore specifying exactly where all the money is going to. We plan to raise probably $50,000 that night. Purely for the environment. If people are curious as to where it is going, they can read this from Nancy and I saying how people, what they do inside their own home. Not a big scary governmental finger shaking thing. Just like, tips that normal people can do in normal ways in their homes, to make a difference. It's just like a very middle-class kind of idea. It's not aimed at anything except every man."

CH: "Almost at the grass roots level. OK, how about the show itself?"

Ann: "What people can expect to see, really, is Heart at its peak, at it's stride in 1990. What began in the Moore Theatre way back in March is now like a big monster. We took the Moore for two weeks to get the show together and like rehearsed everything and get used to being on stage and stuff. So what you are going to see is the latest generation of lighting technology that is not technology any more. It's more like art. It's just like the colors we are using in the air right now are rich, thick jewel colors and it's -almost like the music is only half of the beauty. It's something to see and it's something to hear. Nancy is back playing acoustic guitars along with electric guitars. We are doing a couple of songs that aren't even on a record."

CH: "Cool, covers? Or are they unreleased originals?"

Ann: "One of them is called 'You're the Voice', which we have released in Russia only so far. The rest I want to be a surprise. I don't want to wreck the whole thing."

CH: "After the benefit you only have a couple of stops left on the tour, right?"

Ann: "Then we are going to come home and be people and have Christmas with our families. After that, we're going to just be people for a while and then start writing songs. Nancy and I are going to write, songs for the next Heart record. We're also very excited about doing a dual solo album. Only Anne and Nancy. I mean not to the breakup of the band or anything but just two of us doing what we like to do that's not appropriate for Heart. Which is more acoustic stuff, more... deeper lyrical content, bluesy stuff."

CH: "As though there were room for anymore, what else ya got going?"

Ann: "When we get back to Seattle after Christmas, we'll be way into that. We are going to build a world class studio in Seattle at last."

CH: "Now, will that be something that's in your homes or is it going to be available to local musicians that have money to rent it?"

Ann: It will be for everybody to use but it will be to our specifications. Seattle so far has been very backward when it comes to state of the art, up to the minute, recording studios. We are so sick of having to always go away to L.A to record and living in that place down there. We feel like it actually infringes on our edges as musicians. So that's why we are making the [Bad Animals] studio in Seattle finally."

CH: "Best city ever."

Ann: "Capitol Hill is really an amazing area. It's full of artists and full of rock people. That's where I live when I'm not on the road. Our drummer lives in San Francisco and our bass player lives in L.A but the core of the band Howard, Nancy and I still

> *live in Seattle. People in Seattle have always coexisted with us and let us just be ourselves and not made our lives miserable. Like, there is always a few kids hanging around my gate but they are loving people, they are not nutso or weirdos necessarily. It's where we were raised and where we intend to be with our families."*

Speaking of families, you may have heard something a while back about Ann pursuing an adoption. Seems the rumor's true and she may be a mother as soon as February. Yet another good reason to make Seattle home. We're glad that they're proud of their home and we'd like to thank them for their efforts that will benefit everyone.

We'd also like to wish Heart (and everyone else) a happy holiday season and a rippin' nineteen ninety-one!

> *CH: "How long do you see Heart going on? You've just renewed your Capitol contract for five more albums."*
>
> *Ann: "That's impossible to say. Heart will exist as long as it's meaningful to do it. As long as it's appropriate. If it turns into a nightmare, we'll knock it on the head. But, if it keeps on being cool, then..."*
>
> *CH: "Is that Nancy laughing in the background?"*
>
> *Ann: "Yeah, Nancy's laughing. She thought that was a funny way to put it. Like Nancy says, 'well knock it on the head, well clean it. cook it and eat it.'"*

CH: "Alright some fisher woman."

Ann: "Yeah, fisher woman, fisher folk. Fish wives. But anyway, so I think we've got a few more years left in us, you know?"

CH: "We agree!"

Billy Idol & Faith No More - In Concert, Hot Flashes, City Heat

This was a Halloween not soon forgotten, and a concert equally memorable. 18,000 crazed goblins, pregnant nuns, ghoulish beings and just plain night owls gathered to spend All Hallow's Eve with kindred spirits.

Pre-show, I asked Faith No More's Jim Martin if his festive self was dressing up for the occasion.

> *An enthused, "Of course!" was followed by, "I'm planning to change my t-shirt."*

Though visibly road-weary, Faith No More smashed open pumpkin night with *From Out of Nowhere*, using all the tenacity and power that makes their stage show a must-see.

Polaroid: Karen Mason

Center stage, sporting gorilla fur pants, red flannel shirt and a Doris Day wig, Michael Patton went immediately into his flinging, flailing, stomping routine that I overheard one very un-PC mother describe as a 'good imitation of a retarded person'.

IN CONCERT

BILLY IDOL
FAITH NO MORE

This was a Halloween not soon forgetten, and a concert equally memorable. 18,000 crazed goblins, pregnant nuns, ghoulish beings and just plain night owls gathered to spend All Hallow's Eve with kindred spirits. Pre-show, I asked Faith No More's Jim Martin if his festive self was dressing up for the occasion. An enthused "of course!" was followed by "I'm planning to change my t-shirt."

Though visibly road-weary, FNM smashed open pumpkin night with "From Out of Nowhere", using all the tenacity and power that makes their stage show a must-see. Center stage, sporting gorilla fur pants, red flannel shirt and a Doris Day wig, Michael Patton went immeditately into his flinging, flailing, stomping routine- that I overheard one mother describe as a good imitation of a retarded person. Next up was their most current cool cut, "Falling To Pieces". They crammed "Underwater Love", "Surprise, You're Dead", "The Real Thing", and the only number from a previous album, "We Care Alot", into their formidable opening set- highlighted by joyously cheeky renditions of the Nestle's Alpine White jingle and "The Edge Of The World".

This being the combination of both Halloween and the last date of FNM's stint on the Charmed Life tour, we were in for some surprises. In the midst of thumping out their "Epic" hit, Mr. Idol's road crew thumped the band with a huge amount of smelt from the lighting rig. After flinging fish into the crowd and taking their bows, FNM returned to the stage for a cover of The Commodore's "Easy (Like Sunday Morning)" with the help of three housewives in robes, singing backup and opening their robes to flash mammoth false breasts. An unfalse B.A. from the girls accompanied the curtain call. And there was more fun in store.

As soon as Idol hit the stage with "Cradle Of Love", it began. A gorilla came dancing around stage right, surprising the beautiful duo singing backups. Then it joined along with their dance steps, all the while, Billy Idol was oblivious to the show-stealing going on behind him.

Mr. Idol gave an energetic performance that seemed little-affected by his recent lameness. Limp and barely noticeable, he posed and sneered and swaggered like in top form. He rattled off his long list of hits from the latest, back to Gen X days with "The Untouchables". Songs from an MTV generation: "Eyes Without A Face", "White Wedding", "Rebel Yell", and "Flesh For Fantasy" (which featured a pretty neato robotic, chest-baring dance step from the Idol one).

The real kicker, however, came in the midst of his encore, "To Be A Lover". Heads covered with masks, paper bags and towels, five guys- assumed to be FNM- circled Idol, and danced around him butt-naked. Pretty scary.

Living Colour
LIMBOMANIACS

On November 17th, a near sellout crowd filed into the Paramount to watch Living Colour prove themselves live, and (excuse the expression)- In Living Colour!

Included on the Living Colour ticket is the Limbomaniacs, a funk/rock/rap outfit recently signed to Combat/Relativity records. These guys are the latest band to come out of the recent San Francisco label signing frenzy and I had the dubious honor of chatting with two of the main maniacs: guitarist Mirv (no last names please) and bassist/vocalist Butthouse (don't ask!). Trying to get a straight answer out of them was like pulling teeth,so you be the judge:

CH: So how long have you been out with Living Colour?

Mirv: 2 days, last night in Portland and tonight here. After this we go back to San Francisco for some shows with Bootsy Collins.(their only serious answer)

CH: So what's the typical Limbomaniacs audience like?

Butthouse: Pretty diverse, the usual youngsters, people show up just to see what Mirv's gonna wear on stage each night.

Mirv: Yeah, tonight I'm going to dress like bozo, the clown!

CH: Well what would your ultimate audience be made up of?

Butthouse: Dirtbags, bikers, and homocidal maniacs. (laughs)

CH: Seattle has it's own music scene with it's own sound, do you consider yourselves part of the San Francisco sound?

CITY HEAT December 16

Next up was their most current cool cut, *Falling To Pieces*. They crammed *Underwater Love*, *Surprise! You're Dead!*, *The Real Thing*, and the only number from a previous album, *We Care A Lot*, into their formidable opening set - highlighted by joyously cheeky renditions of the Nestle's Alpine White jingle and *The Edge Of The World*.

This being the combination of both Halloween and the last date of Faith No More's stint on the Charmed Life tour, we were in for some surprises. In the midst of thumping out their *Epic* hit, Mr. Idol's road crew thumped the band with a huge amount of smelt from the lighting rig.

After flinging fish into the crowd and taking their bows, FNM returned to the stage for a cover of The Commodore's *Easy (Like Sunday Morning)* with the help of three housewives in robes, singing backup and opening their robes to flash mammoth false breasts. An unfalse B.A. from the girls accompanied the curtain call.

Thank you! And there was more fun in store.

As soon as Idol hit the stage with *Cradle Of Love*, it began. A gorilla came dancing around stage right, surprising the beautiful duo singing backups. Then it joined along with their dance steps, all the while, Billy Idol was oblivious to the show-stealing going on behind him.

Mr. Idol gave an energetic performance that seemed little afflicted by his recent lameness. Limp barely noticeable, he posed and sneered and swaggered like in top form.

He rattled off his long list of hits from the latest, back to Gen X days with *The Untouchables*. Songs from an MTV generation: *Eyes Without A Face*, *White Wedding*, *Rebel Yell*, and *Flesh For Fantasy* (which featured a pretty neat-o robotic, chest-baring dance step from the Idol one).

The real kicker, however, came in the midst of his encore, *To Be A Lover*. Heads covered with masks, paper bags and towels, five guys (assumed to be Faith No More) circled Idol, and danced around him butt-naked.

Now, that's....

Pretty scary!

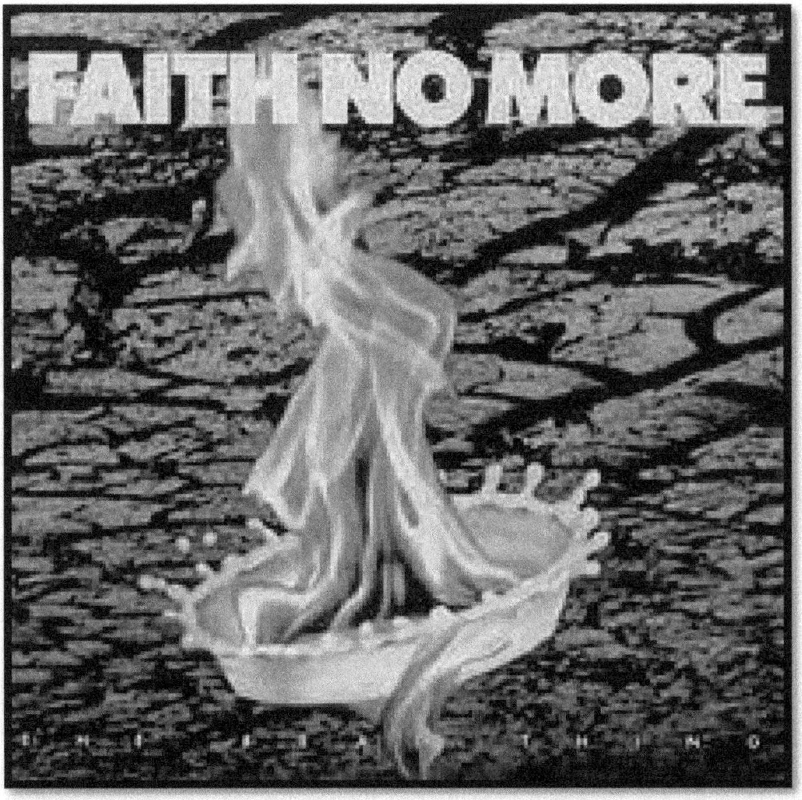

What scared me even more, after the fact, was the way Mike Patton was staring down my dorkie porn stash pirate routine in that pre-show Halloween photo op at Seattle Center Coliseum.

That dude is not to be trifled with!

Reprise

In a lovingly typical Seattle hometown story with heart, *Polish* was about to take *Pain* under wing and make *everything beautiful*, if maybe misunderstood, as SAP soon poured from Seattle's sonic giants (established and establishing).

See the next titles in Seattle's Music Scene series covering the years 1991 and 1992 for more Chain links in that story.

And if you're reading this on paper, check out the Kindle Link**eBook** version to really taste the history, to make it last for hours.

Because when you read the Link**eBook** version…

the story continues!

I'll even send you one myself!

E-mail evidence of your paperback purchase to linkebook@michaeledwardbrowning.com with the words "Kindle Copy" in the Subject or Body and get the digital version in return. Then you'll have both!

Thanks for reading! Thanks for rockin' by!

About The Author

Photo: Shannon Jones

Michael Edward Browning was born November 25th, 1966 in Weisbaden, Germany. He grew up and graduated high school in Eugene, Oregon. Michael moved to Seattle in May of 1988 and lived there until the late 90's writing for many international travel and entertainment publications.

Starting at **City Heat: Seattle's Music Magazine** in the summer of 1989, he was promoted to Editor in the fall of 1990. Freelance work for **RIP, Rock Beat, Blender, Face II Face, Watt, Hype, Rock Power, Melt Down, MovieMaker** and **Entertainment Weekly** as well as Seattle's two dailies followed, along with a gig for **Tower Records' Pulse Magazine** as Seattle Newsline Correspondent.

In the latter half of the 90s, Michael was on the team producing live shows Eye On Seattle and Pirate Television, airing on cable channel 29 around Puget Sound. In 1998, **Pirate Television** won a Live Programming Award of Excellence from the Alliance for Community Media.

Bright Films & Video is Michael's production company. Check out some Candlebox and Sweet Water show vids or have a look at a few Ninkasi Brewing branding concepts or a couple of 48 Hour forays.

DO NOT HESITATE to contact Michael about development funding for a couple of original features he has in mind, featuring Northwest music of course! If you know affluent fans of Everclear or Mother Love Bone, they would love these ideas!

Michael thanks you for reading.

You're invited to please visit him in his messy space over at michaeledwardbrowning.com to hear interview snippets, read unreleased interviews, see where you can ride (mountain bike, snowboard, wakeskate, whatev!) with him this season and get the true skinny on living the life you want to be living.

'Cause he sure still is!

(Love) Rock On, People!

City Heat Magazine - December 1990 Issue

Foreshadowing the ensuing SAP collaboration, this celebratory year-end issue of City Heat featured Heart on the cover while Alice In Chains' Christmas Card photo (another ingenious Karen Mason creation) adorned our December concert and club calendar.

City Heat Issue 29 is reproduced here, in its entirety, as a tribute to Zine culture - and the year 1990!

Time travel **IS** possible!

Enjoy the trip.

CITY HEAT
Music Magazine
HEART

Local Dirt

By J. Hollywood

Season's Greetings to all and may the Christmas wind blow happiness your way. The Christmas season brings many a celebration but the one most dear to us is our 3rd Annual City Heat Christmas Party, scheduled for Dec. 19th at the Sea Tac Hilton. With live music by War Babies, Paisley Sin and Love Brother 9, it promises to be the gala event of the year! Speaking of Paisley Sin, the band just released a two song 45 that's available everywhere on KMA Records. San Prova is in the studio recording a six-song demo that will eventually be released as an EP. Sub-Pop Records announced the release of a single by the Butthole Surfers due out before the end of the year, the Walkabouts are in the studio recording their next album. Local Superstar Heart and special guest Cheap Trick play the Coliseum Saturday, Dec. 8th for "Puget Sound 'Live'". A concert whose proceeds benefit the cleaning up of our Puget Sound, how ironic. We thank these princesses of NW R&R (Ann & Nancy Wilson) for giving of their time and talent, and hope you're one of the fortunate who can be in attendance.

Inflate Dates, Rick Williams, and Pat Elliott have added yours truly, J. Hollywood, to their line-up and we'll keep you posted on the power trios' progress in the near future. Well, I've got some serious Christmas shopping to do — until next year everyone — stay clean, you feel better and have money to see more live music!

Rainy City

Sports Bar & Grill

&

CITY HEAT

MAGAZINE
PRESENT

THE SUNDAY NIGHT HARD ROCK JAM

Bands:bring in any promo picture & get discounts on pitchers of brew.

Guitarists bring your axe **Drummers bring your sticks**

FOR BOOKING INFO. CALL THE RAINY CITY AT 933-9500

2306 California Ave. S.W. West Seattle 933-9500

(take I-5 to West Seattle Freeway, Take the Admiral Wy exit up the hill to California Ave. Take a right and you are there!!)

CITY HEAT December 2

CITY HEAT
An Aird Hooker publication

Executive Publisher
Matthew Aird

Publisher
Robert E. Barr

Editor
Michael Browning

Associate Editors
Claude Flowers
Shay McGraw

Editorial Consultant
Jeff Lageson

Account Executive
Angela Metcalf

Contributing Writers
Katie McMillan
Jimmy St. Buchin
Michelle Klosener
Andrea Long
David Sterling
Jana Skillingstead
Linnea Freed
J. Hollywood
Kellee Francis
Nadia Felker

Fashion Editor
A.R. Stuart

Photography
Charlie Hoselton
Karen Mason

Art Director
Mark Cole

Concert Desk
Lori DeLano

Distribution Manager
Ted Treichler

Computer Consultants
Doug Kammerer

CITY HEAT is published monthly at 929 SW 152nd St. Seattle, WA 98166. CITY HEAT accepts no responsibility for unsolicited materials. Subscriptions are available for $12/year U.S. $15/year first class or foreign. All contents © 1990 Aird Hooker Publishing. All inquiries please phone 206.242.3852.

Editorial

GIRL, YOU KNOW IT'S TRUE- Fab and Rob of chart-topping pop-rock group and international dance club success Milli Vanilli didn't sing a single note on their debut release on Arista Records, Girl You Know It's True. The band's bogus album chalked up four number one Billboard singles; and soared to platinum status, having sold over seven million copies since its release last year. Even more astounding is the fact that they were presented with a Grammy Award last year as being the year's "Best New Band", which the band unduly accepted appreciatively and sincerely, maintaining their more-than-deserving composure all the while. Little did anyone know then that they deserved the award no more than you or I.

Now that Milli Vanilli have been forcibly stripped of their Grammy, I feel that the award should be reissued- but this time to the studio musicians who really did sing on the album- just to set the records straight. After all, they did earn it. And can they be so incredibly hideous that they require this "false front" in order to convey their music? For most, the absence of vocalization on the part of these two Rastafarian look-alike con-men doesn't call for the loss of a night's sleep. It's more a question of "Where do we draw the line?"

It's public knowledge that studio musicians have been prevalent and widely-accepted in the studio for quite some time, but Milli Vanilli offer an entirely different dimension to their usage. Techno-poppers and others have introduced the use of implements such as electronic drumbeats, instrumentals, and sampling in the last decade; and dubbing, re-dubbing, and over-dubbing are virtually a given on the recording end of the business- just to name a few. Not that I'm some hell-bent conservative, determined to uphold the ideals of a generation gone by, but I feel that a band should be capable of reproducing at least adequately what they offer the consumer in their finished and marketed product. If you look at the bands that have stood the test of time, you'll find that for the most part, they're the ones who can do this. The others are something that, just like a bad haircut, will pass with time. This episode, by no means carries with it the implications of Watergate, but should be regarded as fraudulent; and legal measures should be taken against the band's record label, the bandmembers, and any other parties involved. I mean, what entitles them to the money earned from this hoax more than you or I?

Reportedly, this is a moment the dethroned duo had both feared and hoped for quite some time, says their manager. "They couldn't stand to lead this lie forever." Yeah, and bums cringe at the sweet taste of fortified wine. Having read a Rolling Stone interview with Rob and Fab of Milli Vanilli last year, I saw no indication that they didn't plan on going on like this forever. The band were so conceded as to say that they were not only better musicians, but more musically-inclined than the likes of rock legends such as Bob Dylan and The Rolling Stones. Everyone is entitled to their own opinion, but if they aren't even going to perform their own material, they may as well tuck their hair up in colorful knit hats and smoke the ghanja or spend their days cliff-diving under the hot Jamaican sun. If the band's producer wouldn't have come forward and said, "Hey, these geeks couldn't hold a note in a washtub", they would have gone on riding the gravy train as far as it would take them. If Rob and Fab would not have been found out, they would have gone on making records; and the success and shared net profits of their albums would have been due to the studio musicians who actually sang on them, with almost no emphasis on the addition of Rob and Fab's pre-packaged image, which consists of no more than a little fancy footwork and matching hair-dos- not to mention their heavy English accents that ensures their singing career to be nothing more than a dead-end venture. Milli Vanilli are merely a novelty item- typical of a Maurice Starr project, which include the likes of The Perfect Gentlemen, of The New Kids on the Block (who don't write their own music).

There had been some controversy in the past regarding Milli Vanilli lip-syncing during their live performances, but no one beside a select handful of corporate big-wigs and record execs suspected that the roots of the sham were buried this deep. It has been said in the past that "entertainment is an illusion", but where do we draw the line between illusion and all-out deception- or even worse, conspiracy? Music should be true to its audience- at least for the sake of the longevity of the entertainment industry. This isn't the first instance of this kind of deception occurring, however. Janet Jackson and others also utilize lip-syncing at their so-called "live" shows. In other instances, computerized background vocals; sampling of pre-

(Cont on Page 15)

CITY HEAT MAGAZINE

DECEMBER 1990 · ISSUE 29

Features

Departments

HEART

PHOTO: GREG GORMAN / 1992

"Like Chief Seattle said, 'Everything is connected.' If you think that you can just be a consumer inside your own little world and not affect the world outside you, you're nuts. All the new people moving up who don't have environmental consciousness are acting like flood waters eroding the area. I'm not trying to be anti-California or new people at all. What we are trying to do is just educate everybody that we have a great area. When you move into the area, slow down, take a look around, recycle and change your way of thinking."

Many other Washingtonians share the sentiments of the Wilson sisters and are actively involved in this education process. Even if you fancy yourself to be more of the 'inactive' type, you're helping out just by attending Heart's benefit concert on the 8th. Since we all know who Heart are, I'll keep the history to a minimum.

Way back in the late 60's, Ann Wilson was in love with a draft evader named Michael Fisher. His brother Roger and Steve Fossen had a band called The Army (Somewhat ironic, eh?). Ann joined and they called it Hocus Pocus. When they ran to Canada they re-named it Heart. Nancy had been playing coffee houses in college and when she came in the line-up included Howard Leese and Michael DeRosier circa '75. Around the turn of the decade Ann, Nancy and Howard enlisted the talents of Mark Andes on bass and Denny Carmassi on drums, and that's been Heart ever since.

CH: "Let's talk about the benefit. Who came up with the idea?

Ann: "Actually we've been trying to do this for a few years. We got to thinking what could we possibly do for our area. We have been all over the world and we always come back to Seattle. There is something about it that is so different and so sweet, fresh, and special to us that we wanted to make a gesture and so we thought what we can do is just not blow through town like usual and take the money and run. How about if we give our services. Do what we do best. Make the money and turn around and put it back into the hands of the city, but for a certain purpose which is cleaning the water, cleaning the air, the wetlands especially. Puget Sound is only the front yard. The mountains and the forests are the backyards so what we're doing is trying to get the whole area, keeping it stable by putting all this money into various groups that know what to do with it. Nancy and I first came up with the idea about four years ago and tried to get it together in Seattle then and we couldn't even make anyone bat an eyelash then because it wasn't hip."

CH: "And probably the need hadn't been realized."

Ann: "Right. It was before the big influx of people from California and all that kind of stuff. And so now we just kept on pushing and we finally were able to get some business people around town to put in some money and get the whole thing moving and also our other sister Lynn is married to Ted Pankosky, who is the president of the Washington Environmental Council and so all of a sudden it is like a family thrust, you know. So it's also about now that it's

CITY HEAT December 4

sold out in the round and it's going to be quite an exciting night."

CH: "So who will this benefit and in what ways?"

Ann: "It's a push to make money for local environmental groups, especially the Washington Council and at the concert there is going to be literature galore specifying exactly where all the mo... We plan to raise probably ... 00 that night. Purely for the environment. If people are curious as to where it is going, they can read this from Nancy and I saying how people, what they do inside their own home. Not a big scary governmental finger shaking thing. Just like, tips that normal people can do in normal ways in their homes, to make a difference. It's just like a very middle class kind of idea. It's not aimed at anything except every man."

CH: "Almost at the grass roots level. OK, how about the show itself?"

Ann: "what people can expect to see, really is Heart at its peak, at it's stride in 1990. What began in the Moore Theatre way back in March is now like a big monster. We took the Moore for two weeks to get the show together and like rehearsed everything and get used to being on stage and stuff. So what you are going to see is the latest generation of lighting technology that is not technology any more. It's more like art. It's just like the colors we are using in the air right now are rich, thick jewel colors and it's almost like the music is only half of the beauty. It's something to see and it's something to hear. Nancy is back playing acoustic guitars along with electric guitars. We are doing a couple of songs that aren't even on a record."

CH: "Cool. Covers? Or are they unreleased originals?"

Ann: "One of them is called 'You're the Voice', which we have released in Russia only so far. The rest I want to be a surprise. I don't want to wreck the whole thing."

CH: "After the benefit you only have a couple of stops left on the tour, right?"

Ann: "Then we are going to come home and be people and have Christmas with our families. After that, we're going to just be people for a while and then start writing songs. Nancy and I are going to write songs for the next Heart record..We're also very excited about doing a dual solo album. Only Anne and Nancy. I mean not to the break up of the band or anything but just two of us doing what we like to do that's not appropriate for Heart. Which is more acoustic stuff, more deeper lyrical content, bluesy stuff."

CH: "As though there were room for anymore, what else ya got going?"

Ann: "When we get back to Seattle after Christmas, we'll be way into that. We are going to build a world class studio in Seattle at last."

CH: "Now, will that be something that's in your homes or is it going to be available to local musicians that have money to rent it?"

Ann: It will be for everybody to use but it will be to our specifications. Seattle so far has been very backward when it comes to state of the art, up to the minute, recording studios. We are so sick of having to always go away to L.A. to record and living in that place down there. We feel like it actually infringes on our edges as musicians. So that's why we are making the studio in Seattle finally."

CH: "Best city ever."

Ann: ""Capital Hill is really an amazing area. It's full of artists and full of rock people. That's where I live when I'm not on the road. Our drummer lives in San Francisco and our bass player lives in L.A. but the core of the band Howard, Nancy and I still live in Seattle. People in Seattle have always coexisted with us and let us just be ourselves and not made our lives miserable. Like, there is always a few kids hanging around my gate but they are loving people, they are not nutso or wierdos, necessarily. It's where we were raised and where we intend to be with our families."

Speaking of families, you may have heard something a while back about Ann pursuing an adoption. Seems the rumor's true and she may be a mother as soon as February. Yet another good reason to make Seattle home. We're glad that they're proud of their home and we'd like to thank them for their efforts that will benefit everyone. We'd also like to wish Heart (and everyone else) a happy holiday season and a rippin' nineteen ninety-one.

CH: "How long do you see Heart going on? You've just renewed your Capitol contract for five more albums."

Ann: "That's impossible to say. Heart will exist as long as it's meaningful to do it. As long as it's appropriate. If it turns into a nightmare, we'll knock it on the head. But, if it keeps on being cool, then..."

CH: "Is that Nancy laughing in the background?"

Ann: "Yeah, Nancy's laughing. She thought that was a funny way to put it. Like Nancy says, 'we'll knock it on the head, we'll clean it, cook it and eat it.'"

CH: "Alright some fisher woman."

Ann: "Yeah, fisher woman, fisher folk. Fish wives. But anyway, so I think we've got a few more years left in us, you know?"

CH: "We agree"

BY MICHAEL BROWNING

5 *December* *CITY HEAT*

FOR THOSE WHO REALLY LIKE TO ROCK!
TOO COOL
BITCHIN'
Z ROCK
ROCKIN'
BAKIN'
AM 1590
ROCKS HARDER!
MAJOR
TOO OUTRAGEOUS FOR FM!
CRUCIAL
HOT
HIP
ROCK. BE ROCKED. OR STEP ASIDE!
Z ROCK
Z ROCK
BLAZIN'
AM 1590

Tapes Available at
Cellophane Sq.
Peaches
Tower
FANTAZIA
For more info:
Delisio
5102 Shorecrest Dr.
Anchorage Ak 99515
(206) 874-6317
Appearing Live
Dec 4th
Ballard Firehouse
Dec 16th
The Riv
Write to:
Fantasia
P.O. Box 4547
Kent, Wa
98032
Call and request us on Z-ROCK AM 1590 421-1590
Prominent Northwest musicians Scott Delisio (Legend) & Tony Delisio (Fantasia) collaborate to present one of the hottest tapes of the year. DONT MISS IT
Available at these locations:
Peaches
Easy Street
Tower Records
Cellophane Square
DeLisio
December CITY HEAT

Dogma Cipher

Phillip Craft has programmed his digital watch to record important dates in his life. One of these is "3/20/88", the day that he and girlfriend Janice Durham formed their band Dogma Cipher. The ensuing eighteen months have been marked by loss and achievement, but the future of the band looks bright- with a new bass guitarist, forthcoming mini-LP, and a major-label benefactor in New York observing their progress.

Photo: SHOT IN THE DARK

Drummer Phillip was born in San Rafael, and has been back and forth between California and Washington ever since. He got a snare drum at a young age, and his parents bought him a full set when he was in fifth grade. He served in a bunch of garage bands which most people have probably never heard of ("I hope not!"), and his interest in music led to music theory classes in college, work in jazz bands, and a curious tenure with Gene Malone, cousin of the Go-Go's Charlotte Caffey. He admits to taking the job because,"Gene had lots of money and resources up the Yin Yang!" As is often the case, the cash wasn't enough of an incentive to play lifeless Top-40 music, and Phillip split after a Canadian tour.

Singer Janice describes herself as a "military brat." Raised in Fort Sill, Oklahoma and Kansas,she joined the navy, and in Japan, hooked up with some musician pals. "We knew seven songs and played for two hours," she grinned,"and at first we didn't have a name! A club owner told us, 'you need one, mighty quick!' So we said, okay,call us Mighty Quick!" Eventually she, too, migrated to Seattle, played in some Top 40 bands, and then looked for more satisfying work.

Yano C. and original Dogma Cipher bassist Zybnek Pavlicek (nicknamed Z) have even more exotic histories- they're Czechoslovakian refugees who escaped to America during the pre-*Peristroika* era and settled in the Northwest. The duo teamed up with Janice and Phillip, and as Dogma Cipher, the quartet created its own niche within the Seattle scene.

Neither a metal band, nor grunge, funk, rap, ad infiritum, Dogma Cipher has built its reputation on its idiosyncratic style. Janice's gentle yet powerful voice resonates with feeling. She can make it soar, quiver, or sustain notes for what seems to be an eternity. Yano is a master of the "space guitar" stylings of his heros: David Gilmour, Joe Satriani, and Eric Johnson. Grounding the music created by these sonic acrobats are Phillip's tumbling, jazzy drums and Z's throbbing bass. The combination defies description, but has proven to be a crowd pleaser. All four group members were nominated in the 1989 N.A.M.A. Awards for performer categories. Dogma Cipher made the ballot as "Best New Northwest Band."

This first lineup of the band is preserved on the cassette "Dogma Cipher." Independently produced and distributed by the group, it features five tracks that deal with the band's favorite topics- politics and people. Although the cover art and some of the lyrics seem cynical or tragic at first, it is actually full of hope and fighting spirit.

One of the most interesting outcomes of releasing "Dogma Cipher" is that it has earned the group a fan base behind the iron curtain. Yano said this happened because of a friendship the band struck with Czech musician Vlasta Tresnak: "Tresnak was in Seattle to do a concert, and we opened the show. Z did a really long interview with him, and it, along with the demo, was broadcast over (the transeuropean shortwave station) Radio Free Europe." Although the band never was able to pick up the transmission, Phil says, "we do get an occasional fan letter from Czechoslovakia. We give them to Yano to translate."

Another result of the tape is that it established what the bandmembers call their "New York Connection." "A big person in CBS Records," Phillip said cryptically, "is aware of us." The group is going to send a forthcoming demo to it's "Connection," and there are high hopes of obtaining a record contract.

Photo: SHOT IN THE DARK

Those hopes should be realized. Comprised of both new material and Dogma live standards, the forthcoming collection is jam-packed with infectious melodies, and Janice's poetic, dreamy lyrics.

CITY HEAT December 8

The latter are often so personal its a wonder she'd even disclose such feelings to the public. "There Goes Another Friend," is written about the deaths of two loved ones - their pal Eugene, and Phillip's grandfather. The tape is dedicated to their memories.

The most astounding track on the cassette is called "Danton." Janice wrote it after watching the film of that name; a biography of a political moderate who tried to get rebels and royalty to come to a peaceful settlement during the French Revolution. For his troubles, Danton was beheaded at the guillotine. The song has a brilliant arrangement, ending with a militaristic snare drum cadence. And this rendition features a really breath-taking vocal performance.

The tape, which is to be released around the turn of the year, also features the debut of new bassist Gerald Harmon. He stepped in after Z quit the band earlier this year. Phillip says, "Z just wanted to play simpler, raw music. It was a beautiful parting. He played until we found (a replacement)." Z is visiting relatives in Czechoslovakia, but will return to the states and begin working with Ivan Kral, who has played with Iggy Pop, Patti Smith, and Blondie.

Gerald, in typical Dogma Cipher tradition, has an untypical background. He was born in France, spent his early childhood in Germany, and moved to Washington in 1964. He has a degree in microtechnology (!) and plays both bass and guitar. He says Rush is his favorite band and is always trying to master new instruments. "I want to be as versatile as possible," he says, "right now, I'm learning to play five-string bass. One day I want to get an upright bass, but good ones cost twenty to thirty grand."

He shouldn't worry; Dogma Cipher won't be "starving artists" for much longer. But the money- and satisfaction- will come from making music of the heart.

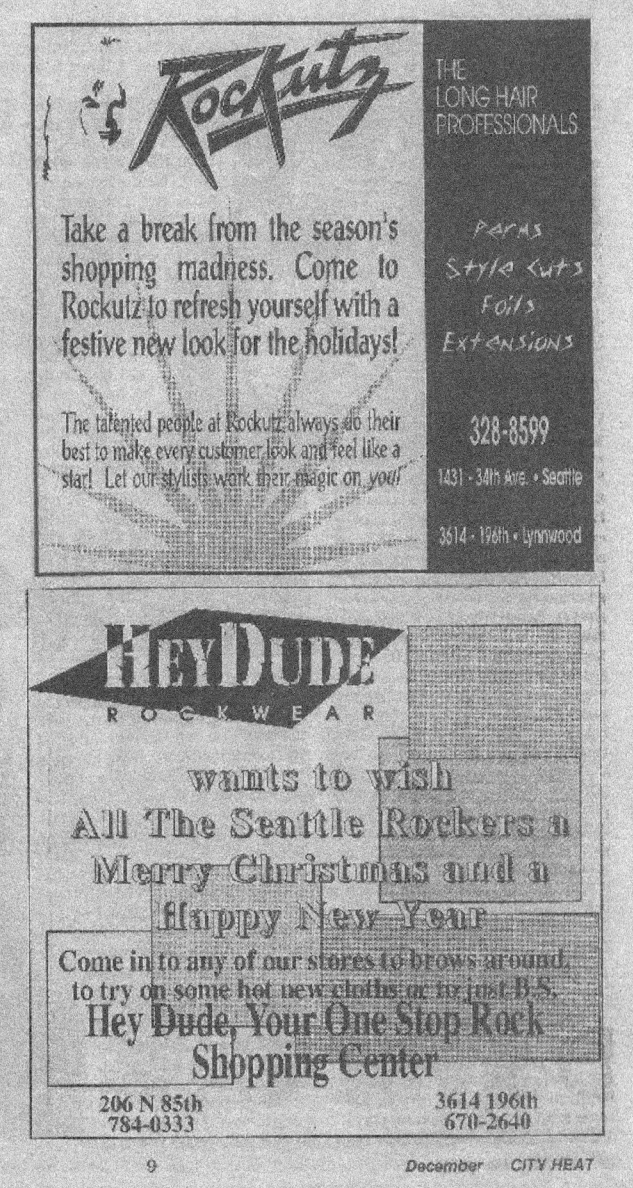

By Claud Flowers

Mad Mad Nomad

"But it's not like we're totally serious," said Caz Murphy as the front man for the Seattle based alternative rock band, Mad Mad Nomad. "We have emotional music, and somewhat intense lyrics, but we also get great joy out of the intensity of things instead of taking things lighthearted, and being a beer drinking kind of band."

Murphy talked briefly about his band of two years, and speculated on why they have been getting noticed favorably more often int he past year of live shows. "I hope to have the prolificness in music be more accepted, rather than formulized music. I think that's happening in the '90s, and that's why I feel we're a real '90s kind of band because in the '80s it was like a band would get their one formula and every album would kind of sound the same. An it seems now that there's quite a few bands who are not limited to saying they are this one kind of band. Usually they say now that they are pop with a reggae influence, and they are this and that...and that's why I say that we're really focusing in because we also have that read widespread view, but now we're gearing in so that we have our few different types of sounds so that also blend together."

Murphy described the other four members in the band, beginning with the drummer, Michael Martin. "Mike is a real serious musician, he's a funny guy and he's real lighthearted in a lot of ways but he studies drums like he's under some kind of guru. When he plays drums he seems to want to have his own song of the drums, it's not like he just wants to do just a back beat. Then we've got John Studamire our bass player, really funny guy...in a way he's the connector of the whole band. He's a real charismatic guy, people follow him around, and everyone seems to like him. John once said that at the age of thirteen he called his mother to say that he wouldn't be able to go to school the following day (in Seattle), and when his mom asked why he said it was because he had just joined a band and was on the road in Denver. So he's been a hard-core bass player for a real long time now." Murphy continued describing his friends/co-musicians by saying, "O.K. then we've got Mark Nelson on guitar, he's a real hard worker, and a real congenial person who is trying to learn new things all the time. He catches on really fast and sometimes when we're having a disagreement he'll have a real good opinion that he'll put in. And then Jackie Grad on keys and violin, she in a lot of ways runs the band...she basically does most of the booking, most of the management and a lot of the production. She also does a lot of the arrangement, she has great musical ideas...I've been writing all of the music up until now. Recently the band has begun to take more interest so we're co-writing a few things and are trying to get a flow of our sound. I'm still going to be writing most of our material, but we're going to have a few where we all write them and that's at different levels, maybe two of us will write some, or whatever. Jackie has a real strong influence, she has a real great sense of simplicity, like when I write something that's a little too much, she'll suggest the best word to drop.

Murphy best described himself unknowingly, as he told me about the root of the alternative rock that Mad Mad Nomad plays. "The way I see it (and express "it" with his guitar/vocals) is almost as if you hear African folk music, and it's got a real funk type of rhythm, but the melody over it is like a melancholy (Scots or Irish) fold melody. What we're trying to put into an American stream is sort of playing funk music, but over it is a more melodic-pop-folk type of rock."

"I met Jackie about five years ago in New Zealand, and we ended up doing a year tour of the Orient. Everything from Tokyo, and the major clubs there to the hill tribes in China, Bali, Thailand, and places like that. The name Mad Mad Nomad comes from a song I wrote during the tour, when we were in Thailand and it goes....HELLO SUSIE WHATCHA DOIN' UP IN WONDERLAND, I'M THE MAD MAD NOMAD FROM NEW MEXICO, AND I'M COMIN' TO TAKE YOUR HAND. I'M GONNA MARRY YOU AND WE'RE GONNA LIVE ON THE BEACH...The song goes on like that, and it's a silly song, but we were trying to figure out a name for the band, and it works for us...."

By Katie McMillan

CITY HEAT *December* 10

SHOT
IN THE DARK
PHOTOGRAPHY
Music Photography
7TH HEAVEN
TEACHERS PET
SHOT IN THE DARK
Seattle Trade Center • 2601 Elliott Avenue Studio 5114 • Seattle 98121 • 206.441.5532

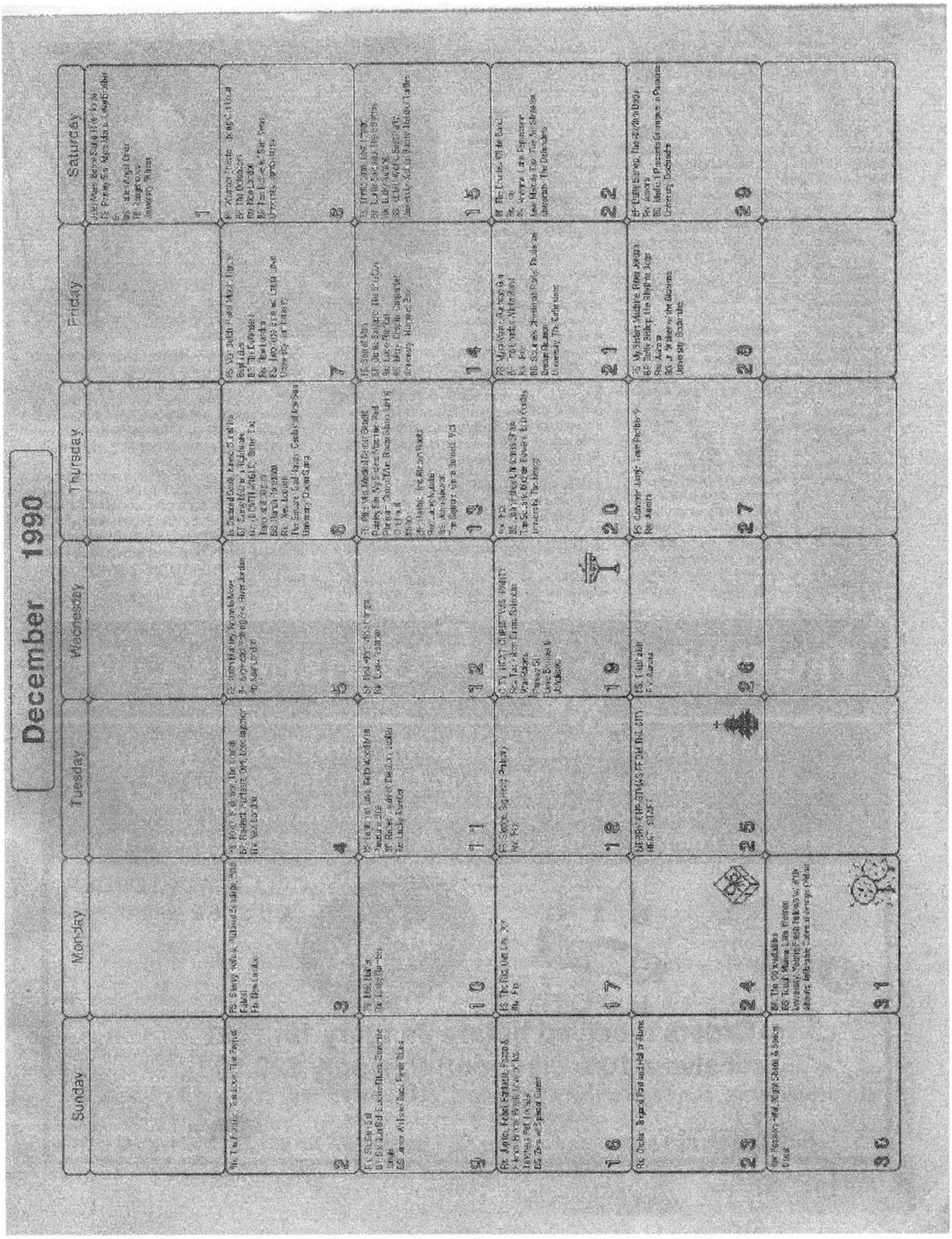
December 1990
Sunday
Monday
Tuesday
Wednesday
Thursday
Friday
Saturday

INDUSTRY PROFILE

Our newest feature at City Heat is **"Industry Profile"**. Each month we will focus on an indevidual who has considerably contributed to the Seattle music scene. This month's candidate is **Jay Boone, Manager of Seattle Music.**

Humbly, Jay started out as a musician in Seattle, playing guitar, bass, and singing. He was a prominent musician in bands such as Dick Tracy and Widow. You may remember Widow as having recorded 3 albums under CBS records. In Widow Jay gained valuable experience as an opening act for such established national artists as Bryan Adams and INXS.

When Jay decided he'd like to make more money than his band was bringing in, he opted to go into retail for two basic reasons:he thought it was cool, and he was good at it, having completed two years of junior college in business. He then helped to start Guitars Etc. in Bellevue by working as floor manager. When Guitars Etc. owner Dan Wallace purchased Seattle Music, Jay was soon to migrate to the new store where he has been working for six years, and has served as manager for one.

Contributing to the family atmosphere at Seattle Music is the fact that Jay has key employees to rely on. One such employee is Evan Sheeley of TKO and Q5 fame.

To keep up with the new technology in the competetive field of music retail, Jay attends seminars including the National Association of Music Merchants (NAMM) convention held twice yearly in Anaheim, California. Jay also has manufacturers representatives give his employees private seminars, keeping them up to date on the latest equipment. Seattle music also hosts instructional clinics featuring national artists.

When asked what advice he would give to people wanting to break into this field, Jay replied, "when your starting out you should get as much sales experience as possible, treat people well, and service them." Jay and Seattle Music strive to be service oriented by treating musicians straightforwardly and giving good deals. Jay tells us that such local heavies as Alice in Chains, Mother Love Bone, and Queensryche shop at Seattle Music.

On the personal front, Jay is married, with children and still enjoys playing in two bands: MO Fo Bro, and Spike and The Continentals. His goals are to continue to write music and to eventually own his own music store.

For those musicians who haven't ventured into Seattle Music, here;s why you should in Jay's own words."Give us a shot and see why we are Seattle's premiere guitar store." Drop by Seattle Music and say Hi to Jay and see why he will continue to be a prominent member of the Seattle music scene.

By Kellee Francis

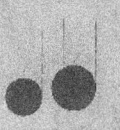

CITY HEAT December 14

club scene

The Central

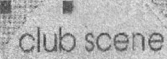

Requiem of a Landmark

In a way The Central Tavern is the Seattle music scene. It's a club, a landmark, a home away from home for some. With the closing of the club on November 30th, like it or not, there will be a void left in the music scene.

The Central Tavern has supported the local music scene for a long time. It's a place that has embraced us [illegible] as much as we've embraced it. It's a place where memories are made, friends are introduced, and bands are weaned into full-fledged rock stars.

The people that frequent The Central wear denim and leather and they drink beer... very Seattle. Nightspots come and go, open and close, and are bought and sold, as the case with The Central. The powers that be aren't saying much about the [illegible] but we do know that it will reopen as a "yuppie" restaurant, probably in about 8 weeks. Okay, I know you're thinking it so I'll just go ahead and say it: it sucks! Just what we need, another yuppie bar. Due to the fact that the club is in the historical district, the name The Central can't be changed, only the [illegible] part will change. We'll be calling it The Central Saloon, The Central Eatery, The Central Restaurant and Grill, or something [illegible] like that...

Speaking realistically, there will still be places for bands to play. There are clubs that serve better drinks. Face it, The Central is not exactly designed for comfort. It's the people who go, and the bands who play that make The Central what it is. It's dingy, it's sweaty, but it's real.

The memories are that we've watched our favorite national acts in an intimate setting. We've watched our favorite local bands grow, mature and prove themselves as [illegible] enough to grab them up. We've also witnessed the brotherhood of Seattle bands coming together (sometimes at the very last minute) for benefits to help out fellow musicians and people in need. Because of a benefit, The Central has a new stage... Basically, we've all had a small part in the buzz that people across the nation are calling the hippest music scene in the country, and we've known it all along.

So will the new Central have music also? Current manager Teri McKinley will only say that it's being discussed. When we asked Teri about some of the more memorable shows at the club, she told us, "Hothouse Flowers and Soundgarden, billed as Vinos and The Nude Dragons stand out as being really successful shows."

A tribute to The Central wouldn't be complete without comments from the musicians who've appeared on stage for us... I asked them to comment on anything they felt about the closing of The Central. I'll leave you with those comments... Goodbye Central Tavern, we'll miss you.

Trevor, vocalist, Sedated Souls: "It sucks that they're closing The Central because it's the only place in the heart of downtown that really supports the local original scene."

JR., guitarist, Sedated Souls: "The dude that works the door is a cool guy."

Jeff Rouse, bassist, Rhino Humpers: "It sucks that it's closing but things will move on."

Brian Coloff, guitarist, Rhino Humpers: "The Central's a place where if you can make it there, you can make it anywhere."

Mark, guitarist, Sunshine: "It's a great place, you can feel the [illegible] done down there, they've always been supportive of the scene and had the best national acts. The new owners should keep the old crew, they're good people."

Jeff Ament, bassist, Mother Love Bone: "I don't think it will be any huge loss. People are making a huge fuss about there not being any place to play but I don't think it's any big deal."

Tom McMullin, guitarist, Warbables: "The Central has been a catalyst for new bands. Just about every band that has made it has been seen by the [illegible] at The Central. What do I think about it closing? It sucks!"

By Kellee Francis

15

EDITORIAL
(Cont from page 3)

programmed rhythms, vocals, and instrumentals occurs- both in the recording process, as well as in live performance.

It seems that after Milli Vanilli had received such a healthy dose of mass media punishment and assorted other embarrassment, that Rob and Fab would have humbly stepped down and taken their lickings like men. Now it is said that the two Sillis seek further embarrassment, and plan to release a second album in which they actually do sing the lead vocals. They should have thought about doing that the first time around, before they lost the respect of the masses. Speculation on my part will cause me to second-guess the validity of this release as well, providing there ever is one.

This entire incident not only makes a joke out of the two dancing dorks, but also humiliates both the American Music Association, who presented the award; and also demands some skepticism from the listener as to the extent of honesty on the part of the music and entertainment industry as a whole. Since I didn't care for the band to begin with, there's no lost love on my part, and this is welcome news. But for others who I feel indebtedly sorry for- namely Milli Vanilli fans- this is a time for feelings of betrayal and discouragement. This may well be the music industry's hoax of the century... up 'til this point at least!!!

Shay McGraw

December *CITY HEAT*

IN CONCERT

BILLY IDOL
FAITH NO MORE

This was a Halloween not soon forgotten, and a concert equally memorable. 18,000 crazed goblins, pregnant nuns, ghoulish beings and just plain night owls gathered to spend All Hallow's Eve with kindred spirits. Pre-show, I asked Faith No More's Jim Martin if his festive self was dressing up for the occasion. An enthused "of course!" was followed by "I'm planning to change my t-shirt."

Though visibly road-weary, FNM smashed open pumpkin night with "From Out of Nowhere", using all the tenacity and power that makes their stage show a must-see. Center stage, sporting gorilla fur pants, red flannel shirt and a Doris Day wig, Michael Patton went immeditately into his flinging, flailing, stomping routine- that I overheard one mother describe as a good imitation of a retarded person. Next up was their most current cool cut, "Falling To Pieces". They crammed "Underwater Love", "Surprise, You're Dead", "The Real Thing", and the only number from a previous album, "We Care Alot", into their formidable opening set- highlighted by joyously cheeky renditions of the Nestle's Alpine White jingle and "The Edge Of The World".

This being the combination of both Halloween and the last date of FNM's stint on the Charmed Life tour, we were in for some surprises. In the midst of thumping out their "Epic" hit, Mr. Idol's road crew thumped the band with a huge amount of smelt from the lighting rig. After flinging fish into the crowd and taking their bows, FNM returned to the stage for a cover of The Commodore's "Easy (Like Sunday Morning)" with the help of three housewives in robes, singing backup and opening their robes to flash mammoth false breasts. An unfalse B.A. from the girls accompanied the curtain call. And there was more fun in store.

As soon as Idol hit the stage with "Cradle Of Love", it began. A gorilla came dancing around stage right, surprising the beautiful duo singing backups. Then it joined along with their dance steps, all the while, Billy Idol was oblivious to the show-stealing going on behind him.

Mr. Idol gave an energetic performance that seemed little-affected by his recent lameness. Limp and barely noticeable, he posed and sneered and swaggered like in top form. He rattled off his long list of hits from the latest, back to Gen X days with "The Untouchables". Songs from an MTV generation: "Eyes Without A Face", "White Wedding", "Rebel Yell", and "Flesh For Fantasy" (which featured a pretty neato robotic, chest-baring dance step from the Idol one).

The real kicker, however, came in the midst of his encore, "To Be A Lover". Heads covered with masks, paper bags and towels, five guys- assumed to be FNM- circled Idol, and danced around him butt-naked. Pretty scary.

Living Colour
LIMBOMANIACS

On November 17th, a near sellout crowd filed into the Paramount to watch Living Colour prove themselves live, and (excuse the expression)- In Living Colour!

Included on the Living Colour ticket is the Limbomaniacs, a funk/rock/rap outfit recently signed to Combat/Relativity records. These guys are the latest band to come out of the recent San Francisco label signing frenzy and I had the dubious honor of chatting with two of the main maniacs: guitarist Mirv (no last names please) and bassist/vocalist Butthouse (don't ask!). Trying to get a straight answer out of them was like pulling teeth,so you be the judge:

CH: So how long have you been out with Living Colour?

Mirv: 2 days, last night in Portland and tonight here. After this we go back to San Francisco for some shows with Bootsy Collins.(their only serious answer)

CH: So what's the typical Limbomaniacs audience like?

Butthouse: Pretty diverse, the usual youngsters, people show up just to see what Mirv's gonna wear on stage each night.

Mirv: Yeah, tonight I'm going to dress like bozo, the clown!

CH: Well what would your ultimate audience be made up of?

Butthouse: Dirtbags, bikers, and homocidal maniacs. (laughs)

CH: Seattle has it's own music scene with it's own sound, do you consider yourselves part of the San Francisco sound?

CITY HEAT December 16

Butthouse: A lot of people might think we jumped on the bandwagon, and we plan to ride the bandwagon to fame and fortune. Ha ha(more laughter)

CH: What would you like to tell the people of Seattle?

Mirv: Hi Seattle, come see us, we're fungi!! (even more laughter)

Fans were conservative in their reaction to the Limbomaniacs. The band played a 30 minute set of songs from their debut album Stinky Grooves, including "Buttfunkin", and their own nasty version of the Commodores hit "Brick House". All in all, a good set, but the crowd was anxious for Living Colour to take the stage, and take the stage they did as lead singer Corey Glover danced, twirled, and gyrated to a collection of songs from their debut album Vivid, and their latest release Times Up, for which they are touring in support of. The stage was a back to basics approach, with the band preferring to let the music do the talking. The only hints of extravagance in staging were drummer William Calhoun's pyramid shaped drum cage, a colorful tapestry hung high above the band, and a reader board situated behind guitarist Vernon Reid.

Unfortunately, the sound wasn't very good, but the youngish crowd didn't seem to mind. Living Colour stormed through each song with intensity, barely taking any time in between songs to chat with the audience. Not quite halfway through the set the band took time out to dedicate the song "fight the Fight"" to an organization called Students Against Violence Everywhere.

Guitarist Vernon Reid's playing was outstanding, although at times the freestyle improv jamming was long and made the crowd grow restless. I was expecting a guitar solo, but to no avail.

Finally, after more songs from the Times Up album (which seemed to go right over the top of the audience' collective heads), the band launched into "Glamour Boys" bringing the crowd to it's feet again. Singer Corey Glover made reference to Milli Vanilli being the ultimate glamour boys, and had everyone cheering. "Open Letter To a Landlord" was next and despite sound difficulties, was a definite crowd pleaser. Rounding out the set was "Elvis is Dead" in which the band had everyone singing the chorus, intersting, but morbid if you ask me.

Saving the best for last, Living Colour returned to the stage for the obligatory encore of "Cult of Personality", leaving the audience content.

The memorable part of the show for me was the "Living Colour Hero" crusade in which the band encourages the fans to bring food to the show to help out the homeless, a noble cause indeed. **KF**

17 December CITY HEAT

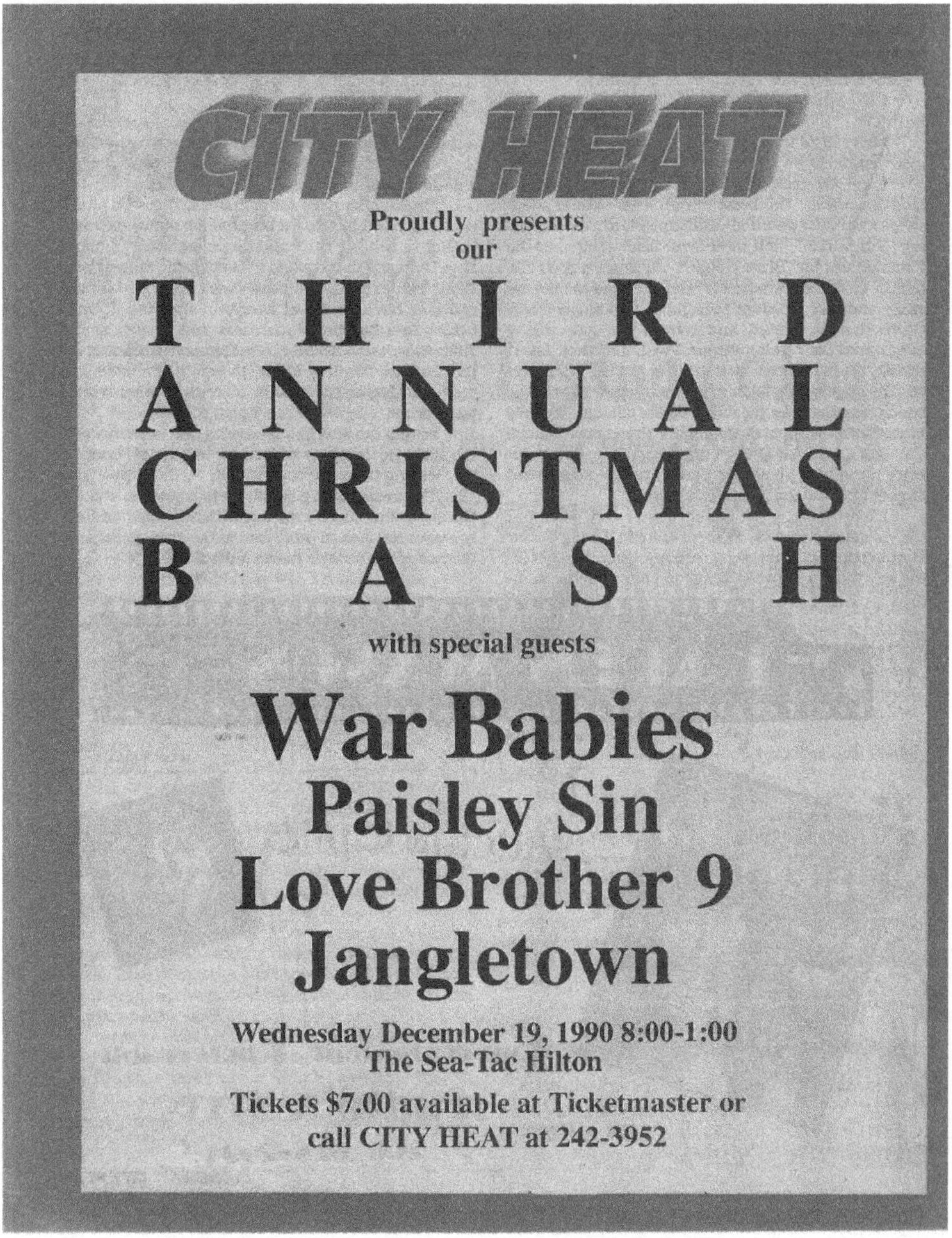
CITY HEAT
Proudly presents
our
THIRD
ANNUAL
CHRISTMAS
BASH
with special guests
War Babies
Paisley Sin
Love Brother 9
Jangletown
Wednesday December 19, 1990 8:00-1:00
The Sea-Tac Hilton
Tickets $7.00 available at Ticketmaster or
call CITY HEAT at 242-3952

TATU BODY ART

Paul
248-6232
1502
1st Ave. S.

- Sterile Conditions
- Black Work
- Custom Design
- Cover Ups

Don't Get Ripped Off!!!

Get a VIPER car alarm for only... $179.95

NORTHWEST AUTO SECURITY

AND GET A FREE PARKING LIGHT ALARM OPTION WHEN YOU MENTION THIS AD (A $40.00 VALUE)

For fast MOBILE INSTALIATIONS call (206) 763-1614

GREENER THAN YOU ARE.

MAD MAD NOMAD

New record out now, OK?

GIVE Musical Instruments FOR CHRISTMAS

Vintage, Professional and Student Models

★ GUITARS ★

- Gibson • Fender
- Martin • Guild
- Epiphone

★ BASSES ★ BANJOS ★ MANDOLINS
★ VIOLINS ★ KEYBOARDS
★ AMPS ★ STEREO EQUIPMENT

Lay-away NOW for Christmas!

Hours: Tues thru Sat. 10-5:30

AL'S GUITARVILLE

19258-15th N.E. 363-8188

Visit our new stereo and violin rooms.

AURORA

Debut Release

"On The Edge"

Merry Christmas & Happy New Year to all our Rock & Roll Fans!!!

Hotline.........781-8010

C.D. PACKAGE INCLUDES:

- Replication
- Art Preparation
- 2 Color C.D. Imprinting
- 4 Color Tray Card & Booklet Cover
- 4 Page Booklet
- Jewel Box
- Completely Packaged & Shrinkwrapped

SOUND PRODUCTIONS

19 December CITY HEAT

Hot Flashes

The Traveling Wilburys
"Volume 3"
Wilbury Records

Beatle George and ELO's Jeff Lynne produced "Volume 3," but Bob Dylan and Tom Petty enjoy all the funniest moments. The Zimmer Man laments, "she likes to stick her tongue right down my throat," while Petty enunciates such phrases as "sinking birdies" in that weird way of his so that it comes out "sinking burrdies." Anyone familiar with the more poker-faced work of either man will chuckle out loud.

"She's My Baby" explodes with guitars (lead by Gary Moore), "Inside Out" and "The Devil's Been Busy" are protest songs with great vocal harmonies. "Cool Dry Place" is a Petty number that offers a sassy new way of saying "shove it up you ass," and "New Blue Moon" is a tribute/parody of the old "Blue Moon." The best moments, however, come during "The Wilbury Twist." If you want to impress your relatives, try this dance during a holiday meal. They'll never forget it (in fact, they might have you arrested!). **C.F.**

The Human League
"Romantic?"
A & M Records

After the disappointing evil twin albums "Hysteria" (only one *inspired* song- "The Lebanon," which was better in its 12" remix format, anyway) and "Crash" (glossed and drained of spontaneity by exacting producers Jimmy Jam and Terry Lewis), the Human League seemed to have lost their path.. "Romantic?" finds them back on track, making electronic dance music with soul. Although the album is a bit short (about 45 minutes), it is consistently entertaining and devoid of filler. And whatever restored the band's muse has also restored much of its good humor. Even "Heart Like A Wheel," with its ostensibly serious lyrics, bristles with giddy energy. Recommended. **C.F.**

Nora Michaels
"Seattle, U.S.A."
Independent

The opening song on this collection by local r & b singer Nora Michaels, "Cleaning Woman Blues," deserves a N.A.M.A. award for the lyrics- a pun extravaganza that ends with Nora running off with Mr. Clean and his "easy poring spout." Sneaky mad genius that she is, Nora follows this lighthearted track with the demur "I Need Your Love So Bad," and keeps the surprises coming for the duration of the E.P. I tend to play this whenever I'm bummed out and it cheers me right up. Write her care of 4842 35th S.W., Seattle, 98126 for ordering info. **C.F.**

Bedlam Rovers
"Frothing Green"
Heyday Records

2 Black 2 Strong
"Burn Baby Burn" cass. single
In-Effect

Both the acoustic folk band Bedlam Rovers and rapper 2 Black 2 Strong attempt to point out the injustices of the world on their new releases. Unfortunately, their muckraking (whining, actually) is too unfocused to be convincing, and they never offer any advice or solutions. "Burn Baby Burn" is redeemed by the "Imperialist Inferno" remix, which fuses "Pump Up the Jam," "Disco Inferno," and "Revolutionary Situation" into a dance groove set at 4/4 time, but the Bedlam Rovers are so sloppy that their work is unbearable. **C.F.**

Two-Bit Thief
Another Sad Story In The B ig City
Combat

Two-Bit Thief takes you to the street to hang out with them and drop you off in the sewer with the dope-dealers and the bums. Each song is a chapter in their novel entitled "Another Story... In The Big City". The introduction, "City Boys," kicks your ass into the picture, as you find yourself caught up in their tale of the concrete jungle in Anytown, U.S.A. It's aimed at the young, drunk, and rebellious; takes its cues from Guns 'N Roses; and shovels up the combined feelings and styles of other gutter-grown bands like Johnny Crash, Circus of Power, and Dangerous Toys.

In the chapters that follow, you're bombarded by the darker side of the daily news and human existence: drugs, crime, and our defective government. The sadder, disheartened side of Two-Bit Thief is what shines through the filth; where you actually see some true emotion, aside from the hardened, street smart image. "Broken Hearts" is a soothing, up-lifting ballad that lifts you from the sludge, and leaves you standing wearily out on that same street corner where you began your journey.

As you wipe the crud from your face and begin to regain consciousness, a heavy rendition of Johnny Cash's "Folsom Prison Blues" grabs you by the arm and yanks you in with a splash. For the most part, the lyrics lack originality; and rely too heavily on rhyming, cliches, and rehashing dead, stereotypical issues. Two-Bit Thief have some good, dirty musicianship but it's the continuous pursuit toward an overall scummy, street-level sound and status, and the lack of true, heart-felt writing that really limits this band's full potential. Watch where you step. **SM**

Limbomaniacs
"Stinky Grooves"
In-Effect

O.K., the first song is called Butt Funkin', and the singer goes by the name Butthouse. There's more songs about butts, sex, and

CITY HEAT December 20

Hot Flashes

drugs. For classification purposes, it falls into the rap category, although a more exact terminology might be "alternative funk-rap". The Limbomaniacs definitely fall into a groove all their own. And doesn't it stink? The only current band that comes to mind as similar in sound and style, for comparative purposes, is Lockup. The Limbomaniacs break away from your average bass-thumpin' rap, and combine their rhymes with some twangy bass; funky motown grooves and hooks that you might hear on Soul Train; and assorted synthesizers and instrumentals that, unfortunately, just wind up losing your interest before they find it. Although the Limbomaniacs have a unique sound and good intentions, this cherry of an idea is sour as a lemon. **SM**

Lizzy Borden
"Master of Disguise"
Metal Blade

I was prepared to give 'em the axe but Lizzy Borden have redeemed themselves in my eyes. This, by far, exceeds anything I can recall hearing from them in the past five years. It's a little over-produced, but rocks hard nonetheless. Holy smoke! Is it just me, or does the singer sound more and more like Bruce Dickinson on each album? On a few tunes, it seems that the whole band is taking on the semblance of a slightly commercially-enhanced Iron Maiden. However, Lizzy Borden's "rock-ier" roots and overall sound are far too colorful to be paired with those of Iron Maiden. They've got a theatrical Phantom of the Opera-type theme going about fifty per cent of the time- complete with haunting organs and other assorted sound effects. It all sounds like a well-orchestrated movie soundtrack. This tape was definitely created with headphones in mind. A couple tracks off this tape are performed live, and they sound great. The vocals are crystal clear, and there's some good instrumentals as well. The more I listen to this tape, the more I like it. It's pleasantly surprising.

One obvious element of the theme, "Phantoms", opens like something Queen might have done in their early "glam"days. "Love is a Crime" is about phone sex. It sets off with some heavy breathing, and then climaxes with some great vibes. It sounds corny, but it's not. Lizzy Borden are finally headed in the right direction. This tape is really good... I'm not kidding. **SM**

Mucky Pup
"Now"
Torrid

I tried to like it- but to be brutally frank, your little brother could have written most of the lyrics for this tape. Mucky Pup appear to be a cruel combination of the rap of The Beastie Boys and the hard-edged metal of M.O.D.- the lyrics being more typical of the latter. Songs like "Hippies Hate Water", "Three Dead Gophers", and "She Quiefed" are just and pointless and slow-witted as their names imply. In "Jimmys", a song that laughs at the drug-related deaths of Jim Morrison and Jimi Hendrix, the vocals are similar to those of Joey Belladonna. On the second side, "Face" has some good, heavy Anthrax-style riffs with a lot of crunch, but the song ultimately flows into the Beastie Boys meet M.O.D. sound once again in "Hotel Penitentiary". The less prevalent, heavier side of this band tells me that they would make a better punk or speed metal band than anything else. And although they don't show much talent on this aberration, there is some there... somewhere. Maybe they'll discover where it is one day. But if you want to look for it, you're going to have to dig deep. **SM**

Every Mother's Nightmare
"Every Mother's Nightmare"
Arista

So you wanna be Skid Row? This tape has a pretty bland consistency seeing that most of the songs sound roughly alike. In each case, Every Mother's Nightmare meld some foot-stompin' Southern roots rhythms and guitars with the straight-ahead rock sound of Skid Row. It really didn't strike any special chord in me; and isn't anything that a number of their rival competitors aren't currently dwelling on. E.M.N. are Arista's version of MCA's recent discovery Sweet F.A.- but Sweet F.A. even leave these guys lying face down in the dirt, with their shitkickers on.

"EZ Come, EZ Go" is a hoedown, Southern rock barnstormer that ends up in the barn. A couple times when you think a song's going to be cool- it disappoints. In the beginning of "Walls Come Down," the guitars are heavy, and the energy leaks out somewhere again. I think this is the singer's doing. These guys would be better off as a three-piece. In any case, a new singer is in order. Withstanding some very minor exceptions, the name of this band and their debut release are understood. **SM**

Kill For Thrills
"Dynamite From Nightmareland"
MCA

Kill For Thrills. Deadly name, harmless band. With titles like "Ghosts And Monsters", "My Addiction", "Misery Pills," and "Something for the Suffering" you get the impression that this might be a black and brooding LP for crappy moods, (and maybe it is) but the sounds that come from it are at times light as a posie. Up, catchy riffs coupled with some drugged out, depressing lyrics. Very listenable, and sometimes makes you think. Can't be all bad.**MB**

21 *December* ***CITY HEAT***

Hot Flashes

Show Reviews

Dharma Bums
Green River Comm. Coll.
November 10, 1990

The Dharma Bums strode onstage at Green River Community College's Lindbloom concert hall not quite with the Godlike confidence of MacArthur into occupied Japan, but certainly with the finesse natural to any band that's toured North America and earned rave reviews all along the way. For a while, their jaunty manner seemed deserved-soon into the first song, moshers formed a circle and ring-around-the-rosied in glorious abandon. But inexplicably, boredom set in for much of the audience (and apparently, even the band), and what could have been a transcendent experience was much less fulfilling.

It's not that the band has gotten lazy. Instead, they are working too hard to *impress*. Singer/guitarist Jeremy Wilson is prone to make sweeping gestures onstage with his arms, all smiles, thumbs up, as if he's Mr. Rock and roll idol incarnate, but his persona comes across as false, as *show-business*. His actions seem motivated by an urge to make the audience like him, as if the fans wouldn't like him if he was more static and reserved. I think they *would*.

The most telling moment came after the concert proper was over. As King County policemen cleared the auditorium of spectators, the Dharma Bums remained onstage and jammed out "Maybe Baby" and "Let's Go To the Hop." They looked happier and more at peace than they had all night, perhaps because they were making music for their own pleasure, not for anyone else's. And for that very reason, the performance was perhaps the most enjoyable one they gave all night. **C.F.**

All Star Jam
The Off Ramp
November 13, 1990

November thirteenth was a good night for Seattle music fans to be out and observant. This particular night at the Off Ramp seemed to be a main event. Bathtub Gin, Inspector Luv and 'special guests' brought out a major crowd from the show's beginning to end.

The show couldn't have had a better start than Bathtub Gin. Although they haven't fully emerged from the swamp of Seattle's music scene yet, hopefully it won't be long before they're riding high. This distinctly talented band rocks but has a bluesiness that rolls like the Mississippi River itself. Harmonica melodies have been a spirited addition to certain songs recently, and hopefully to continue on. A crowd can't help but groove and smile through a set like Bathtub Gin offers. So keep a look out for further shows.

The next band was very different in sound and style. Inspector Luv successfully added a new feel with their moments on stage. This band has more of the dark, heavy elements that set them on the edge of what is the 'Seattle Sound'. Inspector Luv's growing following was pulled through an undertow of full-force tunes that night.

Finishing the night was an, as of then, unnamed special guest. The lineup was Soundgarden vocalist Chris Cornell and drummer Matt Cameron; Mother Love Bone bassist Jeff Ament and guitarist Stone Gossard, with added guitarist Mike McCready. This union of people offered a set with a vitality all its own. It was intriguing to see these guys working together on a project different from their main successes. Most of the tunes had more of a laid back, tempered down feel, but they held echoes of familiar influences. "Say Hello to Heaven" initiated a tribute to the late Andrew Wood, bonding the project as more than just another jam session. However, a few of the more fast-paced songs were taken on by the crowd with a ready enthusiasm. It's been suggested that this musical combination will be carried beyond a one-time shot. Grab a glass and keep your ear to the wall for further information about these goings-on.

The show was a great display of what the Off Ramp has lately been offering for shows. (The beverages aren't bad, either.) So three cheers for the holiday season and a December full of great entertainment everywhere! **NF**

CITY HEAT December 22

Bitchin's Corner

By Jimmy St.Bitchin

Seasons meatings and best fishes to all!, were Jimmy's final words before he hung up the phone. (By the way, this is his secretary, Bambi Woods) Jimmy is entertaining troops over in Saudi Arabia at the moment, then he said that he was going stop by the north pole to give Mrs. Claus a "BIG" Christmas present while Santa's out of town. He said he will have lot's of fun stories to tell when he get's back. Did I do good Jimmy? Bye love Bambi!

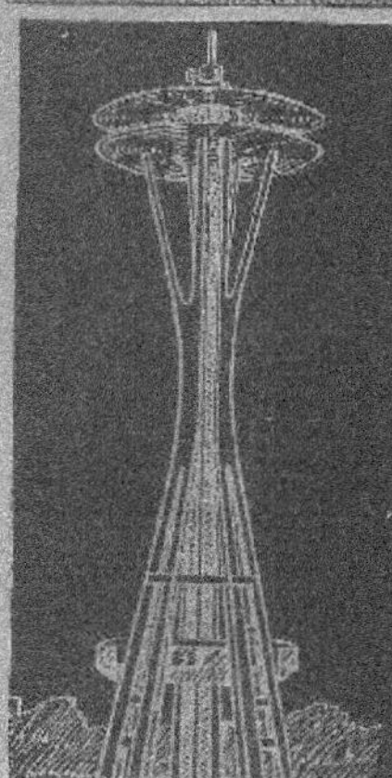

23 *December CITY HEAT*

MEGADETH
RUST
IN
PEACE
COMPACT DISC $11.97
LP/CASSETTE $7.97
Capitol
RECORDS
LP SUBJECT TO AVAILABILITY
Peaches
MUSIC & VIDEO
SEATTLE
I5 & NE 45TH ST 633 2990
BALLARD
2232 NW MARKET 784 9517
SILVERDALE
ON RANDALL WAY, ACROSS
FROM SILO 692 0404

www.ingramcontent.com/pod-product-compliance
Lightning Source LLC
Chambersburg PA
CBHW032224080426
42735CB00008B/705